The New Wider World

Second Edition COURSEMATE

for **Edexcel A** *GCSE Geography*

Lynda Evans

Skills unit developed by
Simon Ross

Written and adapted by Lynda Evans
Skills unit written by Simon Ross

Coursemates content based on *The New Wider World*, Second Edition © David Waugh and Nelson Thornes, 2003

Published in 2005 by:
Nelson Thornes Ltd
Delta Place
27 Bath Road
CHELTENHAM
GL53 7TH
United Kingdom

05 06 07 08 09 / 10 9 8 7 6 5 4 3 2 1

A catalogue record for this book is available from the British Library

ISBN 0 7487 9079 9

Edited by Katherine James
Series Editor Catherine Hurst
Illustrations by Richard Morris and Angela Lumley
Page make-up by Northern Phototypesetting Co Ltd, Bolton

Printed and bound in Great Britain by Scotprint

Acknowledgements

With thanks to the following for permission to reproduce photographs and other copyright material in this book:

Figure 4.9, 4.10 University of Dundee
Figure 9.11 Nexus

Every effort has been made to contact copyright holders. The publishers apologise to anyone whose rights have been inadvertently overlooked, and will be happy to rectify any errors or omissions.

Contents

Introduction iv

1 The physical world 1
River processes produce distinctive landforms in their valleys 1
The characteristics of valleys can be changed by glaciation 6
Coastal processes produce distinctive landforms which are subject to change 9

2 The human world 16
Rates of population change vary from place to place and over time 16
Population structure and characteristics vary from place to place 21
People live in a variety of settlements of different sizes, made up of distinct zones 26

3 The economic world 34
Economic systems vary spatially and over time 34
Farming systems show different characteristics and have been experiencing change 36
The location of industry changes over time 41

4 The natural world 46
Air masses lead to changes in the UK weather 46
Average long-term weather patterns lead to distinct climate types 53
Distinct forest communities develop which are sensitive to human interference 55

5 Managing the environment 61
Coasts are under threat and need to be managed 61
River floods are the result of human and physical factors 64
Fragile environments require sustainable management 69

6 Managing hazards 71
Some places are more hazardous than others 71
Hazards have an impact on people and the environment 75
People can prepare for hazards, and they respond to events in different ways 77

7 Managing tourism 82
The global tourist industry has grown rapidly. Different types of tourists can be identified 82
The rapid growth of tourism has had an impact on people and their environments 85
The impacts of tourism have led to the need for management 86

8 Managing urban areas 89
Urban areas in MEDCs are subject to constant change in their land use 89
Urban areas in LEDCs are subject to very rapid growth 96
Large urban areas face many challenges 101

9 Skills 106
Map skills 106
Interpreting photographs and observing landscapes 112
Graphical skills 114
Looking for patterns 117

Index 119

Introduction

About this book

This New Wider World Coursemate matches the content of *The New Wider World* to your own GCSE Geography specification, and follows the same order. It is a pocket companion for your course and provides a summary of the core information you will need to know and revise for your GCSE Geography examinations.

How the specification is structured

This specification is organised into eight units – four Core and four Option units. Within some of the units, case studies are required.

Core units

- A1 – Physical World
- A2 – Human World
- A3 – Economic World
- A4 – Natural World

You must study all four of these Core units.

Option units

- B5 – Managing the Environment
- B6 – Managing Hazards
- C7 – Managing Tourism
- C8 – Managing Urban Areas

You must study either B5 or B6 and either C7 or C8.

How the specification is assessed

There are three components to the assessment of Edexcel A.

Paper 1 is 1 hour 45 minutes. This exam consists of four structured questions on the UK. One or more questions will be based on a 1:50 000 UK Ordnance Survey map. All questions are compulsory.

Paper 2 is 1 hour 15 minutes. This exam consists of four questions, testing units B5, B6, C7 and C8. You must choose either B5 or B6 and either C7 or C8. Questions are structured and will require specific detail of case studies.

Coursework is worth 25% of the final grade. This should be approximately 2500 words and be based on a fieldwork investigation at a local/small scale. The topic chosen must relate to some part of the specification content. You will be required to use ICT at various stages of the coursework.

How your Coursemate is organised

Your Coursemate follows the same structure and order as the topics in your specification. Most of the information is from *The New Wider World*, so your book acts as a companion to both *The New Wider World* and your own specification. Your Coursemate is organised in the following way:

- The **theme/chapter headings** match those used in the specification.
- The **page references** to *The New Wider World* at the beginning of each chapter tell you which pages in the textbook your Coursemate refers to.

- The **Key Ideas** relate to those which appear in your specification, and the content of your Coursemate is organised around these.
- **Key words to know** – these are the key geographical words and terms you need to know and be able to use.
- **Check this!...** – doing these questions will check that you know and understand the key concepts in each chapter.
- **Back to ...** is a cross-reference to *The New Wider World* for finding more information. It can also be a cross-reference to other information in your Coursemate.
- **Case Studies** are based on the Case Studies and Place Studies in *The New Wider World*, and **Case Study Extras** are new case studies written especially for your specification. Where relevant these will: refer you back to the textbook for more information; tell you how to get the best from your case study; provide links to other topics; provide updates to the case study, which may be websites accessed via a link from the Nelson Thornes website at www.nelsonthornes.com/newwider world *and* include questions which encourage you to learn the case study so that you can use it well in your examination.
- **Exam practice –** these questions are similar to those you will meet in the examination. You can check your answers by going to *The New Wider World Coursemates* website at www.nelsonthornes.com/newwiderworld
- Each **Exam Practice** question is followed by an **Exam Tip** to provide help and advice on answering the question. Exam practice questions are not full exam questions, but are similar in style to the longer, structured questions on your exams.

At the end of this book you will find a chapter on **geographical skills**. This gives information on the basic geographical skills you will need for the interpretation, presentation and analysis of geographical information and data throughout your Geography course and in your examinations.

All references to *The New Wider World* in your Coursemate are to the Second edition.

➪ *The New Wider World*, pp 246–247, 282 285, 292, 300–305, 316–318, 320

1 The physical world

KEY IDEAS

1. River processes produce distinctive landforms in their valleys
2. The characteristics of valleys can be changed by glaciation
3. Coastal processes produce distinctive landforms which are subject to change

1 River processes produce distinctive landforms in their valleys

River and valley characteristics change from source to mouth

There are distinct changes in the width, discharge and gradient of a river channel and in the cross-section of the river valley as it flows from its **source** (where a river starts, usually in an upland area) to its **mouth** (where a river ends, in the sea or, sometimes, in a lake). Figure 1.1 summarises these changes in the **cross-section (cross profile)** and **long section (long profile)** of a river.

Key words to know

Source
Mouth
Cross-section (cross profile)
Long section (long profile)

Figure 1.1 Changes in a river from source to mouth

<table>
<tr><th colspan="2"></th><th>Near source</th><th>Near mouth</th></tr>
<tr><td colspan="2">River gradient (long-section/profile)</td><td colspan="2">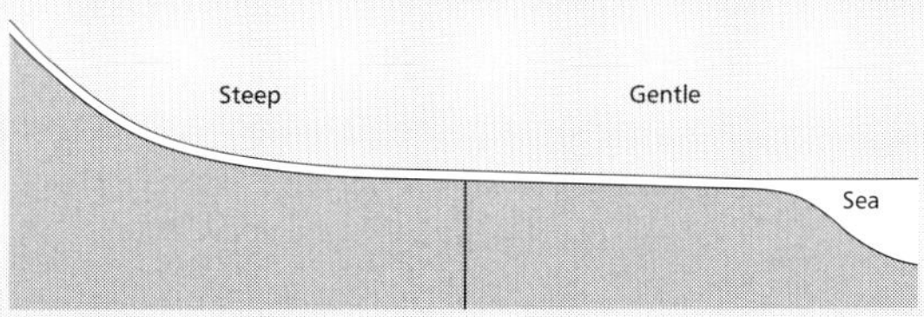
</td></tr>
<tr><td rowspan="3">River channel</td><td>Width</td><td>Very narrow</td><td>Often very wide</td></tr>
<tr><td>Depth</td><td>Shallow</td><td>Can be very deep</td></tr>
<tr><td>Discharge</td><td>Small</td><td>Often very large</td></tr>
<tr><td rowspan="4">River valley</td><td>Shape (cross-section/ profile)</td><td colspan="2">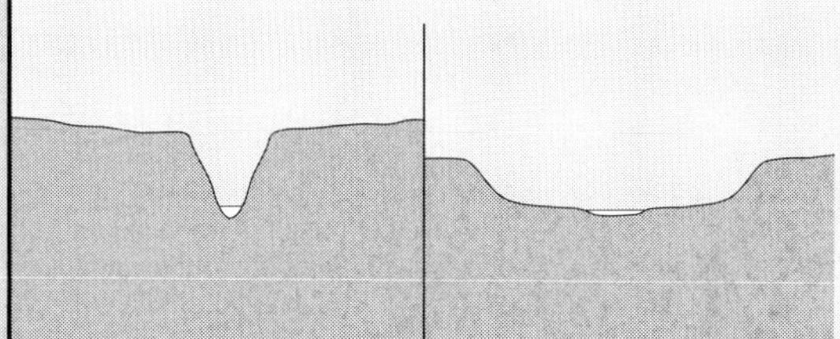</td></tr>
<tr><td>Width</td><td>Narrow</td><td>Can be very wide</td></tr>
<tr><td>Sides</td><td>Very steep</td><td>Very gentle</td></tr>
<tr><td>Floor</td><td>Narrow/none</td><td>Often very wide</td></tr>
</table>

Key words to know

Velocity
Discharge
Wetted perimeter
Confluence
Tributary
Load

Back to …

The New Wider World **page 282** Figure 17.11 which shows the differences between velocity and discharge in the upper and lower course of a river.

There are also changes in energy, **velocity** (speed) and **discharge** (amount of water in a river) from source to mouth. A river uses energy to overcome friction. Under normal conditions, 95 per cent of a river's energy is used in this way. Most friction occurs at the **wetted perimeter** i.e. where the water comes into contact with the river's banks and bed. The channel of a mountain stream, often filled with boulders, creates much friction. As a result water will flow less quickly here than in the lowlands where the channel becomes much wider and deeper.

Following a period of heavy rain, or after the **confluence** (meeting place) with a major **tributary** (smaller river joining a larger one) the volume of the river will increase. As less water is in contact with the wetted perimeter, friction is reduced and the velocity increases. The surplus energy, resulting from the decrease in friction, can now be used to pick up and transport material (or **load**). The greater the velocity of a river, the greater the amount of material, both in quantity and size, that can be carried.

The formation of river landforms

The main river landforms are interlocking spurs, waterfalls, meanders, ox-bow lakes, floodplains, levées and deltas. These are formed by processes of erosion, deposition and transportation.

Key words to know

Attrition
Hydraulic erosion
Abrasion (corrasion)
Solution
Traction
Saltation
Suspension
Solution

River processes – erosion

A river may erode by one of four processes.

- **Attrition** – boulders and other material being transported along the bed of a river collide with each other and break up into smaller pieces. This is more likely to occur when rivers are flowing in highland areas.
- **Hydraulic erosion** – the sheer force of the river dislodges particles from its banks and bed.
- **Abrasion (corrasion)** – smaller material, carried in suspension, rubs against the banks of the river. This process is more likely where the river flows through lowland areas, by which time enough material will have been broken up into small enough pieces to be carried in suspension. River banks are worn away by this sand-papering action.
- **Solution** – sometimes acids in the river water dissolve rocks such as limestone.

River processes – transportation

A river carries its load (eroded material) by one of four processes: **traction, saltation, suspension** or **solution**.

Figure 1.2 Processes of transportation

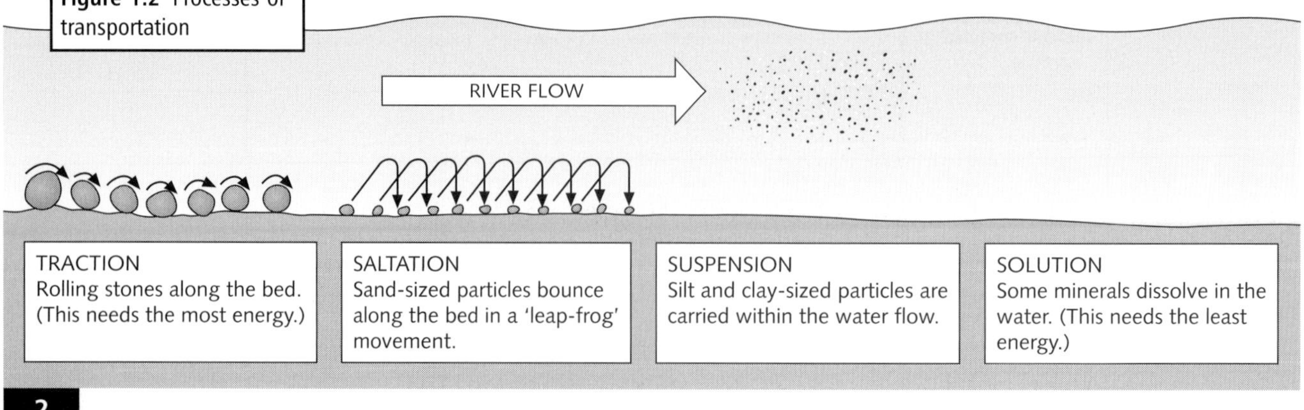

River processes – deposition

Deposition occurs when a river lacks enough energy to carry its load. Deposition, beginning with the heaviest material first, can occur:

- following a dry spell when the discharge and velocity of a river drop, or
- where the current slows down (on the inside of a meander bend, or where the river enters the sea).

Upland river landforms – V-shaped valleys and interlocking spurs

In upland areas a river transports large boulders along its bed. This results in the river cutting rapidly downwards, by **vertical erosion**. Vertical erosion leads to the development of steep-sided, narrow valleys shaped like the letter V (**V-shaped valleys**).

The valley sides are steep as soil and loose rock are washed downhill following periods of heavy rain. The material is then added to the load of the river. The river itself is forced to wind its way around protruding hillsides, known as **interlocking spurs**.

Upland river landforms – waterfalls and rapids

Waterfalls form when there is a sudden interruption in the course of a river due to the action of ice, changes in sea-level, or earth movements. Many waterfalls also form when rivers meet a band of softer, less resistant rock after flowing over a relatively hard, resistant rock. The underlying softer rock is worn away more quickly, and the harder rock is undercut. In time the overlying harder rock becomes unsupported, and collapses. After its collapse, some of the rock is swirled around by the river, especially during times of high discharge, to form a deep plunge pool. This process is likely to be repeated many times, causing the waterfall to retreat upstream leaving a steep-sided gorge. **Rapids** occur where the layers of hard and soft rock are very thin, so no obvious break of slope develops as in a waterfall.

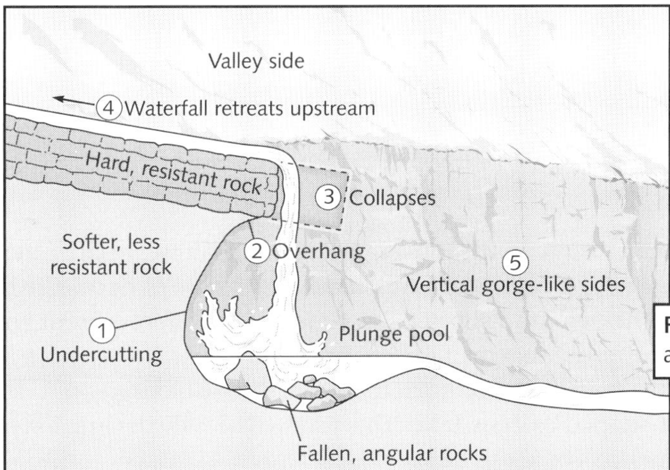

The underlying softer rock is worn away more quickly and the harder rock is undercut. Gradually the overlying harder rock becomes unsupported and collapses. The collapsed rock is swirled around by the river to form a deep plunge pool. The waterfall slowly retreats upstream, leaving behind a steep-sided gorge.

Figure 1.3 Formation of a waterfall and gorge

Check this!...

1 Explain how a V-shaped valley is formed.

2 What are interlocking spurs and how are they formed?

3 How are waterfalls formed?

Check this!...

1 Describe the main changes in a river from source to mouth.

2 Explain the four main processes by which a river erodes the land.

3 How does a river transport its load?

4 When and where does deposition occur?

Back to ...

The New Wider World **page 283** Figure 17.13, a photograph of a V-shaped valley and interlocking spurs.

Key words to know

Vertical erosion
V-shaped valley
Interlocking spurs
Waterfalls
Rapids

Key words to know

Meanders
River cliff
Lateral erosion
Slip-off slope
Ox-bow lake
Floodplain
Levée

Lowland river landforms – meanders and ox-bow lakes

As a river approaches its mouth it develops large bends known as **meanders**. Meanders constantly change their shape and position. When a river reaches a meander most of the water is directed towards the outside of the bend. This reduces friction and increases the velocity of the river at this point. The river therefore has more energy to transport material in suspension and this material is used to erode the outside bank by abrasion. The bank will be undercut, collapse and retreat, to leave a small **river cliff**. The river is now eroding through **lateral erosion**. Meanwhile, as there is less water on the inside of the bend, there is an increase in friction here and a decrease in velocity. As the river loses energy it begins to deposit some of its load. The deposited material builds up to form a gently sloping **slip-off slope**.

Back to ...

The New Wider World **page 284** Figure 17.16, a photograph of a meander.

Figure 1.4 Cross-section of a meander

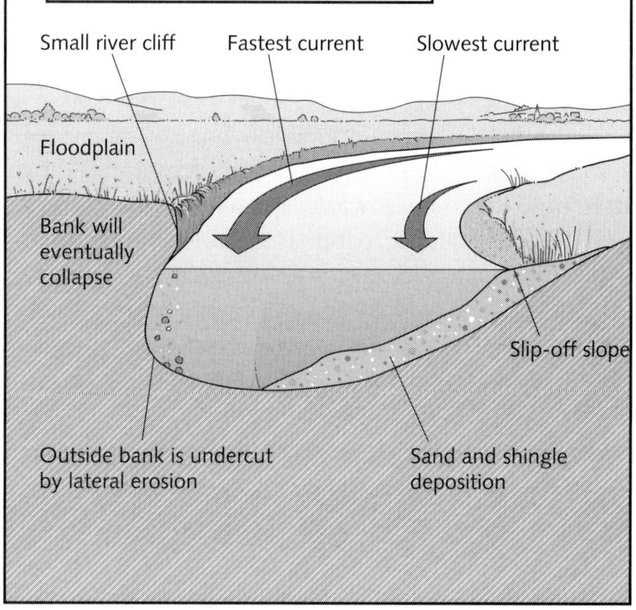

Continual erosion on the outside bend results in the neck of the meander getting narrower until, usually at a time of flood, the river cuts through the neck and shortens its course. The fastest current will now be flowing in the centre of the channel and deposition is more likely next to the banks. The original meander will be blocked off to leave a crescent-shaped **ox-bow lake**. This lake will slowly dry up, except during periods of heavy rain.

Lowland river landforms – floodplains and levées

The river widens its valley by lateral erosion. At times of high discharge, the river has considerable amounts of energy which it uses to transport large amounts of material in suspension. When the river overflows its banks, it spreads out across any surrounding flat land. The sudden increase in friction reduces the water's velocity and fine silt is deposited. Each time the river floods another layer of silt is added and a flat **floodplain** is formed. The coarsest material is dropped first and this can form a natural embankment called a **levée,** next to the river. Sometimes levées are artificially strengthened to act as flood banks.

Figure 1.5 Formation of an ox-bow lake

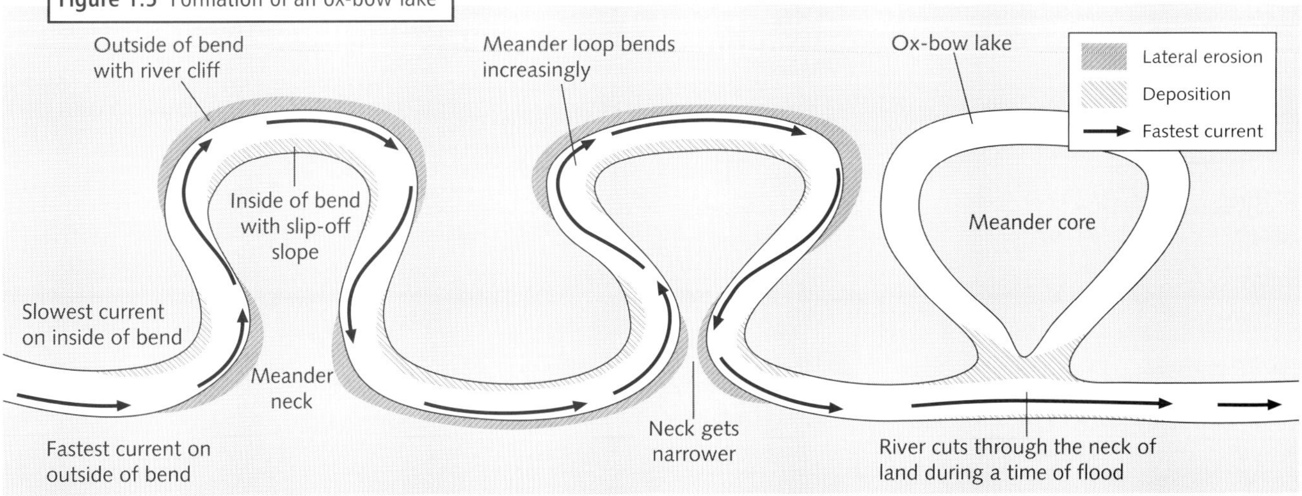

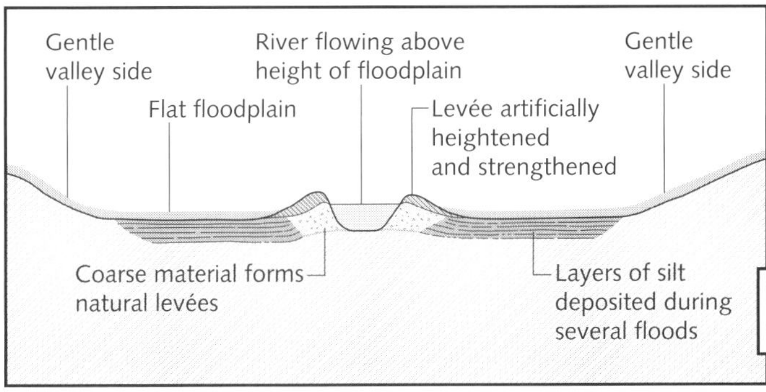

Figure 1.6 Cross-section of a river floodplain

Back to ...

The New Wider World **page 285** Figure 17.20, an aerial photograph of the Mississippi delta.

Lowland river landforms – deltas

As large rivers approach the sea, they have the energy to carry huge amounts of fine material in suspension. On reaching the sea, the river current may suddenly be reduced, allowing the material to be deposited. Sometimes deposition occurs in the main channel, and blocks it. The river has then to divide into a series of smaller channels, called **distributaries,** in order to reach the sea. Over a period of time the deposited material of sand and silt may build upwards and outwards to form a **delta.**

Deltas are only likely to form where the amount of material brought down by a river is too great for sea currents to remove it, or in seas that are virtually tideless. They can also form when a river flows into the gentle waters of a lake.

Rivers and their tributaries are shown as blue lines on OS maps. The shape of a river valley can be worked out by looking at the contour lines on either side of the river to see whether it has a V-shaped valley or a wide floodplain. Waterfalls and rapids are usually indicated by labels. Meanders and ox-bow lakes can be recognised by their shape.

Key words to know

Distributary
Delta

Back to ...

The New Wider World **page 292** for information on river landforms on Ordnance Survey maps.

Check this!...

1 What is a meander?

2 What happens on the outside of a meander bend, and why?

3 What happens on the inside of a meander bend, and why?

4 What is an ox-bow lake? How is it formed?

5 What happens when a river overflows its banks?

6 What is a levée?

7 Explain how a delta is formed.

Check this!...

Use *The New Wider World* **page 202**, Figures 17.38 and 17.39.

1 Name the landforms in the following grid squares:
   a) 0004 (Figure 17.39)
   b) 8628 (Figure 17.38)
   c) 9028 (Figure 17.38).

2 Describe the differences between the two river valleys in grid squares 9031 (Figure 17.38) and 0206 (Figure 17.39).

3 Give a six-figure grid reference for:
   a) the mouth of the River Arun (Figure 17.39)
   b) High Force waterfall (Figure 17.38).

2 The characteristics of valleys can be changed by glaciation

The build-up of ice and the formation of corries

Much of the highland scenery of Scotland, Wales and northern England owes its attractiveness to the work of ice in earlier times. At the height of the Ice Age, northern Britain was covered by a large ice sheet. At other times, glaciers extended down valleys leading from the higher mountains.

The build-up of ice

Ice forms as a result of the accumulation of snow in upland areas. As several layers of snow lie on the ground, air is trapped between the flakes. As more snow falls, the underlying layers are compressed, the air is squeezed out and the snow becomes firmer. As even more snow falls, the underlying layers are compressed into ice, eventually forming a **glacier**. A **valley glacier** forms when ice builds up in a river valley and it may be fed by smaller glaciers in tributary valleys.

Key words to know

Glacier
Valley glacier
Freeze–thaw (frost shattering)

Erosion by ice

A glacier can erode much faster than a river, but only when it has a continuous supply of material within it. The main source of material in a glacier results from the process of **freeze–thaw (frost shattering)**. This process occurs in rocks that have many joints and cracks in them, and where temperatures are frequently around freezing point.

Back to ...

The New Wider World **page 316** for a diagram (Figure 19.1) and a photograph (Figure 19.2) of a glacier system.

Figure 1.7 Freeze–thaw weathering

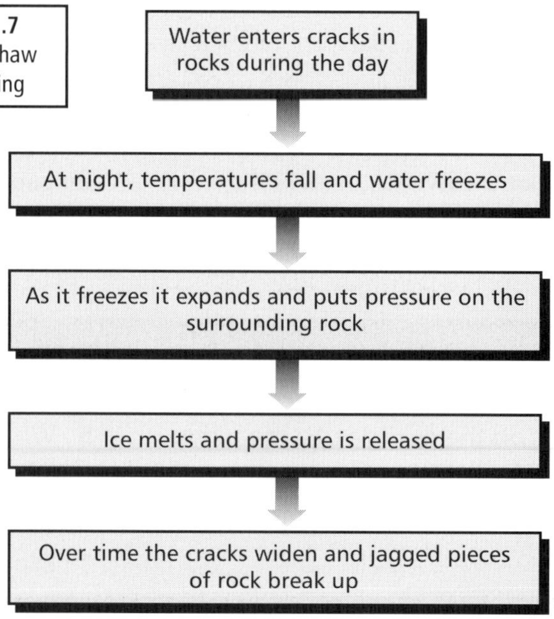

The material broken off from the mountain as a result of freeze–thaw is called **moraine** and is used by the glacier to deepen and widen its valley in two main ways:

- **Abrasion** – as in a river, material carried by the glacier rubs against and wears away the sides and floor of the valley.
- **Plucking** – glacial ice freezes onto solid rock. As the glacier moves away it pulls with it large pieces of rock.

Key words to know

Moraine
Abrasion
Plucking
Corrie (cwm, cirque)
Arête
Pyramidal peak (horn)

Formation of corries, arêtes and pyramidal peaks

Corries, cwms or **cirques** are deep, rounded hollows with a steep back wall and a rock basin.

Figure 1.8 Formation of a corrie

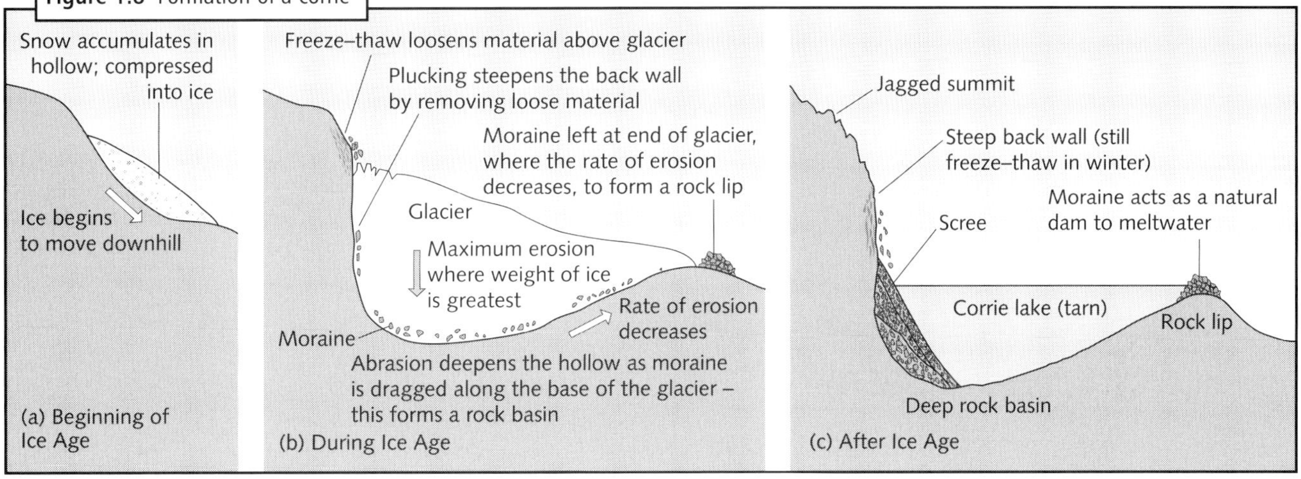

When two or more corries develop back to back (or side by side), they erode backwards (or sideways) towards each other. The land between them gets narrower until a knife-edged ridge, called an **arête,** is formed. Where three or more corries cut backwards into the same mountain, a **pyramidal peak** or **horn** develops. Arêtes radiate from the central peak.

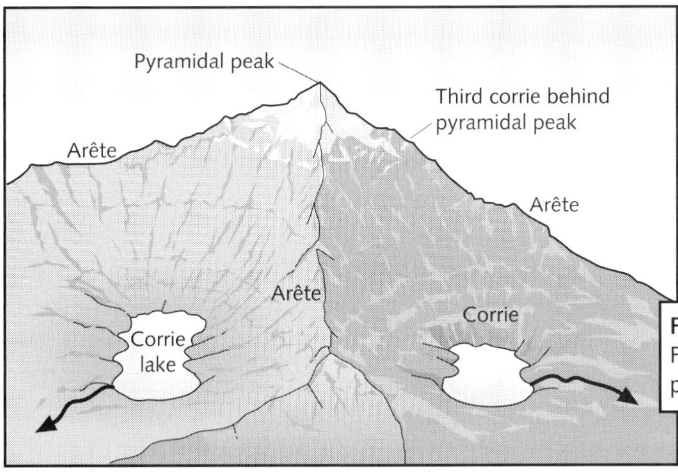

Figure 1.9 Formation of a pyramidal peak

Back to ...

The New Wider World **page 317** for photographs of a corrie (Figure 19.4) and a pyramidal peak (Figure 19.5).

Check this!...

1 Describe how ice builds up to form a glacier.

2 Explain the processes of freeze–thaw and plucking.

3 Draw a sketch diagram to show a corrie, an arête and a pyramidal peak.

4 Explain how a corrie is formed.

Changes to valley characteristics

Glaciated troughs, truncated spurs, hanging valleys and ribbon lakes

Key words to know

Glacial trough
Truncated spur
Hanging valley
Ribbon lake

Glaciers follow river valleys as they move downhill from their source in the mountains. Unlike a river, however, a glacier often fills the whole valley and has much greater erosive power. Instead of having to wind its way around obstacles, such as interlocking spurs, the glacier is able to widen, straighten and deepen its valley.

Figure 1.10 Formation of a glacial trough and associated features

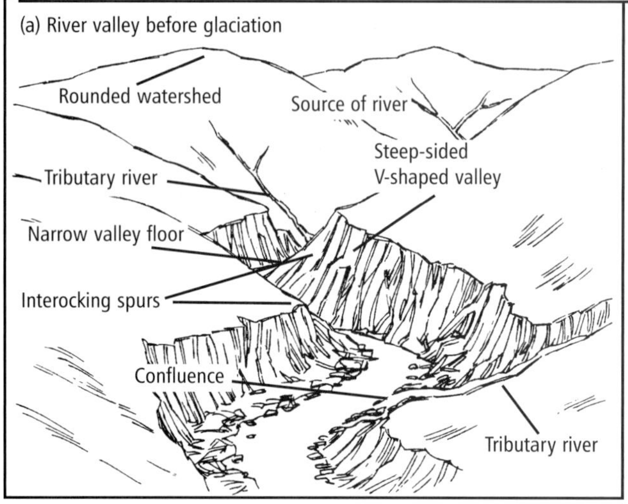

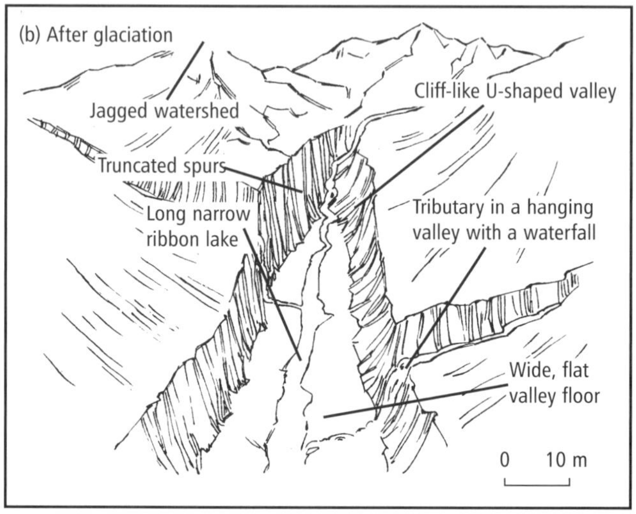

Back to ...

The New Wider World **page 318** for photographs of a glacial trough (Figure 19.8) and a hanging valley (Figure 19.9).

The New Wider World **page 319** for more information on different types of moraine.

- As a result of abrasion, the characteristic V-shaped river valley is changed into the characteristic U-shaped **glacial trough.**
- As the glacier moves down the valley it removes the ends of interlocking spurs to leave steep, cliff-like **truncated spurs.**
- Between adjacent truncated spurs are **hanging valleys.** Before the Ice Age, tributary rivers would have had their confluence with the main river at the same height. During the Ice Age, the glacier in the main valley was much larger than glaciers in the tributary valleys and so it eroded downwards much more rapidly. When the ice melted, the tributary valleys were left 'hanging' above the main valley. Each tributary river now has to descend to the main river by a waterfall.

Many glacial troughs in highland Britain contain long, narrow **ribbon lakes**. These are partly the result of erosion when a glacier over-deepens its valley, perhaps in an area of softer rock or due to increased erosion after being joined by a tributary glacier. They may also be partly created by deposition of moraine across the main valley.

Corries can be recognised by their rounded shape and the fact that they are surrounded on three sides by contour lines which are very close together. Arêtes can often be recognised by the cliff symbol, and many have footpaths along them. Spot heights may identify pyramidal peaks. Long thin stretches of water in areas without contour lines are ribbon lakes in glacial troughs.

Back to ...

The New Wider World **page 320** for information on glacial landforms on OS maps.

Check this!...

1 Draw a sketch diagram to show the features of a glaciated valley.

2 Add detailed annotations to show how the following were formed:
- glacial trough
- hanging valley
- truncated spurs
- ribbon lake.

Refer to *The New Wider World* **page 320**.

3 Give four-figure grid references for:
a) Blea Water (Figure 19.15)
b) the arête named High Street (Figure 19.15)
c) part of a glacial trough (Figure 19.15).

4 Name the features at the following locations:
a) 609543 (Figure 19.14)
b) 624517 (Figure 19.14)
c) 441111 (Figure 19.15).

3 Coastal processes produce distinctive landforms which are subject to change

The impact of erosion, weathering and mass movement on the coast

Erosion

Material along coasts is eroded in a similar way to erosion by rivers.
- **Corrasion (abrasion)** is caused by large waves hurling beach material against a cliff.
- **Attrition** is when waves cause rocks and boulders on the beach to bump into each other and to break up into small particles.
- **Corrosion (solution)** is when salts and other acids in seawater slowly dissolve a cliff.
- **Hydraulic action** is the force of waves compressing air in cracks in a cliff.

Waves are created by the transfer of energy from wind blowing over the surface of the sea. The larger the wave the greater the energy it contains. The largest waves are formed when winds are very strong, blow for lengthy periods and cross large expanses of water. The **fetch** is the maximum distance of water over which winds can blow.

Water particles within a wave move in a circular orbit. When a wave reaches the shallow water, the velocity at its base is slowed by friction with the sea bed and the circular orbit is changed to one that is more elliptical. The top of the wave, unaffected by friction, becomes higher and steeper until it breaks. At this point the remnant of the wave, called the **swash,** moves forward up the beach. The swash transfers energy up the beach and is followed by the **backwash,** which returns energy down the beach. There are two types of wave (Figure 1.11):
- **Constructive waves** have limited energy, most of which is used by the swash to transport material up the beach.
- **Destructive waves** have much more energy, most of which is used by the backwash to transport material back down the beach.

Key words to know

Corrasion (abrasion)
Attrition
Corrosion (solution)
Hydraulic action
Fetch
Swash
Backwash
Constructive waves
Destructive waves

Back to ...

The New Wider World **page 300** Figure 18.1 which shows the formation of a wave.

Figure 1.11 Constructive and destructive waves

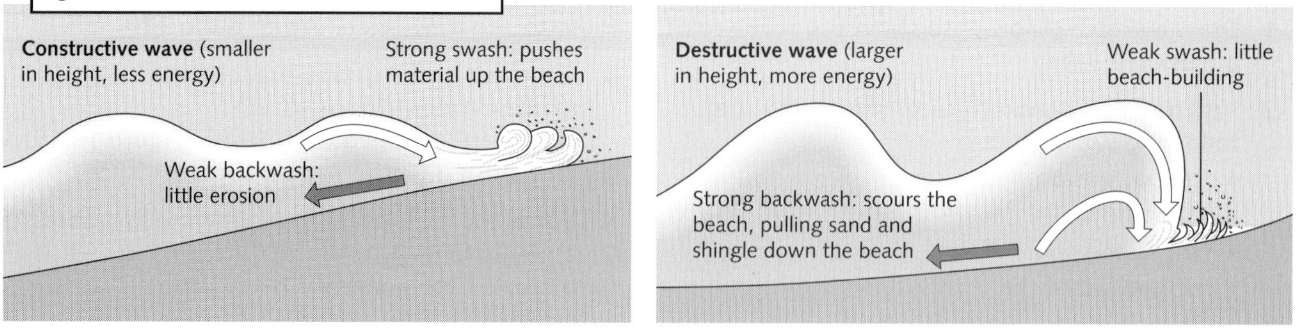

Check this!...

1 Explain how waves are formed.

2 What is the difference between swash and backwash?

3 Describe the two different types of waves.

Features of erosion

These include headlands and bays, cliffs, caves, arches, stacks, wave-cut notches and wave-cut platforms.

Figure 1.12 Formation of headlands and bays

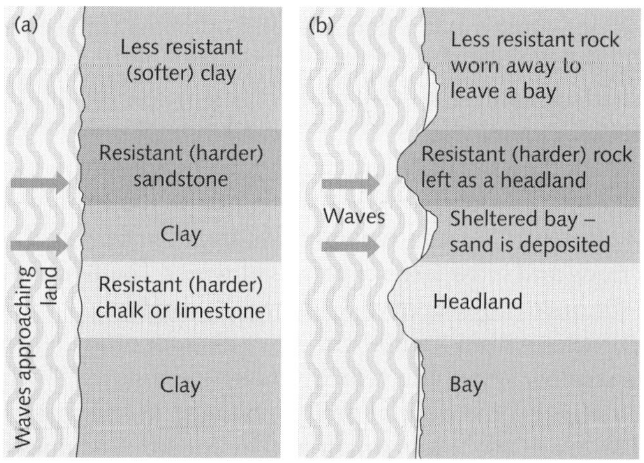

There are alternating outcrops of resistant (harder) and less resistant (softer) rocks.

Destructive waves erode the areas of softer rocks more rapidly to form bays. Headlands are left protruding out to sea and are exposed to the full force of the waves.

Key words to know

Wave-cut notch
Wave-cut platform

Wave erosion is greatest when large waves break against the foot of a cliff. As wave energy is at its maximum, waves undercut the foot of the cliff to form a **wave-cut notch**. Over a period of time the notch enlarges until the cliff above it, left unsupported, collapses. As the process is repeated, the cliff retreats and often increases in height. The gently sloping expanse of rock marking the foot of the retreating cliff is called a **wave-cut platform**. This is exposed at low tide but covered at high tide.

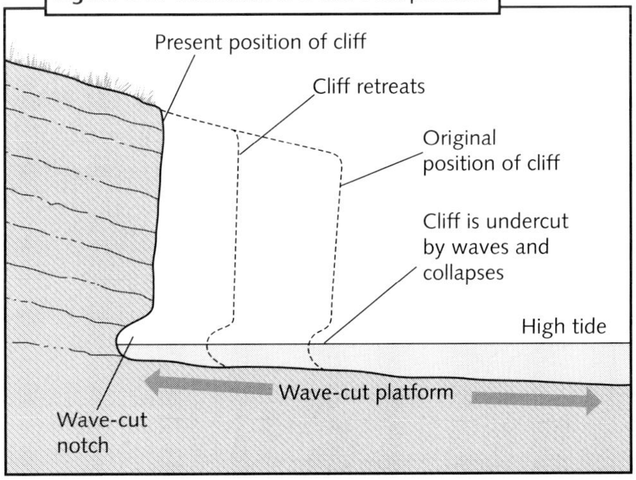

Figure 1.13 Formation of a wave-cut platform

Back to ...

The New Wider World **page 301** Figure 18.5, a photograph of a wave-cut notch and platform at Flamborough Head, Yorkshire.

Key words to know

Cave
Arch
Stack
Stump

Figure 1.14 Formation of caves, arches, stacks and stumps

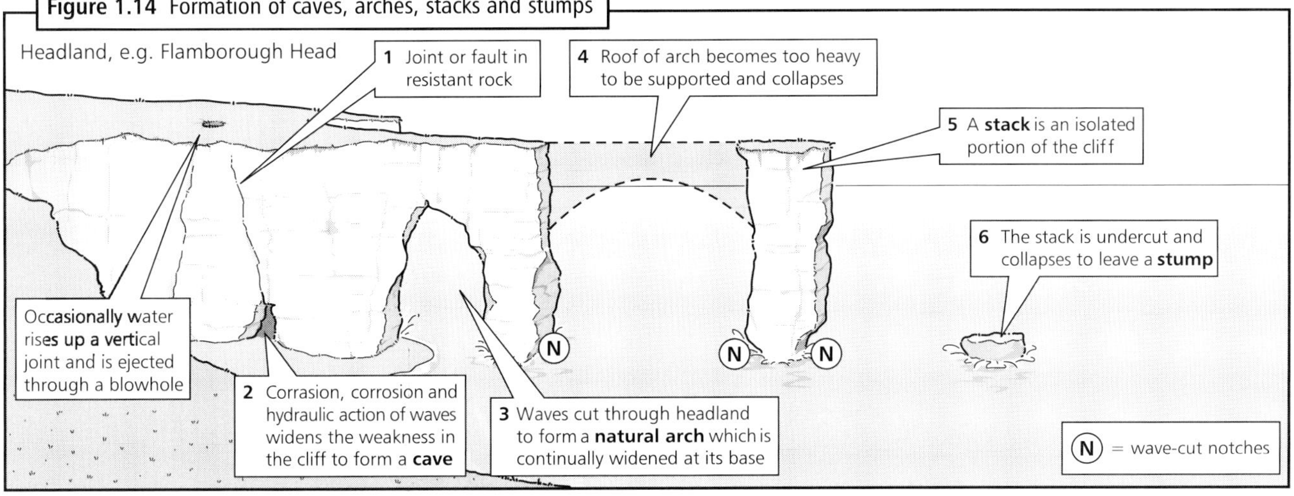

Check this!...

1 Draw an annotated diagram to show the formation of headlands and bays.

2 Describe the difference between a wave-cut notch and a wave-cut platform.

3 Draw a diagram to show the formation of caves, arches, stacks and stumps.

Back to ...

The New Wider World **page 302** Figure 18.7, a photograph of coastal erosion features, on The Foreland, Isle of Purbeck.

Weathering

Rocks that are exposed on the Earth's surface become vulnerable to **weathering** – the disintegration (breaking up) and decomposition (decay) of rocks in situ, i.e. in their place of origin. Unlike erosion, weathering need not involve the movement of material. There are two main types of weathering:

- **Physical weathering** is the disintegration of rock into smaller pieces by physical processes, without any change in the chemical composition of the rock. It is most likely to occur in areas of bare rock, where there is no vegetation to protect the rock from extreme weather conditions. There are three types of physical weathering: **freeze–thaw, exfoliation** and **biological weathering**.

Key words to know

Weathering
Physical weathering
Freeze–thaw
Exfoliation (onion weathering)
Biological weathering

Freeze–thaw	Exfoliation	Biological weathering
• Also called frost shattering • Occurs in exposed, cracked rocks in cold climates • Water enters cracks during day and freezes at night • As it freezes it expands and exerts pressure on the surrounding rock • As temperatures rise, ice melts and pressure is released • The process is repeated and the crack is widened until eventually pieces of rock break off • Broken rocks, called **scree**, collect at foot of cliff	• Also called onion weathering • Occurs in very warm climates as exposed, non-vegetated rock is repeatedly heated and cooled • Surface layers heat and expand more rapidly during the day and cool and contract more rapidly at night than the inner layers • Surface layers eventually peel off, like the layers of an onion, to leave rounded rocks and hills	• Tree roots penetrate and widen bedding planes and other weaknesses in the rock • Blocks of rock become detached

Figure 1.15 Three types of physical weathering

Key words to know

Scree
Chemical weathering
Limestone solution
Soil creep
Terracette
Mudflow
Landslide

- **Chemical weathering** is the decomposition of rocks caused by a chemical change within the rock. It is more likely to occur in warm, moist climates, as these encourage chemical reactions to take place. An example of chemical weathering is **limestone solution**.

Figure 1.16 Limestone solution

Carbonic acid (carbon dioxide in solution) occurs naturally in rainwater

↓

This weak acid solution reacts chemically with rocks such as limestone which contain calcium carbonate

↓

Limestone slowly dissolves and is removed in solution by running water

↓

Solution widens bedding planes and joints

Back to ...

The New Wider World **page 246** Figures 15.8, 15.9 and 15.10, photographs showing some examples of scree, exfoliation and biological weathering.

The New Wider World **page 304** Figure 18.14, a photograph of a collapsing cliff at Holderness, Yorkshire.

The New Wider World **page 247**: Figure 15.11, a photograph of terracettes; Figure 15.12, which shows evidence of soil creep; and Figure 15.13, a photograph of mudflows.

Weathering plays an important part in the formation of coastal features as it can cause cliffs to collapse, especially in areas of less resistant rock. Here, heavy rain can cause material which has been weathered to move downslope where it will be removed by waves and ocean currents.

Mass movement

Mass movement describes the downhill movement of weathered material under the force of gravity. This movement occurs on almost all slopes and is a continuous process, causing the transport of soil, stones and rock. The speed of movement can vary considerably:

- **Soil creep**, where the movement is barely noticeable. It occurs on very gentle, well-vegetated slopes. Although material may move by less than 1 cm a year, its results can be seen as step-like **terracettes** on banks and hillsides.
- **Mudflows** and **landslides**, where the movement becomes increasingly more rapid.

Mudflows and landslides are rapid movements which often take place with little warning. They are most likely to occur on steep slopes. They may occur after periods of heavy rain when loose surface material becomes saturated and the extra weight causes material to move downhill. This often happens at the coast, where soils and softer rock overlie harder, impermeable rock.

Check this!...

1 Describe the three types of physical weathering.

2 Explain how rocks such as limestone can be weathered by chemical reactions.

3 Describe the difference between soil creep and mudflows.

4 Explain how these processes might affect cliffs at the coast.

The impact of transportation and deposition on the coast

Key words to know

Longshore drift
Beach
Spit
Sand-dune

Transportation

Waves carry material up and down a beach but the major movement is along the coast by a process called **longshore drift.**

Figure 1.17 Longshore drift

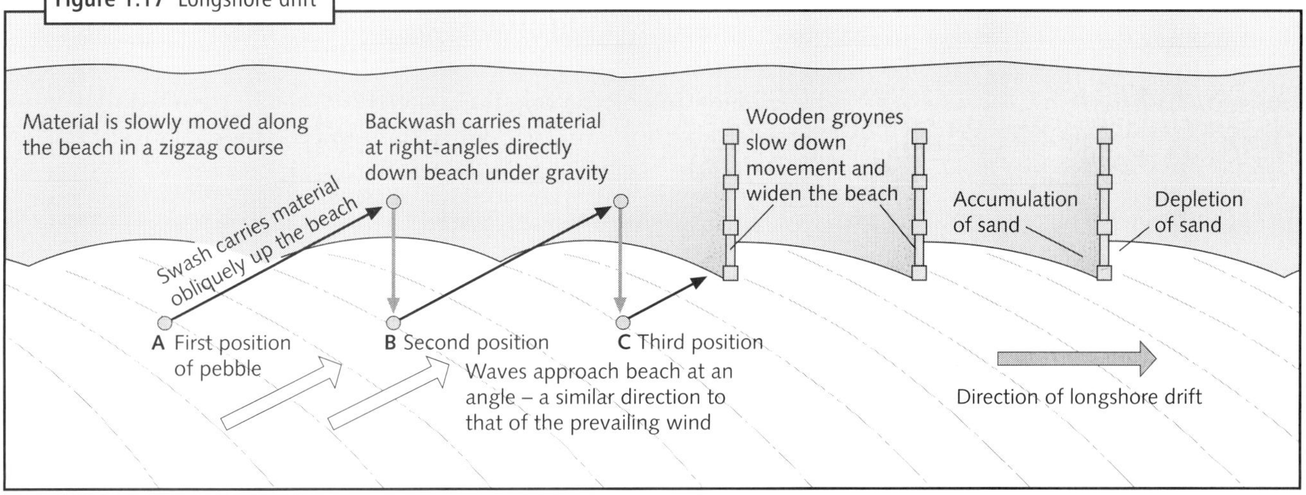

Deposition

Sand and shingle being transported along the coast by longshore drift will, in time, reach an area where the water is sheltered and the waves lack energy, e.g. a bay. The material may be temporarily deposited to form a **beach**. Beaches are not permanent features as their shape can be altered by waves every time the tide comes in and goes out.

A **spit** is a permanent landform resulting from marine deposition. It is a long, narrow accumulation of sand or shingle, with one end attached to the land and the other projecting at a narrow angle either into the sea or across a river estuary. Many spits have a hooked or curved end.

Spits form where longshore drift moves larger amounts of sand and shingle along the coast and where the coastline suddenly changes direction to leave a shallow, sheltered area of water. Spits become permanent when the sand is blown up the beach to form **sand-dunes.**

Back to ...

The New Wider World **page 302** Figure 18.9, a photograph of groynes and the accumulation of sand as a result of longshore drift at Worthing, West Sussex.

The New Wider World **page 303** Figure 18.10, a photograph of Hurst Spit, Hampshire.

Figure 1.18
Formation of a spit

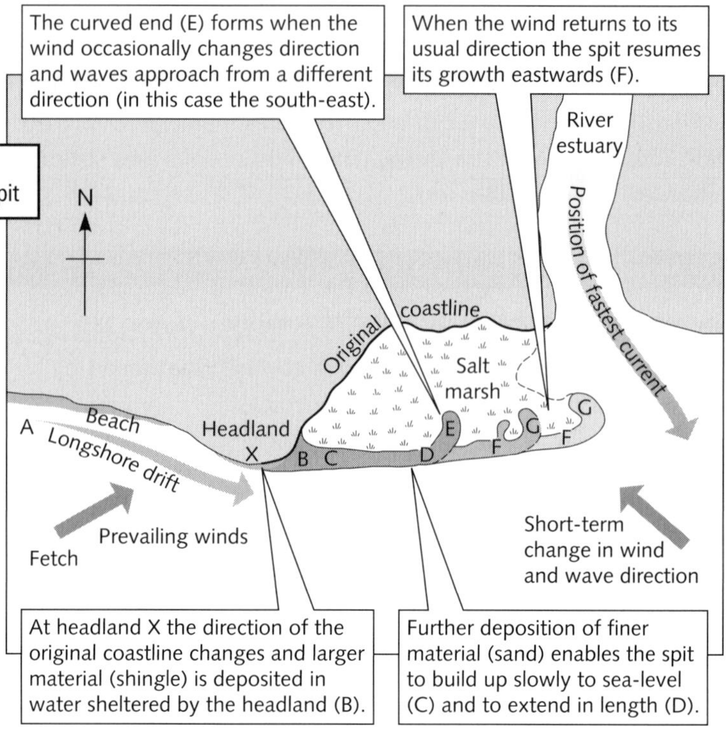

Key words to know

Salt marsh
Bar

In the sheltered water behind the spit a **salt marsh** may develop. The spit is unable to grow across the estuary as the river current carries material out to sea. Should there be no river, the spit may grow across the bay to form a **bar.**

Headlands and bays along the coastline stand out clearly and it is relatively straightforward to identify cliffs and beaches, some with groynes (which are labelled). Smaller features such as wave-cut notches are not identified.

Back to ...

The New Wider World **page 305** to learn about coastal landforms on OS maps.

Check this!...

1 Draw an annotated diagram to show the process of longshore drift.

2 Explain how a spit is formed.

Refer to *The New Wider World* **page 305**.

3 Give a four-figure grid reference for each of the following:
   a) the end of a spit (Figure 18.19)
   b) a beach with groynes (Figures 18.17 and 18.19)
   c) the headland called Peveril Point (Figure 18.17).

4 Name the features found at the following locations:
   a) 055826 (Figure 18.17)
   b) 031770 (Figure 18.17)
   c) 039787 (Figure 18.17).

EXAM PRACTICE

1 Choose either:
a) waterfalls and rapids
or
b) V-shaped valley and interlocking spurs.

Describe your chosen feature and explain how it has been formed by erosional processes. (4)

2 Explain how both erosion and deposition lead to the formation of meanders and ox-bow lakes. Use a series of annotated diagrams to illustrate your answer. (6)

3 Draw a cross-section of a corrie which contains a lake. Add annotations to show how the following processes led to its formation:
a) freeze–thaw
b) plucking
c) abrasion
d) deposition. (6)

4 What is moraine? How does the deposition of moraine lead to the formation of a ribbon lake? (4)

5 Explain the following processes which may occur at the coast:
a) hydraulic action
b) attrition
c) corrosion. (6)

6 Draw an annotated diagram of a spit to show how it is formed by longshore drift. (4)

EXAM TIPS

Features of physical geography (rivers, glaciation and coasts) are often described and explained using diagrams. It is therefore very important that you can draw neat, clear, well-annotated diagrams if necessary in an exam. An annotation is different from a label in that it is more detailed and may often develop a point. For example, on question 2 you will need an annotation linked by an arrow to the outside of the meander bend which explains that the greater speed and force of the water gives it more erosive powers which lead to the formation of a river cliff. If your annotations are not clearly linked to the correct part of your diagram by an arrow the examiner may not be able to award you any marks.

Back to ...

The New Wider World Coursemates website to check your answers to the exam practice questions.

2 The human world

KEY IDEAS

1. Rates of population change vary from place to place and over time
2. Population structure and characteristics vary from place to place
3. People live in a variety of settlements of different sizes, made up of distinct zones

Key words to know

Population explosion
LEDCs
Fertility rate

➪ *The New Wider World*, pp6–15, 17, 22, 25, 27–29, 34–37, 40–49, 81, 86

1 Rates of population change vary from place to place and over time

Global population change

During the last 200 years the world's population has grown at an increasingly faster pace, a process referred to as a **population explosion.**

Figure 2.1 World population growth

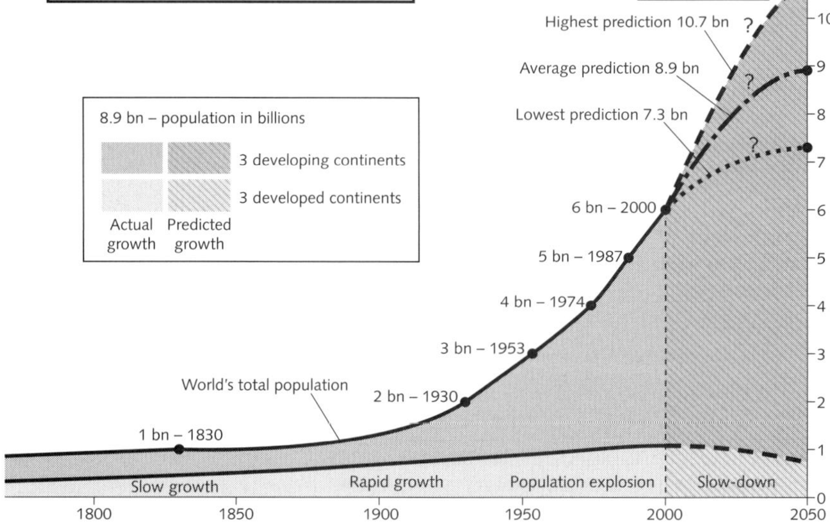

This growth rate, which was even higher in the less economically developed countries (**LEDC**s) caused increasing concern. Early estimates suggested that the world's population of 3 billion in 1960 would reach 7.6 billion by the end of the twentieth century and 11 billion by 2050. In October 1999, however, the world's population reached the 6 billion mark (lower than predicted) and there is continued evidence of a slowing in the total population growth rate. This is due to a number of factors, as Figure 2.2 shows.

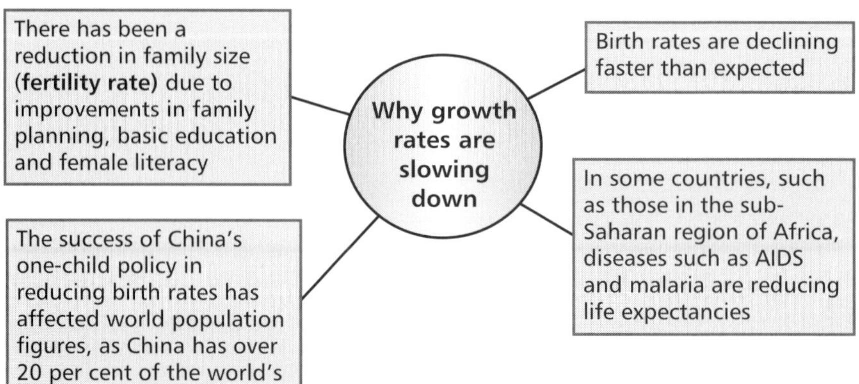

Figure 2.2 Factors reducing world population growth

The balance between birth rate and death rate

Population change depends upon the balance between the **birth rate** (the average number of live births in a year for every 1000 people in the total population) and the **death rate** (the average number of deaths in a year per 1000 people in the population). The difference between the birth rate and the death rate is the **natural increase** (where the birth rate is higher) or the **natural decrease** (where the death rate is higher).

LEDCs generally have a higher birth rate and therefore a greater increase in total population than **MEDCs** (more economically developed countries). This leads to uneven patterns of growth and distribution of population between continents, as Figure 2.3 shows.

Key words to know

Birth rate
Death rate
Natural increase
Natural decrease
MEDCs

Figure 2.3 Population growth and distribution by continent

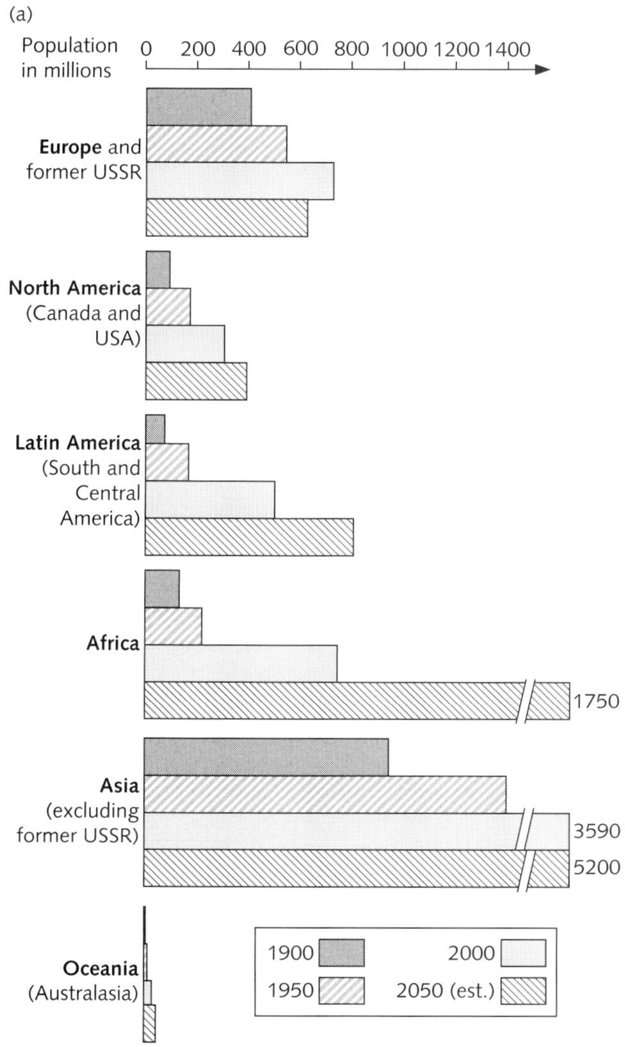

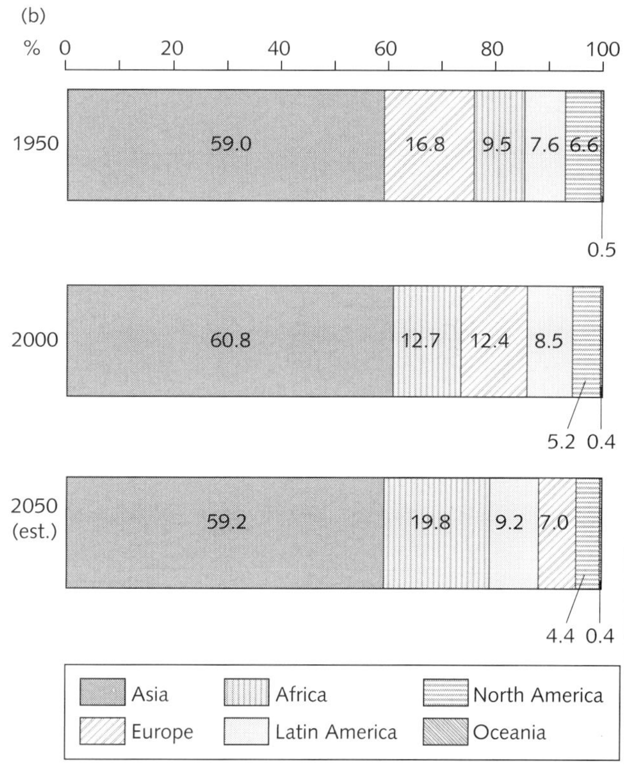

- The developing continents of Africa, Asia and Latin America have the fastest population growth rates.
- Africa has the fastest growth rate despite its high death rate caused by AIDS, crop failure and civil war.
- The developed continents of Europe, North America and Australasia have the slowest growth rates.
- Europe is likely to show a population decrease by the middle of the twenty-first century.
- Most of the world's population live in Asia, with approximately 40% in China and India.

Check this!...

1. What was the population explosion?
2. How did trends in global population change towards the end of the twentieth century?
3. List the factors which are causing a slowing-down of global population growth rates.
4. Describe the differences in population growth rates between MEDCs and LEDCs.
5. Which continent has the largest total population?
6. Describe what has happened to Europe's population contribution (percentage) to the total world population since 1950.

Key words to know

Migration
Economic migrant
Source country
Host country

Back to ...

The New Wider World **page 22** for Figures 2.1 and 2.2 and information on the different types of migration; and Figure 2.3 for examples of major international migrations since 1945.

The New Wider World **pages 28–29** for more detailed information on the movement of Turkish workers into West Germany between 1945 and 1989; and **pages 30–31** for another example of economic migration from Mexico into California.

Change due to migration

Population is also affected by **migration** (the movement of people from one place to another). Migration can be divided into:

- temporary: daily or seasonal movements
- permanent (involving a change in place of residence): both between countries and within a country.

International migration often includes **economic migrants** – people moving voluntarily from one country to another, hoping to find jobs, a higher standard of living and a better quality of life. These migrants are often males aged between 19 and 45. When large numbers are involved, this may alter the population structure and create advantages and disadvantages in both the **source country** (where the migrants came from) and the **host country** (where they moved to).

The movement of Turks into Germany after the Second World War, for example, led to an imbalance between the sexes and the different age groups (Figure 2.4 – see pages 21–24 for more information on population structure).

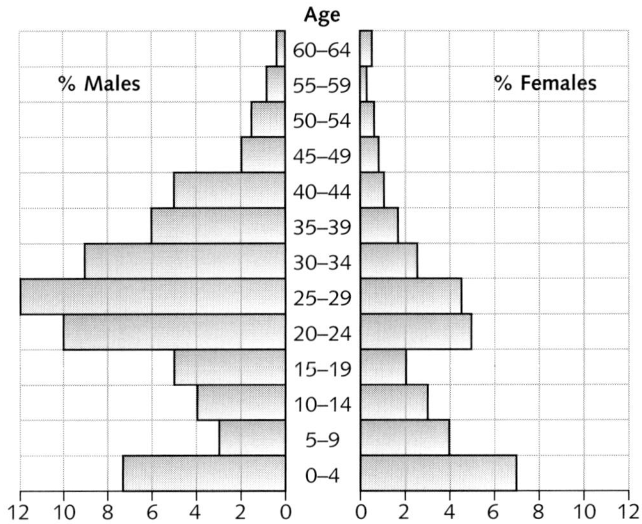

Figure 2.4 Age–sex structure for Turks in the former West Germany

On the source country	On the host country
• Lowers birth rate as migrants are often people of child-bearing age • Loses people in the working age group so the dependency ratio may rise • Loses people most likely to have an education and skills • Many males leave, causing an unbalanced structure • Leaves behind an elderly population with a high death rate	• Overcomes labour shortage • In a developing country, migrants could increase the number of skilled workers • Ethnic groups may not integrate, leading to racial tension • Language difficulties and lack of opportunities for migrants to practise their own religion, culture etc.

Figure 2.5 Effects of migration on population

Check this!...

1 a) What is migration?
b) What is an economic migrant?

2 How can the arrival of large numbers of economic migrants affect the population structure of a country?

3 Describe some other effects of migration on both the source and host countries.

Reasons for changing patterns of birth rates and death rates

The reasons for changing patterns of birth and death rates can be divided into:

- medical
- economic
- social
- political.

Category of reason	Birth rates	Death rates
Medical	As medical improvements lower the **infant mortality rate** (number of babies who die before they reach their first birthday out of every 1000 live births), birth rate subsequently falls as parents no longer need to have more children in the hope that some will survive.	Improvements in medical care lead to a fall in death rates as more diseases are treatable
Economic	Increased wealth is associated with a falling birth rate (as has happened in MEDCs such as the UK) whereas in many LEDCs children are needed to work to grow food for the family, so birth rates remain high.	Sometimes in a wealthy, developed society with an ageing population, death rates from heart problems and cancer may rise.
Social	The changing role of women in society, greater equality and the use of contraception leads to a fall in the birth rate.	Improvements in sanitation and the provision of a clean water supply can reduce death rates in LEDCs.
Political	Strict government schemes, e.g. China's one-child policy, have been accompanied by a fall in birth rates, although in India, where the population comprises people with a variety of cultures, religions and languages, it has not be so easy for the government to influence birth rates.	In a situation of political unrest, or when a country is at war, death rates may temporarily rise.

Figure 2.6 Reasons for changing patterns of birth and death rates

Key words to know

Infant mortality rate
Demographic transition model

The demographic transition model

The **demographic transition model** shows the relationship between birth rates and death rates over a period of time (Figure 2.7).

Figure 2.7 The demographic transition model

	STAGE 1 HIGH FLUCTUATING	STAGE 2 EARLY EXPANDING	STAGE 3 LATE EXPANDING	STAGE 4 LOW FLUCTUATING	POSSIBLE STAGE 5 LOW FLUCTUATING
	Very high, fluctuating birth rates are due to a lack of family planning and the need for agricultural labour. High death rates are the result of high infant mortality, famine, poor hygiene and little medical science. As a result of high birth and death rates population growth is small.	Death rates fall as medical care, sanitation, water and food supply all improve, leading to rapid population growth.	Birth rates fall rapidly due to family planning, increased industrialisation, increased desire for material possessions and the emancipation of women. Population increases slowly.	Both birth and death rates are low, giving a steady population.	Slight fall in birth rate.

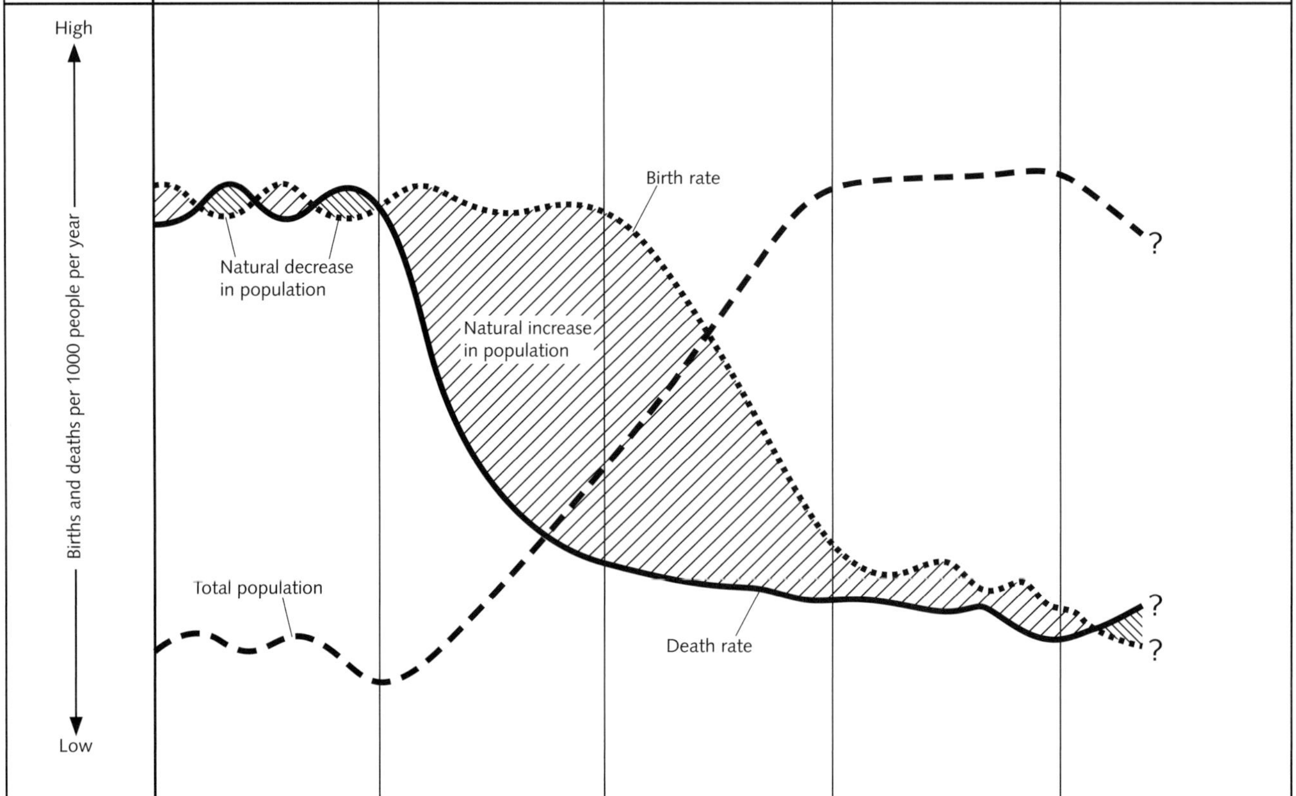

Present world examples	Rainforest tribes	Kenya, Zimbabwe, Bangladesh	Brazil, Mexico, Egypt, India	China, Japan, USA, France	Germany, Italy, Spain
(UK sequence)	(Pre-1760)	(1760–1880)	(1880–1940)	(Post-1940)	?

Back to ...

The New Wider World **pages 6–7** for more information on the demographic transition model; Figure 1.6 for examples of birth rates, death rates and countries at each stage of the model.

Check this!...

1 What different factors affect birth and death rates?

2 What is a natural increase in population?

3 What are the characteristics of each stage of the demographic transition model?

4 Give an example of one country for each stage of the model.

2 Population structure and characteristics vary from place to place

Population can be classified according to age, sex, ethnicity, religion and occupation. Knowing about population structure can help governments to predict changes in the working population and demand for housing, and to plan facilities and services for the young and elderly. Population structures can also be compared between LEDCs and MEDCs, between different settlements and between areas within a settlement.

Key words to know

Census
Life expectancy
Population (age–sex) pyramid

How information on population is collected

In the United Kingdom a **census** is held every 10 years in the form of a questionnaire completed by every household. Apart from an interruption during the Second World War a census has been completed in the UK every 10 years between 1801 and 2001. Although most countries now have some sort of census, their frequency and accuracy varies enormously. In India, for example, it is extremely difficult to obtain proper data, especially in isolated rural areas.

Differences between MEDCs and LEDCs – an overview

There are links between stages of the demographic transition model and population structure.

- Countries at stages 2 and 3 of the demographic transition model are less economically developed and have a higher birth rate than those more economically developed countries which are at stage 4. A high birth rate results in a high proportion of the total population being aged 15 or under. In Africa and much of southern Asia this proportion is likely to be over 40 per cent and in Latin America over 30 per cent. In comparison, in MEDCs it is often under 20 per cent.
- In contrast, in MEDCs there has been a falling birth rate and an increase in **life expectancy** (the number of years that a person born might be expected to live). This means that an increasingly higher proportion of a country's population lives beyond 65, and even beyond 80.

Population pyramids

Population structure can be shown by a **population pyramid,** also known as an **age–sex pyramid**.

Population pyramids produce four idealised types of graph representing different stages of development, as shown in Figure 2.9.

Figure 2.8 Population pyramid for the UK

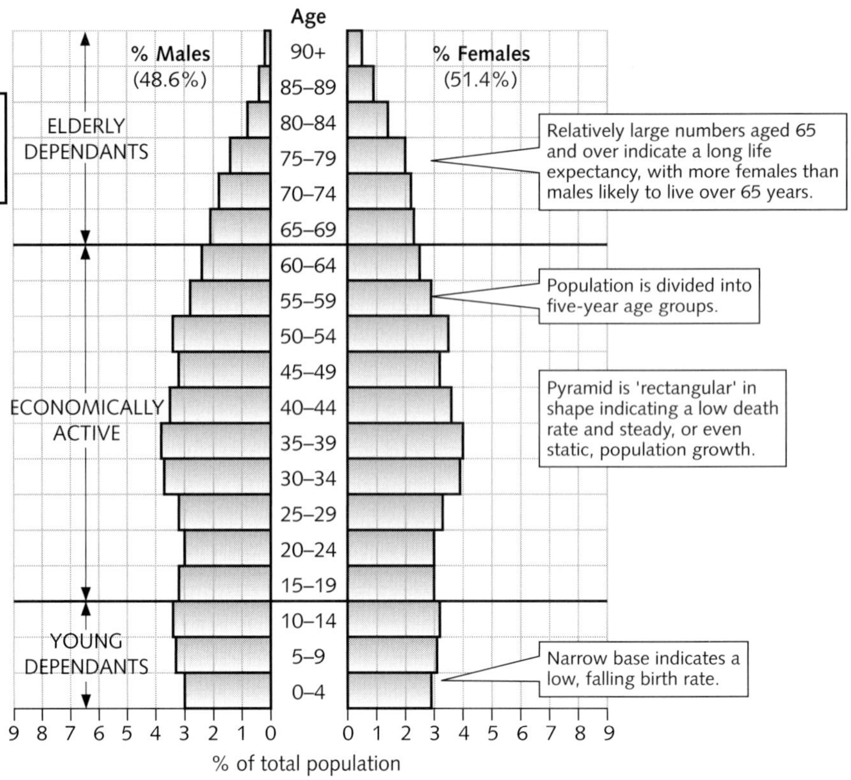

Figure 2.9 Changing population structures

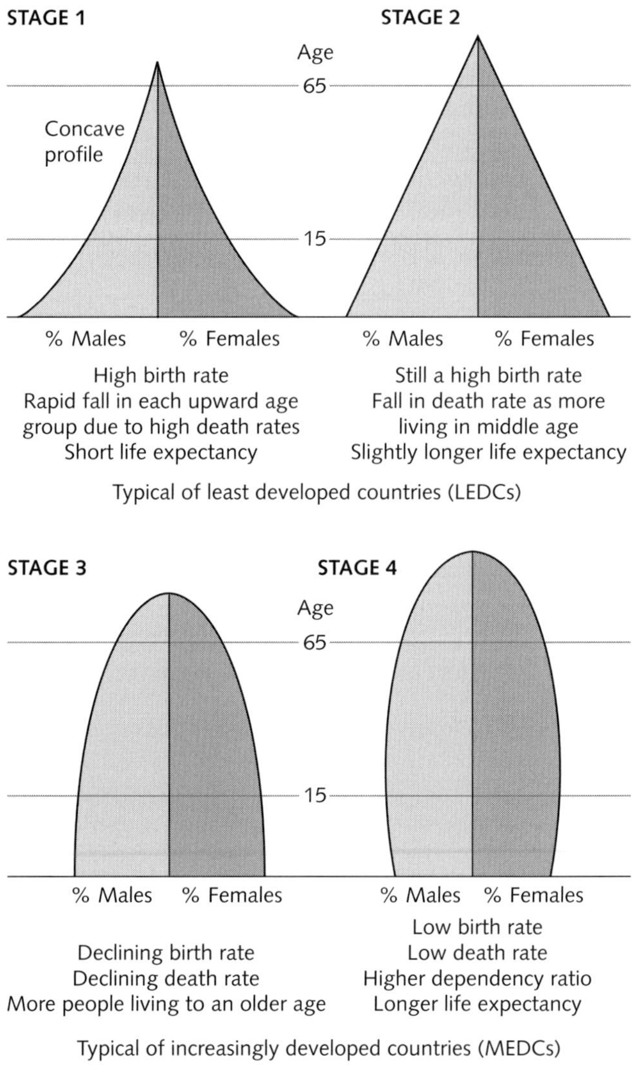

Back to ...

The New Wider World **page 9** Figure 1.9 for examples of population pyramids of countries at different stages of development.

Differences between rural and urban population structures

Differences between rural and urban population structures are often more apparent in LEDCs than in MEDCs. In rural areas, migration to the cities creates a shortage of young adults, particularly males. As a result the urban population structure is likely to show a bulge in the 20–35 age range. In rural areas, most people are employed in **primary** economic activities (those using the Earth's resources, e.g. farming), whereas in urban areas people are more likely to be employed in **secondary** (manufacturing) and **tertiary** (service) activities.

Key words to know

Primary
Secondary
Tertiary

Figure 2.10 Differences in urban and rural populations in an LEDC

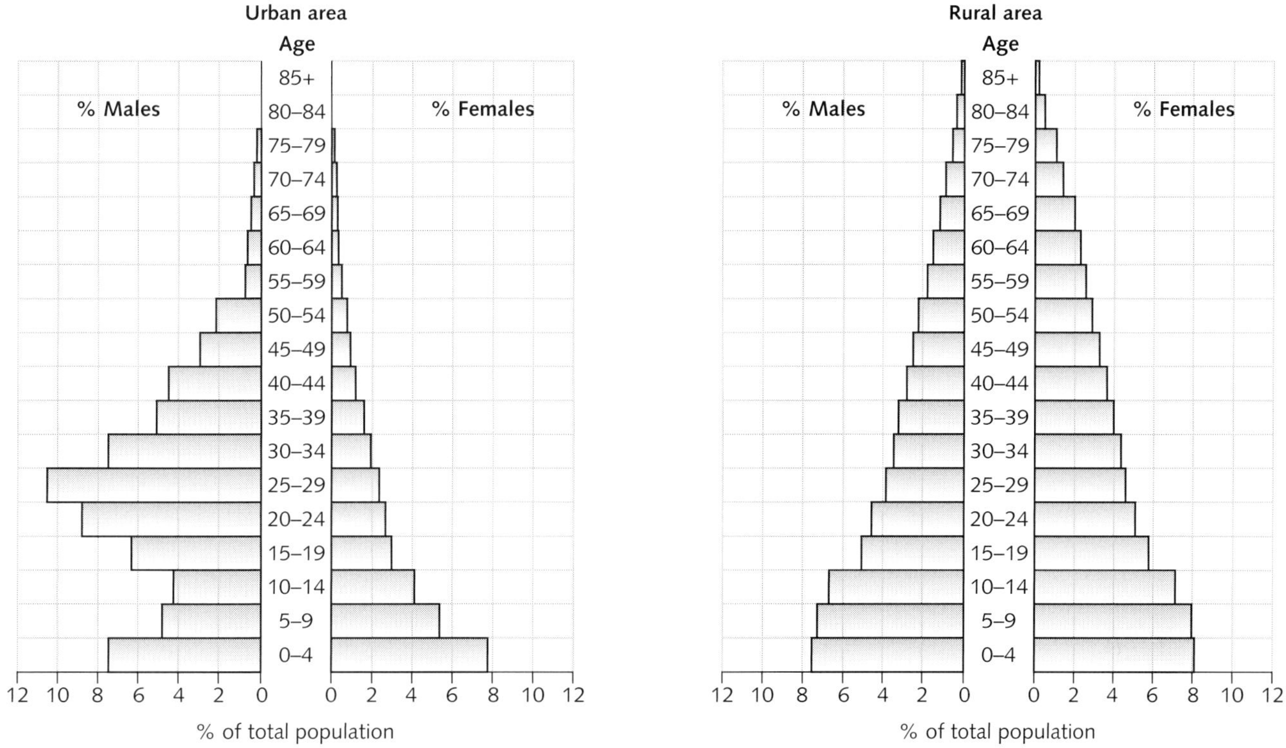

In MEDCs young people also move to the cities in search of employment but additionally there is a movement of people away from urban areas due to:

- a desire for retirement homes in rural areas with a better quality of life
- a desire by people with children for larger homes in a more pleasant environment.

The dependency ratio

Key words to know

Dependency ratio

The population pyramid for the UK (Figure 2.8) shows a relatively smaller number in the 15–64 age group, which is the one that produces children and most of the national wealth. This can be shown as the **dependency ratio:**

$$\frac{\text{Non-economically active (i.e. children 0–14 and elderly 65+)}}{\text{Economically active (i.e. those of working age 15–64)}} \times 100$$

e.g. UK 2001 (figures in millions):

$$\frac{11.105 + 9.341}{38.342} \times 100 = \text{dependency ratio of } 53.33$$

This means that for every 100 people of working age there were 53.33 people dependent on them. Compared with 1971, the dependency ratio had fallen slightly. This was because despite a fall in Britain's birth rate, there had been an increase in the number of economically active people and an increase in life expectancy. Most developed countries have a dependency ratio between 50 and 70, whereas in developing countries the ratio is often over 100 due to the large numbers of children.

Check this!...

1 Why is it useful to know about the population structure of a country?

2 Describe how information on population is collected.

3 Explain what a population pyramid shows.

4 How might the population structure of the UK change in the future?

5 Explain the differences in population structures between rural and urban areas in an LEDC.

6 What is the dependency ratio?

The impact of youthful and ageing populations

Key words to know

Youthful population

If a country has a large percentage of young people and/or older people (i.e. a high dependency ratio) this will affect the provision of social services such as health, education, housing and pensions as well as employment levels. Many LEDCs have a large **youthful population** (high percentages of people aged 20 and below). This means that:

- there is a great demand for child health care and education – two services that LEDCs cannot afford
- in the future, there will be more people reaching child bearing age, possibly leading to a population explosion.

- Many children are needed to help us work on the land, to carry wood and water, and to care for us when we are old.
- A high infant mortality rate means that many children die before their first birthday.
- Religious beliefs may forbid birth control.

- A lack of education, especially for women, has an effect on family planning.
- There is a lack of access to and insufficient money for the supply of contraceptives.
- A large family can enhance a family's reputation for the local community, especially for the husband.

Figure 2.11 Why birth and fertility rates are high in LEDCs

It is now recognised that the way to reduce birth rates is by making improvements in:

- family planning:
  - increasing the knowledge of contraception methods and access to family planning services
  - reducing the cost and increasing the supply of contraception commodities
  - overcoming the disapproval of husbands and the opposition of certain religious groups
- health care – including safer abortions and a reduction in infant mortality
- women's education and status – this delays marriage and gives women the right to decide between having more children or using birth control.

In contrast, MEDCs often have an **ageing population** structure due to better health care. This means that there are more people living who are aged 65 and over.

Figure 2.12 Percentage of population over 65 years, 1950–2020

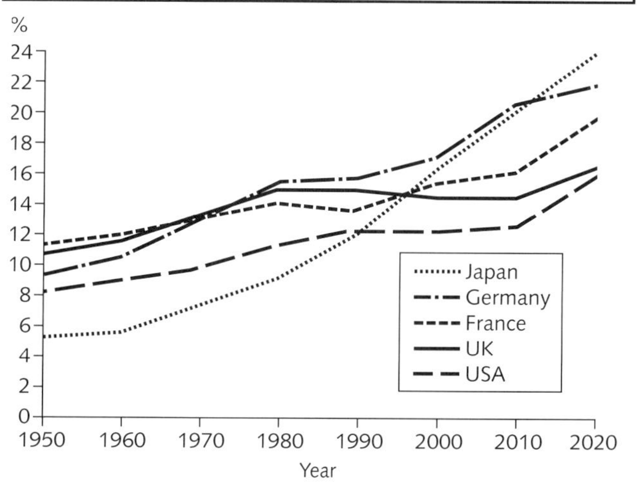

Governments have to plan for future service needs, such as old people's homes. The UK government is already facing the problem of providing pensions and social care for its ageing population. In countries like Germany, Italy and Spain, birth rates are at, or lower than, death rates. The **replacement rate**, which is when there are just sufficient children born to balance the number of people who die, is not being met. This may leave too few skilled workers to keep the economy going and a reduction in the country's competitive advantage in science and technology.

Check this!...

1 What problems are faced by a government in a country with large numbers of children?

2 Why are these problems usually found in LEDCs?

3 What problems are created in a country with an ageing population for:
   a) the government
   b) the elderly people themselves?

Key words to know

Ageing population
Replacement rate

Back to ...

The New Wider World **page 17** for more information on Brazil's youthful population.

The New Wider World **page 13** for the case study on China's one-child policy, an attempt to reduce birth rates.

The New Wider World **pages 14–15** for more detail of ageing populations in Italy and China; Figure 1.19 for the problems of an ageing population.

3 People live in a variety of settlements of different sizes, made up of distinct zones

Key words to know

Settlement
Site
Situation
Wet point site
Dry point site
Nodal point
Bridging point
Dispersed
Nucleated
Linear

A **settlement** is a place where people live. It can be large or small, permanent or temporary. Although each settlement is unique, it is likely to share similar characteristics with other settlements.

Location of settlements

A variety of physical and economic factors affect the location, shape and growth of settlements. Physical factors include:

- drainage
- gradient
- water supply.

Economic factors include:

- transport links
- mineral resources
- port functions.

The location of a settlement is related to its **site** and **situation**.

- **Site** is the point at which a settlement is located. Very often physical factors were important in choosing the initial site of a settlement.
- **Situation** is where the settlement is located in relation to surrounding features such as other settlements, mountains, rivers and communications. It is the situation of a settlement that determines whether or not it will continue to grow to become a large town or city, or whether it remains as a small hamlet or village.

Figure 2.13 Sites for early settlements

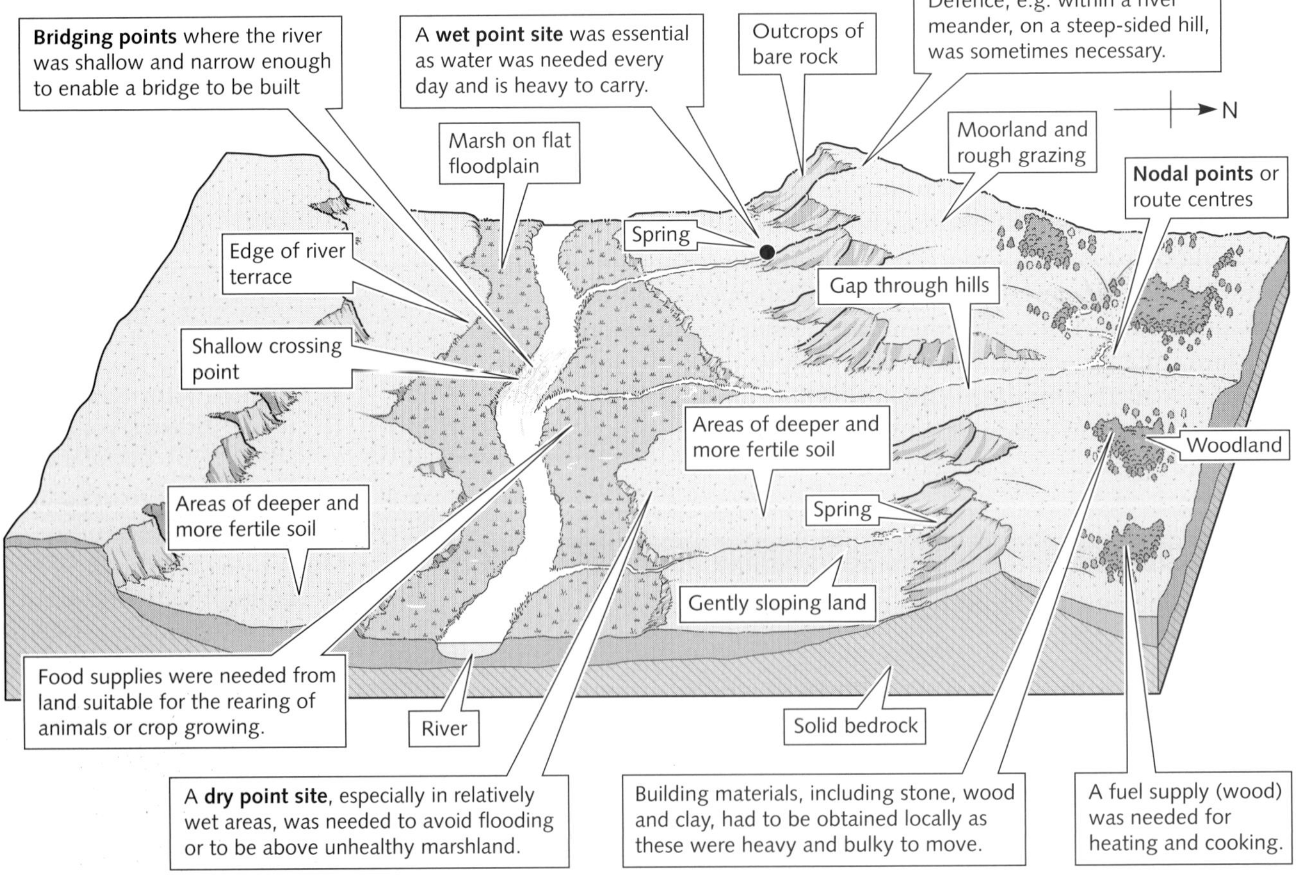

Settlement patterns

Settlements can be divided into three types according to their shape.

Key word to know

Function

Figure 2.14 Settlement patterns

Dispersed: an isolated, individual building, or a group of two or three buildings, perhaps forming a hamlet, and separated from the next group by 2–3 km, e.g. mountainous parts of Scotland.

Nucleated: several buildings grouped together, initially for defensive purposes and later for social and economic reasons, e.g. in the English Midlands.

Linear (street): buildings strung out along a line of communication (e.g. a main road), a river valley (e.g. in South Wales) or a canal or dyke (e.g. English Fens).

Settlement function

The **function** of a settlement relates to its economic and social development and refers to its main activities.

Back to ...

The New Wider World **pages 36–37** Figures 3.7, 3.8 and 3.9, photographs of dispersed, nucleated and linear settlements.

Figure 2.15 Types of function

		UK example	World example
Market towns	Originally collecting and distribution centres for surrounding farming area. Today they may service and process agricultural machinery and produce.	York	Winnipeg
Mining towns	Developed to exploit local mineral or fuel.	Corby	Prudhoe Bay
Industrial–manufacturing	Where raw materials are processed into manufactured goods.	Birmingham	Pittsburgh
Ports	Located on coasts, rivers and lakes for the movement of goods and people from land to sea, or vice versa.	Southampton	Thunder Bay
Route centres	At the convergence of several natural routes, or at nodal points resulting from economic development.	Carlisle	Paris
Commercial	Providing the needs of industry and business.	London	Hong Kong
Cultural/religious	Attracting people, perhaps for a short period, for educational and religious purposes.	Cambridge	Rome
Administrative	Developed to control areas which may vary from a small region (county town) to a country (capital city)	Exeter	Brasilia
Residential	Where the majority or residents live but do not work	Telford	Marne-la-Vallée
Tourist resorts	Includes spa towns, coastal and mountain resorts	Bath	Orlando

Back to ...

The New Wider World **pages 40–41** for information on settlements and OS maps.

Larger settlements tend to be multi-functional (i.e. they have several functions), although one is likely to be predominant, e.g. Cambridge is a university town, Dover is a port. In some cases the original function may no longer be applicable. In other cases, functions have changed over time, e.g. a former South Wales mining town may now be a location for high-tech industry.

Settlements are shaded in brown on the 1:50 000 OS map on page 41 of *The New Wider World*. You can tell from the shape of a rural settlement whether it is dispersed, nucleated or linear. It is sometimes possible to work out the original site factors for a settlement – for example, one reason for the original location of Hedon (2928) may have been the availability of water.

Check this!...

1 What is the difference between the site and the situation of a settlement?

2 Describe the types of sites which were used for early settlements.

3 Using diagrams, explain the difference between dispersed, nucleated and linear settlements.

4 How might the function of a settlement change through time?

Use *The New Wider World* **page 41** Figure 3.18.

5 Give grid references for examples of:
a) an isolated farm
b) a small hamlet
c) a nucleated village
d) a linear village or residential area.

6 Suggest some original site factors for the following villages:
a) Burstwick (2227)
b) Preston (2830, 2930)
c) Elstronwick (2232, 2332).

Key words to know

Urbanisation
Urban land use model
Central business district (CBD)

Settlement growth and structure

Urbanisation means an increase in the proportion of people living in towns and cities. The rapid growth of industry in the nineteenth century led to large-scale urbanisation in the UK. During the twentieth century, people continued to move to urban areas for several reasons:

- more and better-paid jobs
- nearness to places of work and entertainment
- better housing, services (schools and hospitals), shopping facilities and education.

Back to ...

The New Wider World **pages 42–43** for the factors which led to the creation of functional zones within cities.

Land use zones in MEDC towns and cities

The characteristics and location of different functional zones in cities are often compared using **urban land use models**. A model is a theoretical framework which may not actually exist, but which helps to explain reality.

Figure 2.16 Urban land use models

Burgess: the **central business district (CBD)** contains the main retail and commercial functions and is in the centre of a town. Towns grew outwards in a concentric pattern, resulting in circles based on the age of houses and the wealth of their occupants, with newer buildings and wealthier occupants on the outskirts.

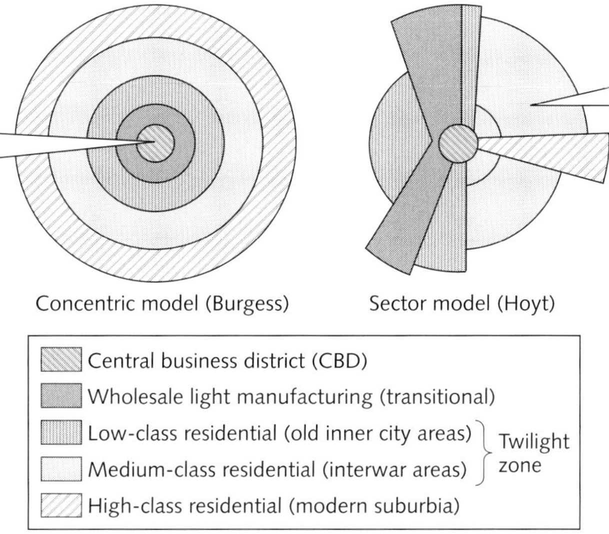

Hoyt: urban areas developed in sectors, or wedges, alongside main transport routes into and out of a city. Different types of industry and associated low-cost housing locate in the same sector.

Case Study

Land use in an MEDC town – Burnley, Lancashire

Back to ...

The New Wider World **page 43** Figure 3.23, a map showing land use in Burnley.

Using your case study

You need to be able to describe the growth, characteristics and land use patterns in Burnley. For example, is there evidence of any outward growth over time? The map can be used to compare Burnley with the two land use models (Burgess and Hoyt) – look for similarities and try and explain any differences.

Case study links

Compare the Burnley case study with that of Rio de Janeiro on page 32 of this book.

Update

Go to *The New Wider World Coursemates* website for a link to look at different scale maps of Burnley, in order to work out its shape and make comparisons with the urban models.

Learn it!

1 Where is Burnley? How and why has it grown?

2 Draw a simplified land use map of Burnley. Add annotations to show which factors are important in determining its layout and to make comparisons with the urban land use models, e.g. wealthier houses have been built on the outskirts as Burgess's model suggests, although they do not occupy a complete ring around the town.

Check this!...

1 What is urbanisation?

2 Why have people moved to towns and cities since the nineteenth century?

3 What is an urban land use model?

Characteristics of land use zones in MEDC towns and cities

CBD (central business district)

The major land users in the CBD are those which need to be accessible to large numbers of people and can afford the high cost of land.

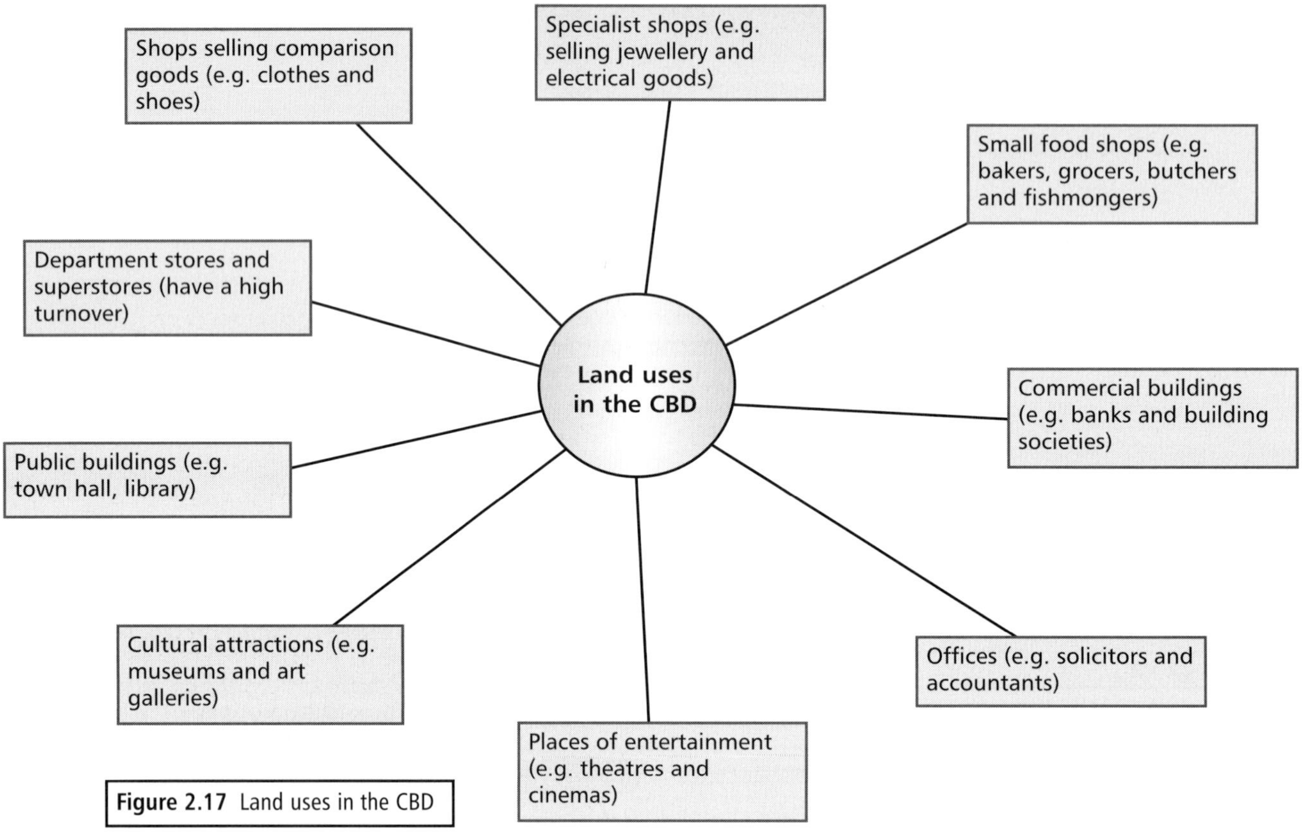

Figure 2.17 Land uses in the CBD

Back to ...

The New Wider World **pages 58–59** for more information on changes in the CBD.

Many CBDs became increasingly congested with pedestrians and traffic which reduced their accessibility and attractiveness as a place to either shop or work. As a result, many CBDs have undergone improvements such as the creation of pedestrianised zones and the development of shopping malls.

Twilight zone

Around the CBD is a zone which is undergoing great change as older, often derelict sites are being redeveloped. Land use is mixed and this zone is also known as the **transitional zone**.

Key word to know

Transitional zone

Industrial areas

Originally industry was found in the inner city areas, where large factories were built during the Industrial Revolution. They were located:

- on the nearest available land to the town centre and where there was enough space for large buildings
- next to canals and, after the 1840s, to railways which were needed to transport the heavy, bulky raw materials and the finished manufactured goods
- beside rivers which, initially used as a source of power, provided water for washing and cooling and a means of disposing of waste
- next to land that could be used to house the large number of workers who were needed.

Since then many factories have been forced to close due to a lack of space for expansion and modernisation, or due to narrow, congested roads. Some factories have been left empty, while others have been pulled down to leave large areas of derelict land. Newer purpose-built industrial estates have developed on the edge of towns and cities where land was cheaper, more was available and access was easier.

Key words to know

High density
Slum clearance
Urban redevelopment
Urban renewal
Suburbia
Urban sprawl
Commuting

Check this!...

1 Where is the CBD and what are the main land uses in this zone?

2 Why have many CBDs undergone great changes?

3 What is the twilight zone?

4 How has the location of industry changed?

Residential areas

Inner city	Suburbs (suburbia)	Rural–urban fringe
• Developed around the CBD alongside industry in the nineteenth century. • People needed low-cost houses close to their place of work. • **High-density** terraces built in straight rows and laid out in a grid-iron pattern. • Few amenities, either in the house (no indoor toilet, bathroom, running water, sewerage or electricity) or around it (no gardens or open spaces). • Attempts made to improve living conditions, in the 1960s by bulldozing large areas (**slum clearance**) and building high-rise flats (**urban redevelopment**) and later by improving existing properties (**urban renewal**).	• In the inter-war period (1920s and 1930s) private, car-dependent suburbs were built in a process of outward growth known as **urban sprawl.** • Houses were semi-detached with bay windows, garages and front and back gardens. • Residents had to travel long distances to their place of work – a process known as **commuting.**	• Private estates with low-density, high-quality housing; large, detached houses with modern amenities both indoors (central heating, double glazing, deluxe bathroom and kitchen) and outside (large gardens back and front, and even a double garage). • Houses built either in a cul-de-sac or along winding roads that were usually tree lined and relatively free of traffic; small areas left as open spaces. • Out-of-city council housing built during the 1950s and 1960s to rehouse people from inner city areas which were being redeveloped. • A mixture of high-rise tower blocks, low-rise flats and single-storey terraces built at a higher density than on the private estates but lower than in the inner city areas. • Houses were small and lacked gardens and garages, but did have indoor amenities including modern kitchens and bathrooms.

Figure 2.18 Residential areas in towns and cities

Check this!...

1 Describe nineteenth-century inner city housing.

2 Why were high-rise flats not the ideal solution to the poor housing conditions in inner city areas?

3 What factors led to the growth of the suburbs?

4 How were housing estates built in the suburbs different from those in inner city areas?

5 Describe the differences between a private housing estate built on the rural–urban fringe and an outer city council estate.

Back to ...

The New Wider World **pages 44–47** for photographs of the different types of residential areas; and pages **48–49** for additional photographs, street plans and statistics of different residential areas.

Key words to know
Shanty settlement

Land use zones in LEDC towns and cities

Cities in developing countries also develop their own distinctive pattern, which is different from that in an MEDC city.

Figure 2.19 Urban land use model for an LEDC

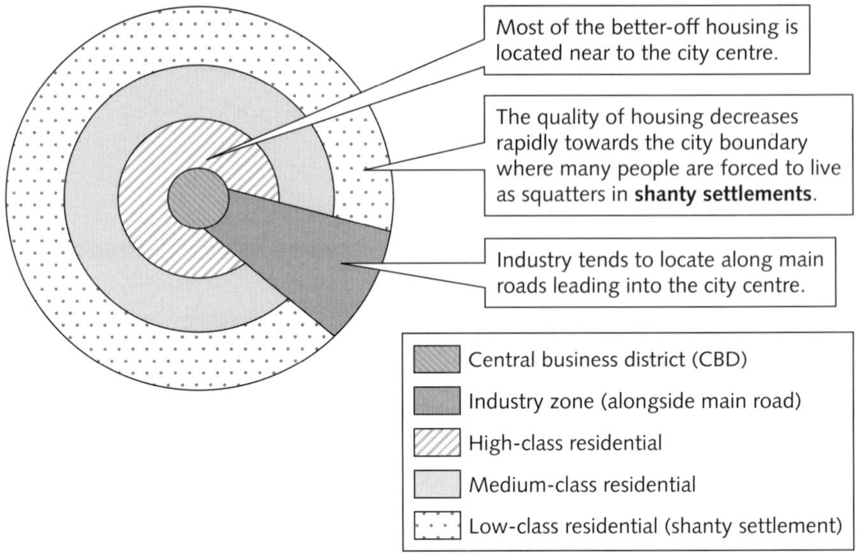

Back to ...

The New Wider World **page 81** Figure 5.10, a land use model for a developing city based on Brazil.

The New Wider World **page 82** for details of housing for the well-off and housing for the poor in São Paulo, Brazil; **page 84** for information on housing in Kolkata, India.

In most cities in developing countries there is an extreme contrast between the living conditions of the well-off, who usually live near the city centre, and those of the poor, who are forced to live near the city boundary.

Case Study

Land use in an LEDC city – Rio de Janeiro, Brazil

Back to ...

The New Wider World **page 86** for a land use map of Rio de Janeiro (Figure 5.22) and some information on the housing in Rio.

Using your case study

You need to be able to describe the growth, characteristics and land use of Rio. The map can be used to compare Rio to the LEDC land use models – look for similarities and try to explain any differences. You should also compare it with the MEDC case study of Burnley on page 29 of this book.

Update

Go to *The New Wider World Coursemates* website for a link giving information on how Rio can be divided into three main zones.

Learn it!

1 Where is Rio de Janeiro? How and why has it grown?

2 Draw a simplified land use map of Rio. Add annotations to try and show the important factors in determining its layout and identifying any similarities to and differences from the theoretical LEDC model shown in Figure 2.19.

Check this!...

How is an urban land use model for a city in an LEDC different from one for an MEDC?

EXAM PRACTICE

1 What is a natural increase in population? (2)

2 Explain how a variety of factors can affect both birth and death rates. (4)

3 What is the demographic transition model? (2)

4 Explain why MEDCs and LEDCs are at different stages of the demographic transition model. (4)

5 Draw the outline of a population pyramid for a country with a youthful population. Add annotations to illustrate some of the characteristics of this type of age structure and some of the problems this causes for governments. (6)

6 Draw an annotated diagram to show nucleated, dispersed and linear settlements. (3)

7 Describe how physical and economic factors affect the location, shape and growth of settlements. (5)

8 With reference to named examples, describe how land use patterns in an MEDC town or city are different from those in an LEDC town or city. (4)

EXAM TIPS

There are a number of factors (medical, economic, social and political) which influence population change and structure. It is useful to be able to categorise these and to use this as a way of structuring your answers, e.g. questions 2 and 4. Some of your annotations for the population pyramid in question 5 need to be identified as social, medical and economic.

Back to ...

The New Wider World Coursemates website to check your answers to the exam practice questions.

3 The economic world

KEY IDEAS

1 Economic systems vary spatially and over time

2 Farming systems show different characteristics and have been experiencing change

3 The location of industry changes over time

The New Wider World, pp92–94, 96–98, 101, 106–107, 109, 112–113, 136, 140, 144, 148–149, 192–193

1 Economic systems vary spatially and over time

Types of economic system

An economic activity can be regarded as a **system** with **inputs** into the activity, **processes** that take place and **outputs** that are produced.

- **primary:** industries extracting raw material from the earth or sea, e.g. farming, fishing, forestry and mining
- **secondary:** industries processing and manufacturing primary products, e.g. steelmaking, furniture manufacture and car assembly
- **tertiary:** industries providing a service, e.g. education, health, office work, retailing, transport and entertainment
- **quaternary:** industries providing information and expertise, e.g. micro-electronics.

The proportion of people working in each of the sectors (primary, secondary, etc.) is called the **employment structure,** with figures for each group given as a percentage of the total.

Changes over time

Key words to know

System
Inputs
Processes
Outputs
Primary
Secondary
Tertiary
Quaternary
Employment structure

Figure 3.1 Changing employment structure in the UK, 1800–2000

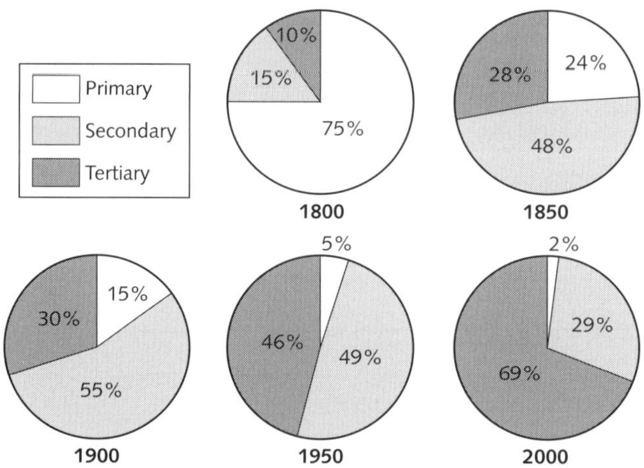

Figure 3.1 shows employment structures for the UK and how they have changed over time. Two hundred years ago, most people worked in the primary sector, as farmers. One hundred years ago, after the Industrial Revolution, many more people worked in the secondary sector in steelworks, shipyards and textile mills. In the twentieth century farming and industry became more mechanised and needed fewer workers. At the same time, more people were needed to work in the tertiary sector, in schools, hospitals, shops, offices and transport.

Differences between places

Figure 3.2 shows:

- changes in employment structure between the economic regions of the UK
- the number of people employed in each region.

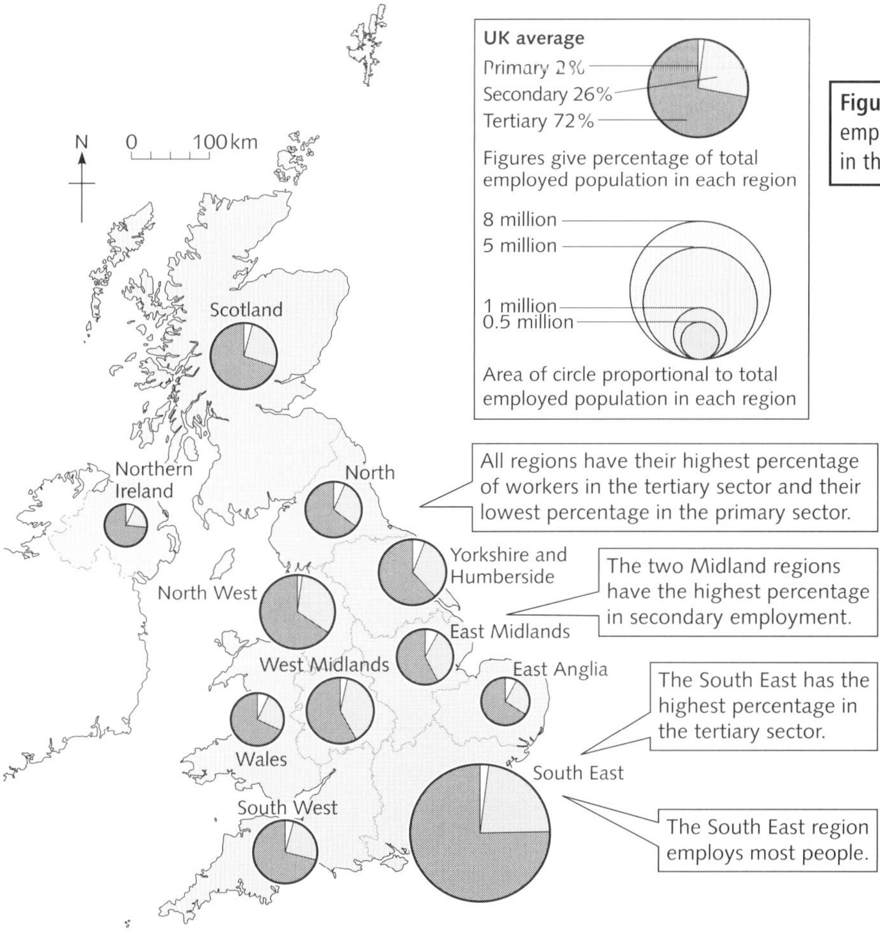

Figure 3.2 Regional employment structure in the UK, 2000

Employment structure and development

There is a link between employment structures and levels of economic development.

Figure 3.3 Employment structure and economic development

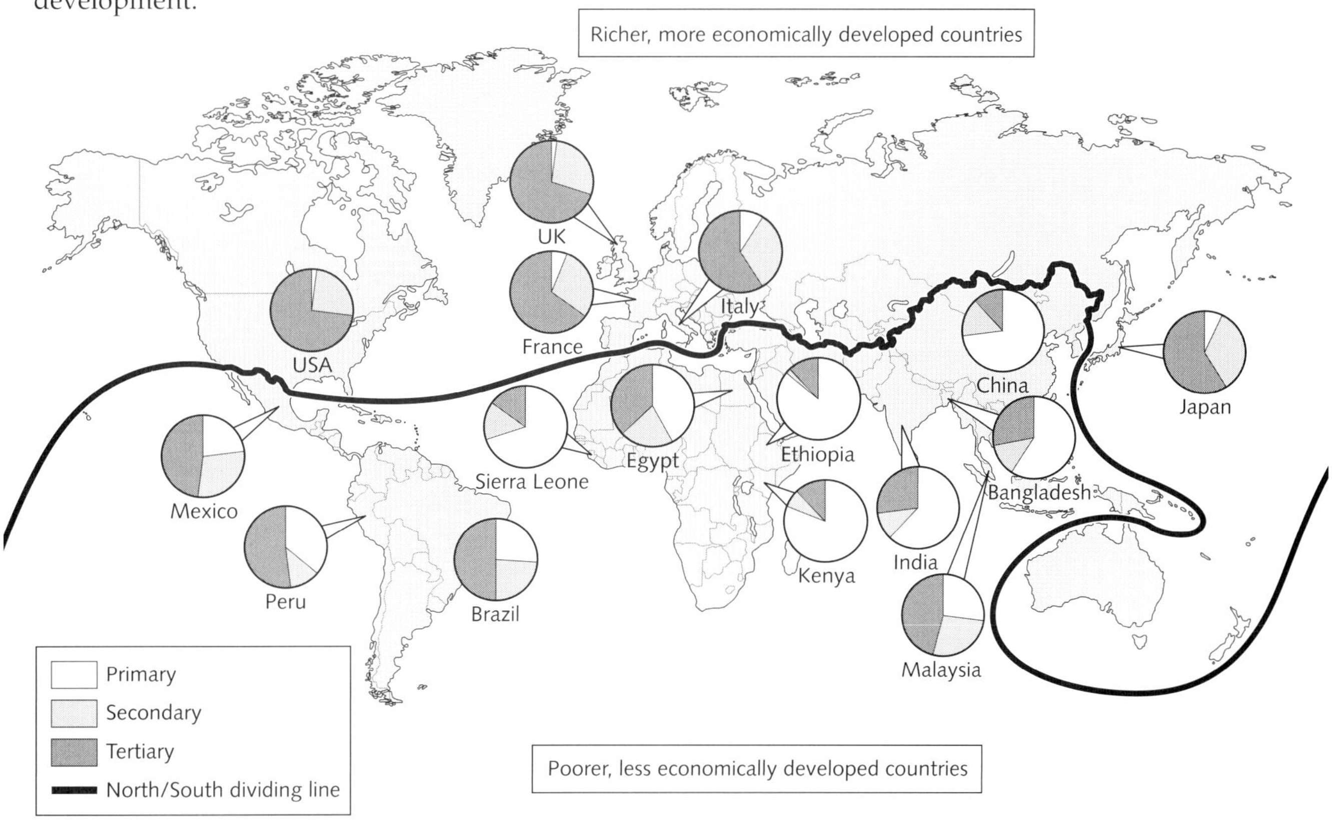

Key words to know

MEDC
LEDC

Figure 3.3 shows that:

- the richer, industrialised and more economically developed countries (**MEDCs**) have a very high percentage in the tertiary sector, a high percentage in the secondary sector and a very low percentage in the primary sector
- the poorer, least industrialised, less economically developed countries (**LEDCs**) have a very high percentage in the primary sector (most are farmers) and a low percentage in both the secondary and tertiary sectors.

Back to ...

The New Wider World **pages 192–193** for information on employment structures in an MEDC (Japan) and an LEDC (Kenya).

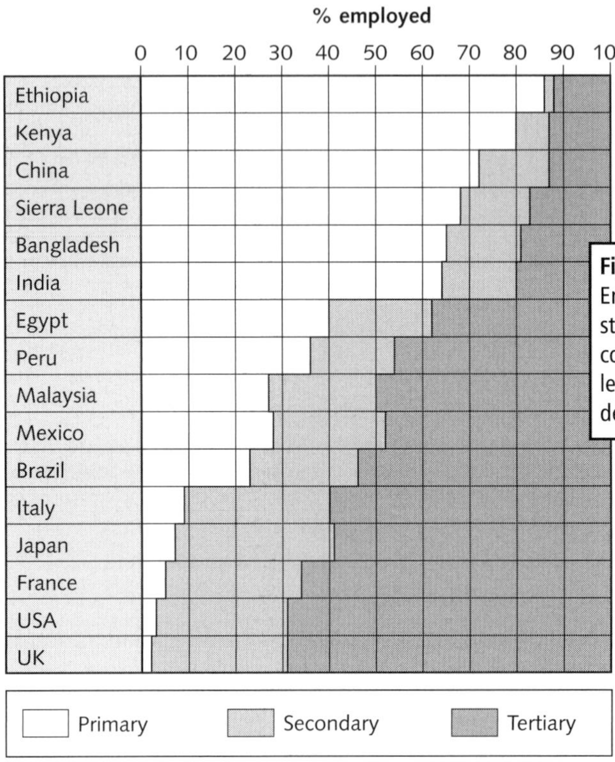

Figure 3.4 Employment structures for countries at different levels of economic development

Check this!...

1. Explain the four types of economic activity.
2. Explain the link between employment structure and levels of economic development.

Figure 3.4 shows a series of countries ranked according to the percentage of the people employed in the primary sector. It is a percentage bar graph, drawn horizontally and with each bar divided into 10 segments. Each bar is then divided into three parts to indicate the percentage of people employed in each economic sector.

2 Farming systems show different characteristics and have been experiencing change

Key words to know

System
Inputs
Processes
Outputs

Characteristics of farming systems

Farming is an industry and operates as a **system**, with **inputs** into the farm, **processes** which take place on the farm and **outputs** from the farm.

There are differences between farming systems in MEDCs and LEDCs, as shown in Figure 3.6.

Figure 3.5 Simplified farming system

INPUTS	PROCESSES	OUPUTS
Physical environment (natural) inputs and human/economic (artificial) inputs	Patterns and methods of farming e.g. growing of crops, rearing of animals	Products for sale e.g. cereals, animal products
Expenditure	Storage	Income

Figure 3.6 Farming systems in MEDCs and LEDCs

In MEDCs, outputs usually exceed inputs, allowing the farmer to make a profit which may then be re-invested.

INPUTS		PROCESSES		OUTPUTS
Skilled labour	Fertiliser	Land	240 hectares	Milk
Electricity	Cattle feed	Animals	40 calves	Pigs
Seeds	Barns for storage		160 cows	Cattle
Rain all year	Low, undulating		50 pigs	Barley
Growing season 8	relief and deep	Crops	Grass	Hay
months	soils		Barley	Manure
Machines			Potatoes	Potatoes
				= Profit

In LEDCs, the output is often consumed by the family with little surplus left for sale.

INPUTS		PROCESSES	OUTPUTS
Plenty of rain	Much labour	2 hectares of land	Rice
Growing season	Hand tools	10 chickens	Some wheat
all year	2 oxen	2 cows	Eggs
Flat land	Rice seed	2 oxen	Chickens
Rich soils		Rice and wheat cultivation	
			= No profit

Farming can be:

- **intensive** (when farm size is small in comparison with either the numbers working there or the amount of money spent on it) or **extensive** (when farm size is very large in comparison with either the amount of money spent on it or the numbers working on it)
- **commercial** (crops grown, animals reared for sale) or **subsistence** (just sufficient food is grown for the farmer's own family)
- **arable** (the growing of crops) or **pastoral** (the rearing of animals).

Key words to know

Intensive
Extensive
Commercial
Subsistence
Arable
Pastoral
Organic farming

Organic farming

Since the mid-1980s some farmers have turned to **organic farming**. Instead of chemical fertilisers and pesticides, natural fertilisers such as animal and green manure and mineral fertilisers such as fish and bonemeal are used. These put organic material back into the soil, enabling it to retain moisture during dry periods, allowing better drainage and aeration during wetter spells and reducing the risk of soil erosion and exhaustion. The advantages of organic farming are:

- less environmental damage
- no nitrate run-off into rivers
- no pesticides to harm wildlife.

There are also some disadvantages of organic farming:

- yields may be lower
- more weeding has to be done
- the extra work involved makes organic products more expensive to buy.

Check this!...

1 Explain how farming can be viewed as a system with inputs, processes and outputs.

2 Describe some of the differences between farming systems in MEDCs and LEDCs.

3 Explain the difference between:
   a) intensive/extensive farming
   b) commercial/subsistence farming
   c) arable/pastoral farming.

4 What is organic farming?

Factors affecting a farmer's choice

Farmer's make decisions on:

- what crops to grow
- which animals to rear
- which methods to use to maximise profits.

These decisions depend on the most favourable physical and human factors although if the farmer has several choices, the final choice may be down to individual preferences. On other occasions, choice may be limited by extreme physical conditions or economic and political pressures.

Figure 3.7 Factors affecting a farmer's choice and the location of farming types

PHYSICAL (ENVIRONMENTAL) FACTORS	
Relief and altitude	Usually the flatter and the more low-lying the land, the more efficient and commercial is the farm (arable in East Anglia). Output tends to decrease as the land gets steeper and higher and farming becomes less commercial and more extensive (pastoral in the Lake District).
Soils	The deeper and richer the soil, the more intensive and commercial the farming (alluvium of the Fens). Ideally soils should be well drained yet capable of retaining water.
Temperature/sunshine	In Scotland, summers are cool and the growing season is too short for most cereals. Moving south, temperatures, the amount of sunshine and the length of the growing season all increase. Aspect is an important local factor (maximum sunlight, protection against frost and wind).
Rainfall/water supply	Areas with adequate and reliable rainfall throughout the year tend to produce good grass for rearing animals (western Britain). Drier areas to the east grow cereals (East Anglia) and fruit (Kent).
HUMAN (SOCIAL) AND ECONOMIC INPUTS	
Land ownership/tenure	Many British farmers own their own farms but some are tenant farmers (the former are usually more commercial). A small, but increasing, number are run by processing companies (frozen foods in East Anglia).
Size of farms/fields	Farms increase in size as larger, more efficient farmers buy up smaller, less successful farms. Field size has also increased, especially where hedgerows have been removed (eastern England). The EU encourages larger farms and larger fields.
Competition for land	Many traditional farming areas, especially near the rural–urban fringe, are under threat from urban sprawl and the demand for new roads, industry, housing and recreation.
Transport and markets	Perishable goods need to be produced near to markets for freshness, and bulky goods near to markets due to their weight. Fruit and vegetables (market gardening) are grown near most large urban areas.
Capital (money)	By world standards, the UK is well-off, so farmers can find money to improve their farm buildings and machinery and to buy fertiliser and good-quality seed and animals.
Mechanisation/ technology	The increased use of labour-saving machinery and computers increases outputs but reduces the need for farm workers. Farms in the south and east tend to be more mechanised than those in the north and west.
POLITICAL FACTORS	
Government/EU policies	Governments have provided grants for new stock and machinery and subsidies to guarantee a fixed income. This now comes from the EU's Common Agricultural Policy (CAP).
Variable inputs	Farmers are vulnerable to changes in government/EU policies, market prices and market demand. They are also affected by changes in the weather (floods, drought and frost) and by disease (foot and mouth, potato blight).

Case Study

Rice farming in the Lower Ganges Valley

Back to …

The New Wider World **pages 112–113** for this case study on wet rice farming in an LEDC: Bangladesh, which is on the Lower Ganges delta.

Using your case study

You need to know the physical and human factors which influence this type of farming in Bangladesh. You should also learn about changes to this type of farming brought about by land reform and the **Green Revolution** (the introduction of high-yielding varieties of crops). Where relevant, learn both good and bad effects of these changes.

Key words to know

Green Revolution

Update

Go to *The New Wider World Coursemates* website for a link giving you a clear summary of intensive subsistence rice farming on the Ganges delta.

Learn it!

1 Where is the Ganges delta?

2 What physical factors (climate, relief, soils) are suited to wet rice cultivation?

3 Wet rice farming is labour intensive – what does this mean?

4 Why is land reform needed in Bangladesh?

Changes affecting farm systems in the EU

Arable farming in East Anglia

The main type of farming in East Anglia is the growing of cereals, mainly wheat and barley, together with root crops (potatoes and sugar beet) and vegetables (peas and beans).

Physical inputs	Human inputs	Variable inputs
Low rainfall (650 mm) which falls mostly during the growing season Warm sunny summers ideal for ripening crops Winter frosts help break up the soil Gently undulating, low-lying land Deep, fertile and well-drained soils	Good road and rail links linking to markets in south-east England Land is ideal for large-scale machinery (combine harvesters, sprayers) Considerable capital available in the region	Possible droughts during the summer Changes in government (EU) policies Disease affecting cereals or other crops

Figure 3.8 Inputs of arable farming in East Anglia

The main processes of arable farming include ploughing, harvesting, weeding, applying fertiliser and pesticides, maintaining field boundaries and machinery. The main outputs are wheat, barley, sugar beet, potatoes, peas and beans.

Recent changes in arable farming include:

- larger farms encouraged by the EU – this has happened in East Anglia as hedgerows have been removed to increase outputs and profits on arable farms
- larger fields for larger machinery due to the removal of hedgerows
- increased use of fertiliser.

However, the result of many of these changes was overproduction and the creation of food surpluses. Consequently the EU introduced further changes, including:

Back to ...

The New Wider World **pages 106–107** for more detailed information on changes in farming in the UK and the EU.

- Reduced subsidies to reduce EU overproduction: these had been an economic burden during the 1970s and 1980s when 70 per cent of the EU budget was spent on supporting farmers. This did mean, however, that farmers lost income.
- An increase in the amount of set-aside land: in order to continue to receive subsidies, farmers were required to take 15 per cent of their land out of cultivation – in other words they are paid not to produce crops. Instead they may leave land fallow or use it for non-agricultural purposes such as recreation and tourism.

Case Study Extra

Lynford House Farm

Lynford House Farm is in the Cambridgeshire Fens, north-west of Ely, and is 570 hectares in size. It is an arable farm on flat, fertile land which is just above sea-level. Average rainfall is 559 mm per year.

- In 2000, 535.6 hectares of land were under arable crops, 6.38 hectares were grassland and 27.1 were set aside.
- The farm employs 2 family members full-time and also 3 general full-time farm workers. At certain times of the year, contractors are employed for muck spreading and lime spreading.
- Large amounts of machinery have been purchased recently, including a combine harvester costing £82,000, a tractor costing £25,000 and fertiliser spreader costing £2,850.
- The farm has specialised buildings for drying grain, cold stores for potatoes and a general farm workshop.
- Some of the inputs needed on an annual basis include fertiliser, which costs £10,495, and pesticides, which cost £43,790.
- The farm belongs to a local cooperative through which chemicals can be bought in bulk to lower costs, and economic advice can be easily obtained.
- The farm produces wheat, sugar beet, potatoes, vining peas and winter linseed. Sugar beet is grown under quota – 4,154 tonnes are allowed.
- Subsidies contribute to 6 per cent of the farmer's total income. These come from the Arable Area Aid, paid on wheat crops, and there are also some payments for the set-aside land.
- Diversification has occurred recently – there are 12 bungalows on the farm which are let out and may be sold in the future. They have become available as fewer farm labourers are needed.

In the future, there may be wind turbines on the farm which will produce enough clean energy for 3500 homes and give the farmer additional income from renting his land to Eastern Generation and Wind Prospect, the two companies involved.

Using your case study

You can use this case study to describe the factors affecting arable farming, i.e. physical factors such as relief and rainfall; human factors such as subsidies and other EU payments. You should also learn some of the inputs, processes and outputs of the farm and how the farmer has diversified to maintain his income.

Update

Go to *The New Wider World Coursemates* website for a link giving more information on Lynford House Farm.

Learn it!

1 Where is Lynford House Farm?

2 List the main physical and human factors which affect land use on this farm.

3 What are the main inputs and outputs of the farm?

4 How has the farm diversified in recent years?

Check this!...

1 Explain, with examples, the main physical factors affecting the type of farming in an area.

2 How can human factors influence farming?

3 The location of industry changes over time

Factors affecting the location of secondary industries in MEDCs

Industry, like farming, can be regarded as a system with inputs into a factory, processes that take place in a factory, and outputs from the factory. For a firm to make a profit and remain in business, the value of its outputs must be greater than the cost of its inputs. Some of the profit should then be re-invested, e.g. in modernising the factory and introducing new technology.

Figure 3.9 Industry as a system

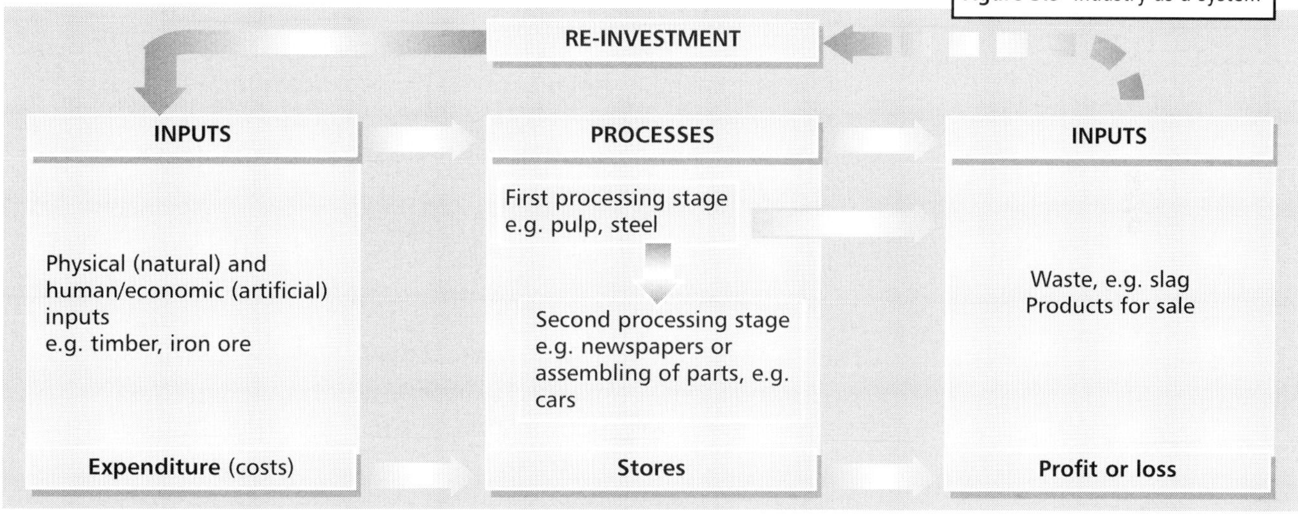

Factories may be built by an individual entrepreneur, a private firm, a nationalised company or a transnational corporation. Decisions are made about the best site for its location, based on physical, economic, political and human factors.

Figure 3.10 Factors affecting the location of industry in the UK

PHYSICAL FACTORS	HUMAN, ECONOMIC AND POLITICAL FACTORS
Raw materials The bulkier and heavier these are to transport, the nearer the factory should be located to the raw materials. This was even more important in times when transport was less developed. **Power – energy** This is needed to work the machines in the factory. Early industry needed to be sited near to fast-flowing rivers or coal reserves, but today electricity can be transported long distances. **Natural routes** River valleys and flat areas were essential in the days before the railway, car or lorry. **Site and land** Although early industry did not at first take up much space, it did need flat land. As the size of plant increased (e.g. steelworks), more land was needed. Ideally such sites should be on low-quality farmland where the cost of purchase is lower. Last century many sites were in today's inner city areas whereas now they tend to be on edge-of-city 'greenfield' locations.	**Labour** This includes both quantity (large numbers in nineteenth century factories) and quality (some areas demand special skills as technology develops). **Capital (money)** Early industry depended on wealthy entrepreneurs. Now banks and governments may provide the money. **Markets** The size and location of markets has become more important than the source of raw materials. **Transport** Costs increase when items moved are bulky, fragile, heavy or perishable. **Economies of scale** Small units may become unprofitable and so merge with, or are taken over by, other firms. **Government policies** As governments tend to control most wealth, they can influence industrial location. **Improved technology** Examples are facsimile (fax) machines and electronic mail. **Leisure facilities** Both within the town and the surrounding countryside, leisure activities are becoming more desirable.

In the nineteenth century, industry in Britain was heavily reliant on the use of coal for power, so many large industrial areas developed on and close to coalfield areas such as South Wales and on the Yorks, Derby, Notts coalfield. Others developed in coastal ports with deepwater estuaries, such as the Mersey and the Thames. The location of Britain's present-day industry is very different:

- Modern industries are high-tech and connected with electronics. As they use electricity from the national grid for power they are said to be **footloose** and have a relatively free choice of location.
- Many new industries have developed in areas where there is a pleasant working environment, large markets nearby and close to major transport routes, such as the M4 corridor.
- Many have been encouraged by government policy to locate in the former industrial areas which often had high levels of unemployment.

Key words to know

Footloose
High-tech industry

Modern, high-tech industry

A **high-tech industry** refers to industries developed in the last 25 years whose processing techniques involve micro-electronics. They are said to be footloose industries because they are not tied to heavy raw materials, so they have a relatively free choice of location. They can be divided into:

- the 'sunrise' industries with a high-tech base
- information technology industries involving computers, telecommunications and micro-electronics.

High-tech industries need a highly skilled, inventive, intelligent workforce and therefore tend to be attracted to areas which the researchers and workers find attractive to live in, from a climatic, scenic, health and social point of view. They also tend to locate near to large markets and major transport routes.

Case Study

The M4 corridor

Back to ...

The New Wider World **page 140** for this case study of a modern, footloose industry.

Using your case study

You need to make sure you know where the M4 corridor is and can name some of the key towns and cities along its route. You need to learn specific examples of how each locational factor is important for footloose industry here – the various forms of transport available, potential sources of labour, opportunities for research such as Oxford University and the type of greenfield sites available.

Update

Go to *The New Wider World Coursemates* website for a link to the 's-cool' revision website. Choose the options: GCSE Revision, Geography, Industry.

Learn it!

1 Draw a sketch map to show the location of the M4 corridor between London and Bristol.

2 Add annotations to show the key locational factors which have encouraged footloose industries to set up in this area.

3 Explain why an attractive environment is such an important factor.

Check this!...

1 Explain how industry can be viewed as a system.

2 Describe and explain the location of industry in the UK 200 years ago.

3 Describe and explain the present-day location of industry in the UK.

4 How are decisions about the location of an industry made?

Formal and informal sectors in LEDCs

In LEDC cities, the number of inhabitants outweighs the number of available jobs. An increasing number of people have to find work for themselves and enter the **informal sector** of employment as opposed to the **formal sector** (the professions, shops, offices and modern industry).

Key words to know

Informal sector
Formal sector

Figure 3.11 The growth of the informal sector of industry

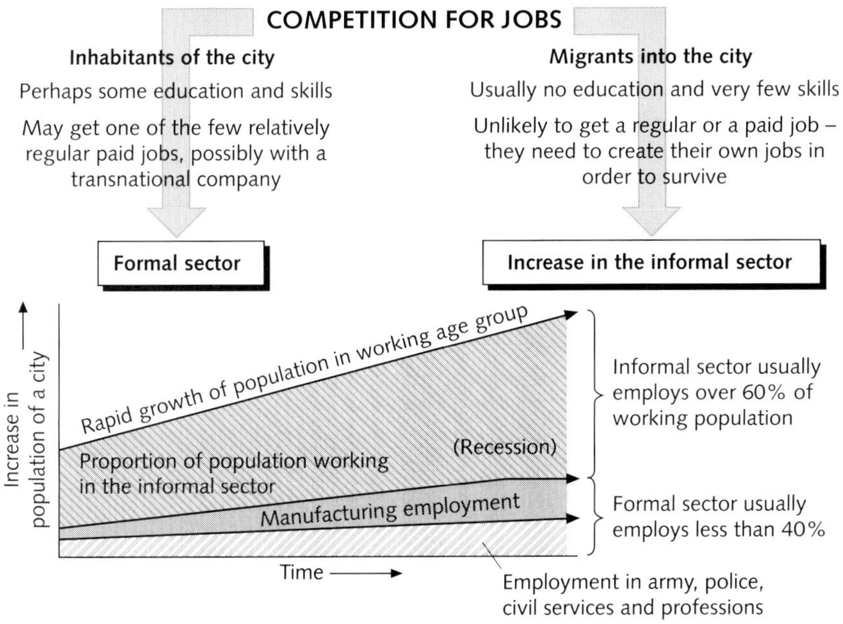

Back to ...

The New Wider World **page 149** for more information on the informal sector.

The New Wider World **pages 144–145** for more information on TNCs.

Figure 3.12 shows the differences between the formal and informal sectors.

Figure 3.12 Differences between the formal and informal sectors

	Formal	Informal
Description	Employee of a large firm	Self-employed
	Often a transnational	Small-scale/family enterprise
	Much capital employed	Little capital involved
	Capital-intensive with relatively few workers, mechanised	Labour-intensive with the use of very few tools
	Expensive raw materials	Using cheap or recycled waste materials
	A guaranteed standard in the final product	Often a low standard in quality of goods
	Regular hours (often long) and wages (often low)	Irregular hours and uncertain wages
	Fixed prices	Prices rarely fixed and so negotiable (bartering)
	Jobs done in factories	Jobs often done in the home (cottage industry) or on the streets
	Government and multinational help	No government assistance
	Legal	Often outside the law (illegal)
	Usually males	Often children and females

	Formal	Informal
Types of job	Manufacturing – both local and transnational industries	Distributive, e.g. street pedlars and small stalls
	Government-created jobs such as police, army and civil service	Services, e.g. shoecleaners, selling clothing and fruit
		Small-scale industry, e.g. food processing, dress repairs, furniture repairs
Advantages	Uses some skilled and many unskilled workers	Employs many thousands of unskilled workers
	Provides permanent jobs andregular wages	Jobs may provide some training and skills which might lead to better jobs in the future
	Produces goods for the more wealthy (cars, food) within their own country so that profits may remain within the country	Any profit will be used within the city; the products will be for local use by the lower-paid people
	Waste materials provide raw materials for the informal sector	Uses local and waste materials

Children make up a large proportion of the informal sector workers. Very few of them go to school and from an early age they go out on the streets to try to supplement the family income.

Key words to know

Transnational corporation (TNC)

Factors attracting a transnational corporation to an LEDC

A **transnational corporation (TNC)** is one that operates in many countries:

- the headquarters and main factory is usually in a more developed country
- branch factories are usually located in less developed countries.

Case Study Extra

Fiat in Brazil

Fiat has a large assembly plant at Betim in the state of Minas Gerais (employing 12,000 workers and producing 650,000 cars a year) and two transmission and engine plants (each employing 1,700 workers). Brazil is now Fiat's second largest manufacturing location and its second largest market. In 1995, 18 per cent of its vehicles were sold here.

Fiat chose to locate in Brazil for several reasons:

- There was a large labour pool with workers prepared to work for lower wages than in other countries (despite pay increases workers earn the equivalent of $7 an hour).
- Brazil's economy was expanding in global markets (it is now the tenth largest economy in the world).
- The government was keen to encourage a market-oriented economy and encouraged foreign investment. Loans, grants and cheap land were offered as incentives which meant that Fiat could build and operate a factory at low cost.
- The government was also very strong, which meant that strikes were unlikely to occur.
- Cheap electricity was available from Brazil's HEP programme, which included the Itaipù Dam project.
- Steel and other necessary products were available in Brazil.

Using your case study

You can use this example to explain the reasons why a TNC such as Fiat decides to locate in a developing country.

Update

Go to *The New Wider World Coursemates* website for a link to a web enquiry which examines the problems and benefits arising from transnationals in LEDCs.

Learn it!

1 Where is Betim? Using an atlas, draw a sketch map to show its location in Brazil.

2 Why did Fiat decide to build a car assembly plant at Betim?

Check this!...

1 Using examples, explain the difference between the formal and the informal sector of employment in LEDCs.

2 Why has the informal sector of employment grown in many LEDC cities?

3 What is a TNC?

EXAM PRACTICE

1 Describe and explain how the numbers of people employed in different economic activities has changed through time. (5)

2 With reference to examples, describe and explain the differences in employment structures between an MEDC and an LEDC. (5)

3 Explain, with reference to a specific example, how the Green Revolution brought both benefits and problems for wet rice farming in an LEDC. (5)

4 With reference to farming in an EU country, explain how changing EU policy has affected activities on the farm. (5)

5 With reference to a specific example, describe and explain the location of a high-tech industry. (5)

6 With reference to an example, explain how TNCs can bring benefits and problems to an LEDC. (5)

EXAM TIPS

In some sections of your GCSE specification, you are required to learn specific case studies. In 'The Economic World', for example, you must learn an example of intensive wet rice farming, a study of farming in the EU, a study of a high-tech industry and an example of a TNC in an LEDC. This means you must learn details – such as facts, figures and dates – which are specific to your case studies. You will need to include these in your exam answers to achieve above a Level 1 answer. In question 5, for example, you need to be able to name the main towns along the M4 corridor, give examples of nearby attractive environments, name nearby airports and sources of labour.

Back to ...

The New Wider World Coursemates website to check your answers to the exam practice questions.

4 The natural world

KEY IDEAS

1. Air masses lead to changes in the UK weather
2. Average long-term weather patterns lead to distinct climate types
3. Distinct forest communities develop which are sensitive to human interference

The New Wider World, pp200–207, 211, 215, 232, 235, 238–240

1 Air masses lead to changes in the UK weather

- **Weather** is the day-to-day changes in temperature, sunshine, cloud cover, precipitation, atmospheric pressure, wind speed and wind direction. It is short-term and can be localised in a relatively small area.
- **Climate** is the average weather condition of a place taken over a long period of time, such as 30 years. It is the expected, rather than the actual, conditions. It is long term and is often applied to sizeable parts of the globe, e.g. equatorial climate.

Key words to know

Weather
Climate
Air mass

The origins and characteristics of the main air masses affecting the UK

Britain is affected by four main **air masses** at different times, giving it a variable climate. An air mass forms when air remains stationary over a place for several days. During this time the air is likely to assume the temperature and humidity properties of that area. Air masses are classified according to:

- the latitude in which they originate, as this determines their temperature, i.e. giving either cold polar (P) air from the north or warmer tropical (T) air from the south
- the surface over which they develop, as this affects their humidity and precipitation, i.e. giving either wet, maritime (m) air from over the sea or dry continental (c) air if over land.

Figure 4.1 shows the characteristics of the four main air masses which affect the UK.

Figure 4.1 Air masses and their associated weather

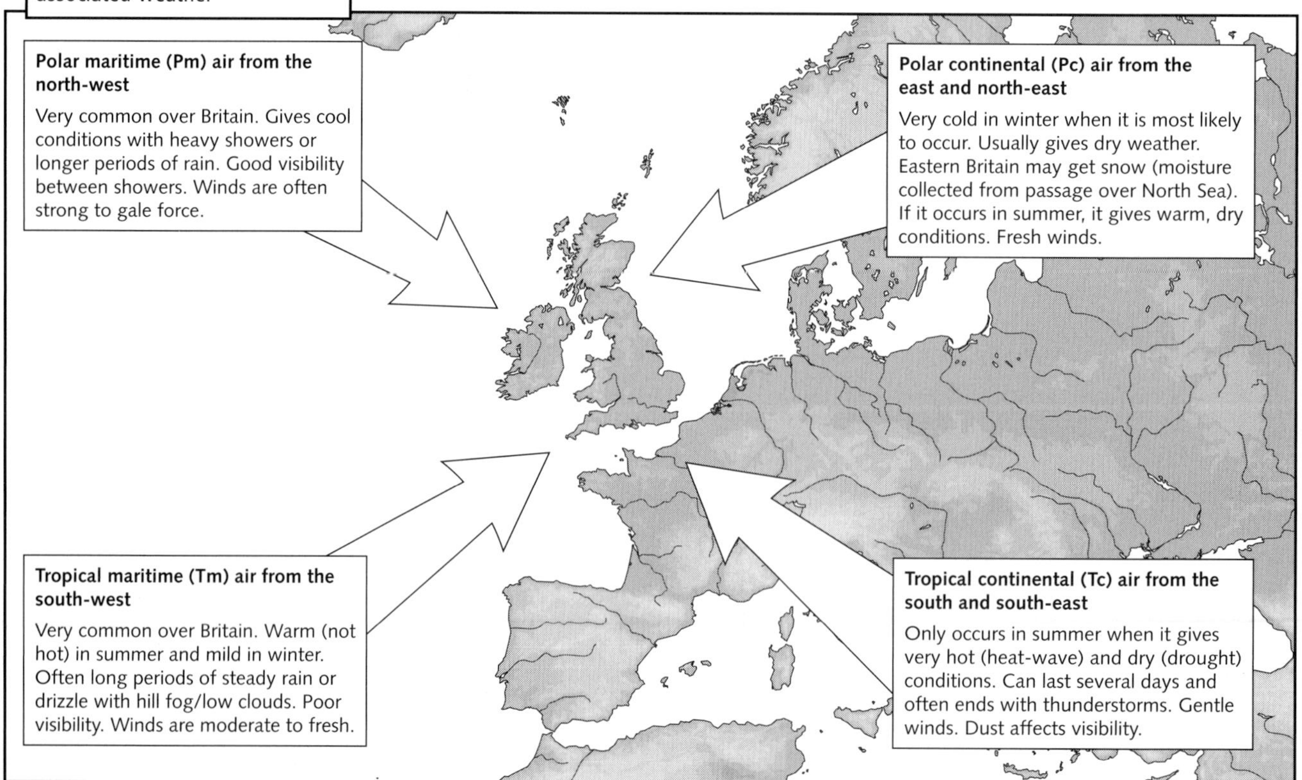

How the air masses influence weather in the UK

Each of the four main air masses brings with it its own characteristic type of weather:

- **Polar maritime (Pm)** air – occurs frequently and brings cool wet weather
- **Polar continental (Pc)** air – not very frequent and gives cooler, drier weather
- **Tropical maritime (Tm)** air – occurs most frequently and brings warm, wet conditions
- **Tropical continental (Tc)** air – the least frequent and gives warm, dry conditions.

Key words to know

Polar maritime (Pm)
Polar continental (Pc)
Tropical maritime (Tm)
Tropical continental (Tc)

Patterns of rainfall in the UK

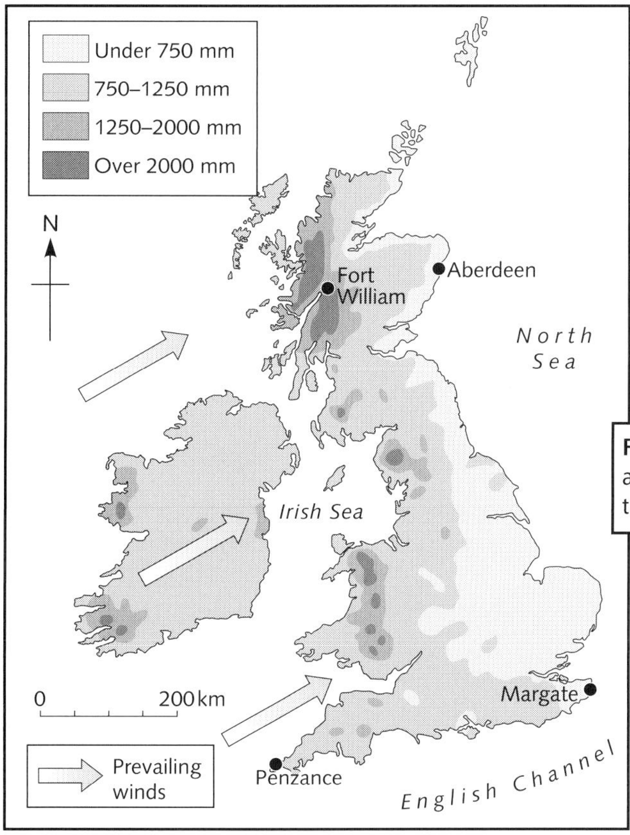

Figure 4.2 Average annual rainfall throughout the UK

Figure 4.2 shows that the distribution of rainfall across the UK is uneven. Places to the west, especially where there are mountains, receive considerably more rainfall than places to the east which are low-lying. The amount of rainfall in parts of the UK is closely linked to the type of air masses affecting the country – the maritime air masses are the most frequent and also wetter than the less frequent, continental air masses. Rainfall results from warm air – which contains water vapour – being forced to rise until it cools sufficiently for condensation to take place (Figure 4.3).

Back to ...

The New Wider World **page 202** for a detailed explanation of the conditions needed for condensation to occur.

Figure 4.3 Formation of rain

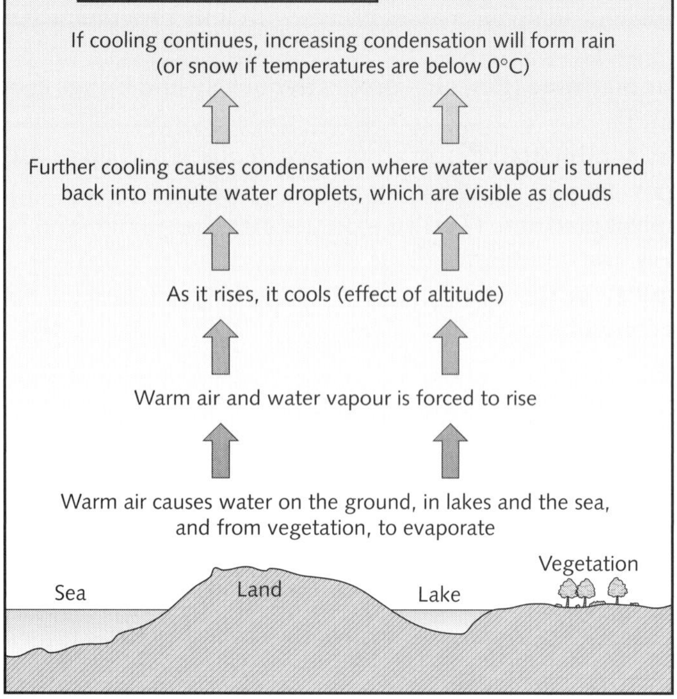

Relief rainfall

Relief rainfall occurs when:

- warm, almost saturated air from the sea is blown inland by the wind
- where there is a coastal mountain barrier, the air is forced to rise over it
- the rising air cools and condensation takes place
- once over the mountains the air descends, warms and, therefore, rain is less likely to occur.

The most frequent air mass over the UK is the tropical maritime, which is warm, as it comes from the south-west and collects moisture as it passes over the Atlantic Ocean. This air mass is forced to rise over the high land which comprises much of the western part of the UK, giving rise to the higher levels of rainfall here (see Figure 4.2).

Figure 4.4 Formation of relief rainfall

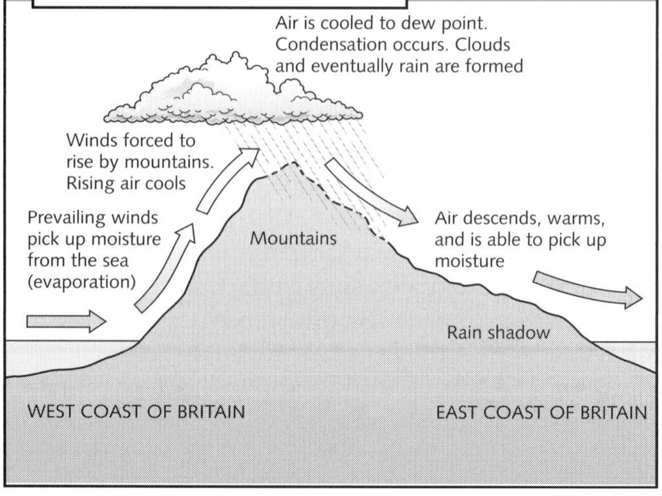

Frontal rainfall

Figure 4.5 Formation of frontal rainfall

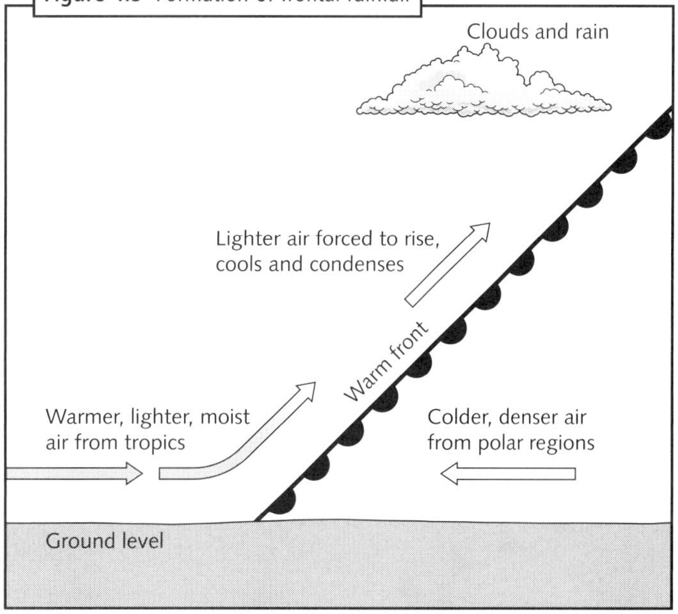

Key words to know

Relief rainfall
Frontal rainfall
Front

Frontal rainfall is associated with depressions and results from the meeting of tropical maritime and polar continental air masses:

- the two air masses have different characteristics and cannot merge
- the warmer, moister, lighter air mass (Tm) is forced to rise over the colder, denser air mass (Pc), setting the condensation process into motion
- the boundary between the warm and cold air is called a **front** – most depressions have two fronts, a warm and a cold front, giving two periods of rainfall (see Figure 4.6).

Britain is influenced by many depressions and their associated fronts each year. Depressions usually come from the Atlantic Ocean, increasing rainfall on the west coast.

Check this!...

1 Explain the difference between weather and climate.

2 What is an air mass?

3 Name the four main air masses which affect the UK.

4 Explain how the following types of rainfall are formed:
a) relief rainfall
b) frontal rainfall.

Characteristic weather conditions associated with depressions

For much of the year the weather in the UK is dominated by the passage of **depressions** – areas of low pressure bringing rain, cloud and

Key words to know

Depression
Warm front
Cold front
Occluded front
Anticyclone

wind. They form over the Atlantic Ocean when a mass of warm, moist tropical maritime air meets a mass of cooler, drier polar continental air. Due to differences in temperature and density the two air masses do not mix, instead:

- when lighter, warmer air moves towards denser colder air it is forced to rise above the denser colder air at a **warm front**
- when denser, colder air moves towards warm air, it undercuts the warm air forcing it to rise at a **cold front**.

In both cases the rising warm air is cooled and some of its water vapour condenses, producing cloud and frontal rain. The cold front travels faster than the warm front, catching it up to form an **occluded front**. Although each depression is unique, the weather they bring to the UK as they travel eastwards tends to have an easily recognisable pattern.

Figure 4.6 Typical weather conditions in a depression

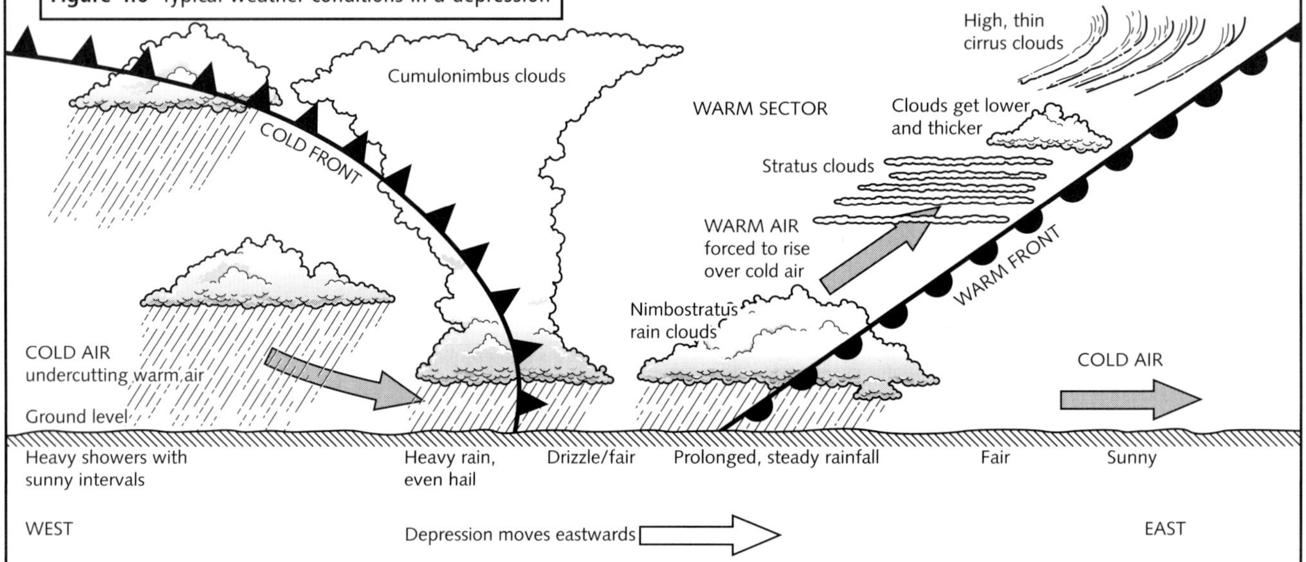

As a warm front approaches:
- clouds begin to form, getting lower and thicker
- winds blow from the south-east, in an anti-clockwise direction, and slowly increase in strength
- atmospheric pressure drops as the air rises.

As a warm front passes:
- there is a lengthy period of steady rainfall
- clouds are low and winds are strong.

In the warm sector:
- clouds are low and sometimes broken
- winds decrease
- there may be light drizzle and dry spells.

As a cold front passes:
- the weather rapidly deteriorates
- winds often reach gale force and swing round to the north-west
- rainfall is very heavy, although of short duration
- temperatures fall rapidly.

After a cold front passes:
- the weather slowly improves as pressure increases
- heavy rain gives way to heavy showers and eventually sunny intervals
- winds are cold and slow to moderate, but still come from the north-west.

Most depressions take 1–3 days to pass over the British Isles.

Characteristic weather conditions associated with anticyclones

In Britain anticyclones are experienced far less frequently than depressions but, once established, they can remain stationary for several days and, under extreme conditions, even weeks. Their main characteristics are the opposite to those of depressions. In an **anticyclone**, air descends and pressure increases. Winds are very light and blow in a clockwise direction. At times they may even be nonexistent and give periods of calm. As the air descends it warms and is able to pick up more moisture through evaporation. This usually results in settled conditions with clear skies and a lack of rain. There are, however, differences between summer and winter anticyclones.

Back to ...

The New Wider World **page 203** Figure 12.10 which shows how convectional rainfall is formed.

Figure 4.7 Weather associated with an anticyclone in summer and winter

Summer	Winter
• Absence of cloud gives very warm, sunny conditions during the day. • At night clear skies allow some of the heat to escape and temperatures can fall rapidly. • As air next to the ground cools, condensation can occur and dew and mist may form. • Thunderstorms are also a risk under 'heat-wave' conditions as convectional rainfall may occur.	• Temperatures remain low during the day due to the low angle of the sun in the sky (see Figure 4.13 in this chapter). • Weather is likely to be dry and bright. • Nights can be very cold due to rapid heat loss under clear skies. • Condensation near to the ground can produce frost and fog which may, due to the sun's lack of heat, persist all day.

Check this!...

1 Describe what happens when a warm air mass meets a cold air mass.

2 Describe the weather associated as a depression passes over:
   a) as the warm front approaches
   b) as a warm front passes over
   c) in the warm sector
   d) as a cold front passes
   e) after the cold front passes.

3 List the main characteristics of an anticyclone.

4 Explain the differences between the weather in an anticyclone in summer and an anticyclone in winter.

The use of synoptic charts and satellite images to show weather conditions

Key words to know

Synoptic chart

The daily weather maps on TV or in newspapers aim to give a clear, simplified forecast. This means they must use symbols which can be easily understood. **Synoptic charts** produced by the Meteorological Office use official symbols to show conditions at specific weather stations (e.g. Valencia in south-west Ireland, the Isles of Scilly off the coast of south-west England, Norwich in East Anglia, Tynemouth in north-east England, a weather ship off the coast of north-west Ireland). These weather stations record a number of elements which are then recorded on synoptic charts by symbols: temperature, wind speed, wind direction, amount of cloud cover and atmospheric pressure. They also record the type of precipitation.

Figure 4.8 Weather map symbols

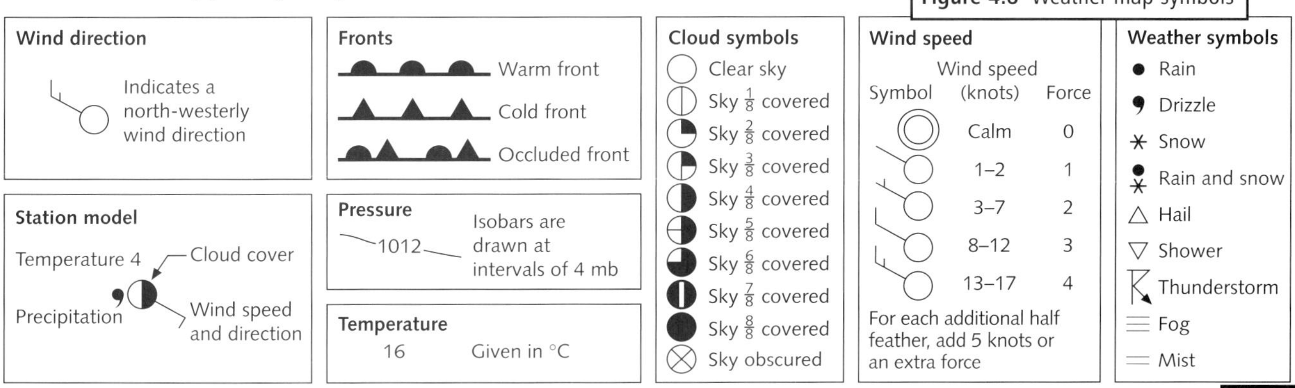

Key words to know

Satellite image

Depressions can be seen on **satellite images** as masses of swirling cloud. Satellite images are photos taken from space and sent back to Earth. They are invaluable when trying to produce a weather forecast or to predict short-term changes in the weather. The three synoptic charts in Figure 4.9 match the three satellite images.

Figure 4.9 Satellite images and synoptic charts for a passing depression

a 0600 hours 4 January

The cloud cover (white) and two fronts are over Ireland. ▼

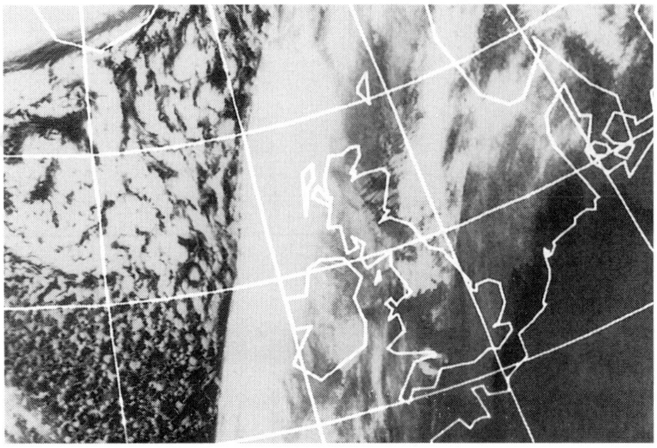

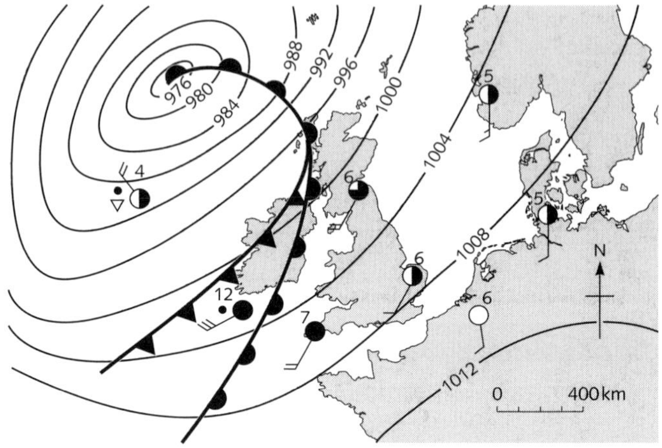

b 1800 hours 4 January

12 hours later the cloud and fronts have moved eastwards over East Anglia and the North Sea. ▼

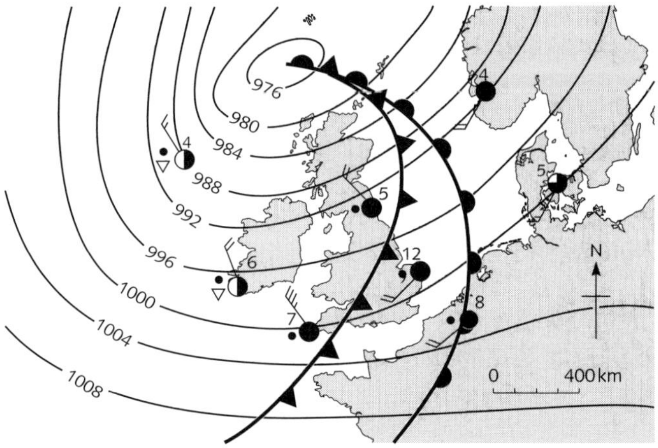

c 0600 hours 5 January

Another 12 hours later, clouds and fronts have moved further east to lie across Denmark and Germany. ▼

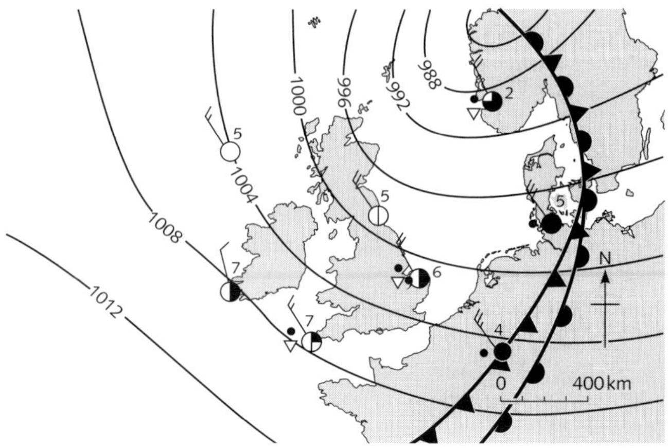

Anticyclones can also be shown on satellite images and synoptic charts.

Figure 4.10 Anticyclones

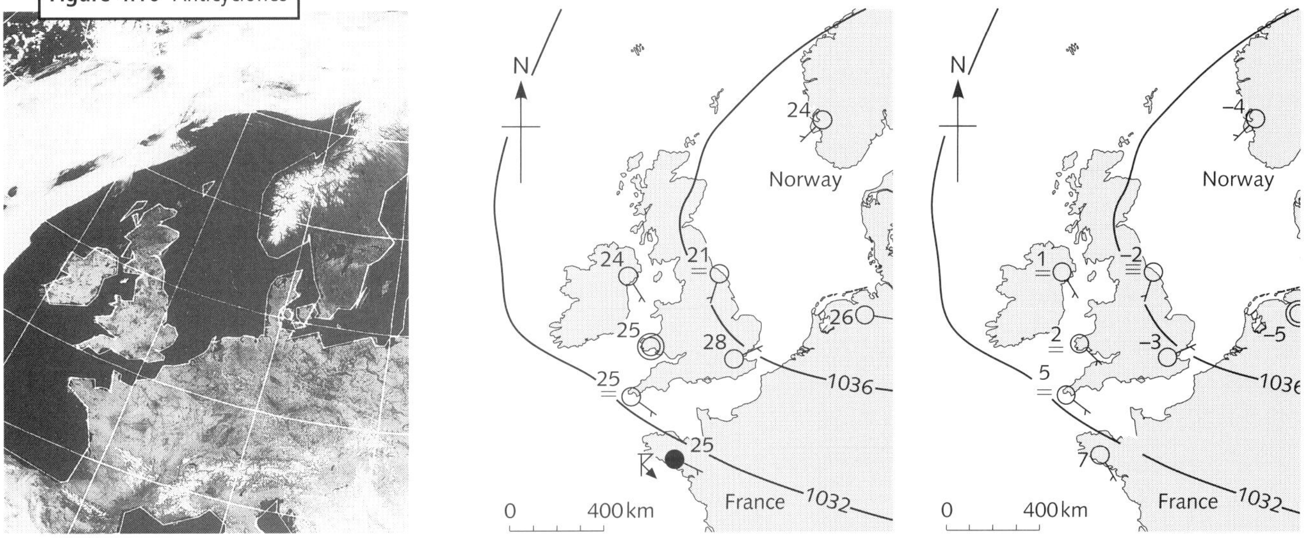

Satellite image: an anticyclone

A summer anticyclone

A winter anticyclone

Check this!...

1 What is a synoptic chart?

2 What are satellite images?

Back to ...

The New Wider World **page 207** Figure 12.18 which summarises the seasonal and regional differences in temperature and rainfall in the British Isles.

2 Average long-term weather patterns lead to distinct climate types

Factors affecting climate type

Climate is the average weather conditions for a place taken over a period of time. In other words it is the expected weather conditions found in a particular place. The type of weather experienced in any one place is influenced by several factors:

- **Distance from the sea:** Land heats up more quickly during the summer and cools down more rapidly in winter than the sea. This means that places towards the centre of continents (e.g. East European interior) will have warmer summers and colder winters than those with a coastal location (e.g. West European maritime).
- **Ocean currents:** Ocean currents may be warm or cold and affect the climate of coastal areas. Warm currents tend to raise winter temperatures (e.g. British climate) while cold currents usually lower summer temperatures.
- **Latitude:** Places in the Tropics, being nearer the Equator, are much warmer than places towards the Poles. This is due to the curvature of the Earth and the angle of the sun. At the Equator the sun is always high in the sky. When it is overhead it shines directly downwards, concentrating its heat into a small area

which can become very hot. In contrast, the sun is always low in the sky towards the Poles. This means that here the heat is spread over a wide area, so temperatures remain lower. The lower the angle of the sun, the greater the amount of atmosphere through which the sun's rays have to pass. This means that more heat is lost to gases, dust and cloud in the atmosphere.

Figure 4.11 Effects of latitude

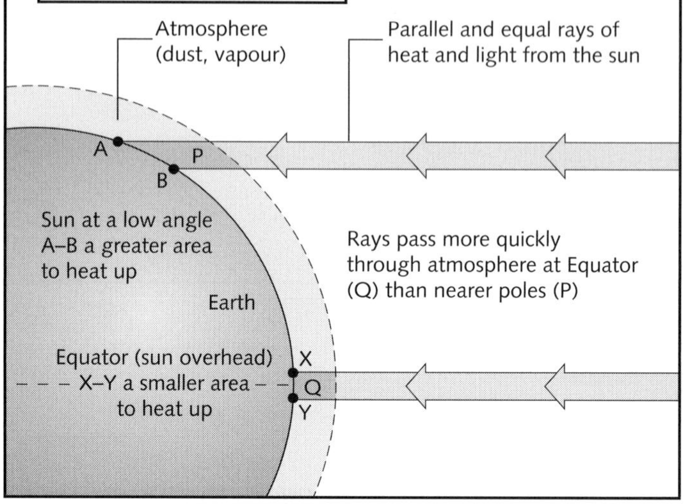

Check this!...

Explain how the following factors affect climate types:

a) distance from the sea
b) ocean currents
c) latitude.

Figure 4.12 Climate graph for Plymouth

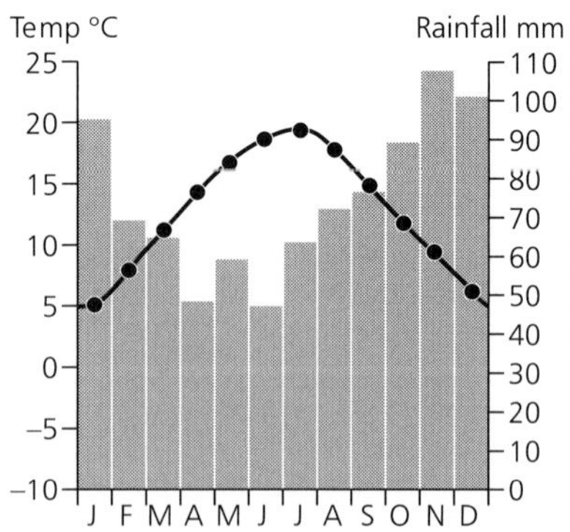

- Small **annual temperature range** of 11°C (difference between highest and lowest temperatures)
- Maximum temperature of 17°C in July and a minimum of 6°C in January
- Gradual changes between the months
- Summers are warm, winters are cool or mild
- Rainfall is regular – annual total 9000–10 000 mm

Two contrasting climate types are the West European maritime climate, experienced by countries such as the UK and Ireland on the western edge of Europe, and the very different East European continental climate, experienced by places much further inland, such as Poland and Russia.

Characteristics of west European maritime climates

Plymouth lies on the south coast of England at 50°N and it has a maritime climate. This means it is strongly influenced by the sea, which keeps places cooler in summer and milder in winter than those further inland.

Characteristics of east European interior climates

Kiev lies in the Ukraine and is on the same latitude as Plymouth (50°N), but its climate is very different because it has an East European continental climate and is not influenced by the sea (Figure 4.13).

Check this!...

1 Use an atlas to check the locations of Plymouth and Kiev.

2 Describe each of the climate graphs in Figures 4.12 and 4.13, commenting on:
   a) total rainfall and seasonality (when does most rain fall?)
   b) maximum and minimum temperatures and annual range
   c) general comments on climate over the year (e.g. dry, mild).

Figure 4.13 Climate graph for Kiev

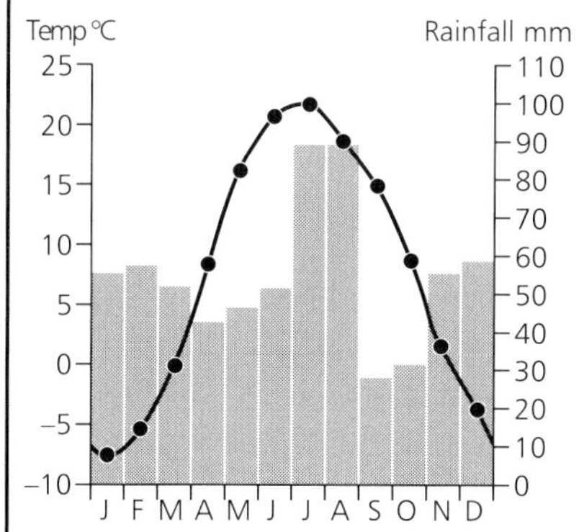

- Large annual **temperature range** of 27°C
- Maximum temperature is 20°C in July, minimum −7°C in January
- Monthly changes in temperature can be quite large – up to 8°C or 9°C
- Warm/hot summers, winters exceptionally cold
- Precipitation is low but falls as snow in the winter months due to the low temperatures
- Thunderstorms common in summer, due to **convection** (rising warm air currents)
- Annual rainfall total 250–425 mm

3 Distinct forest communities develop which are sensitive to human interference

The global distribution of different forest types

There is a close link between climate and natural vegetation. In certain parts of the world forests have developed with different types of trees which are suited to different types of climate. As a result, the trees in the colder tundra regions of northern Canada and Siberia are very different from those in equatorial rainforests. These forest communities are used for a variety of human activities but they can be very sensitive and easily damaged by these activities.

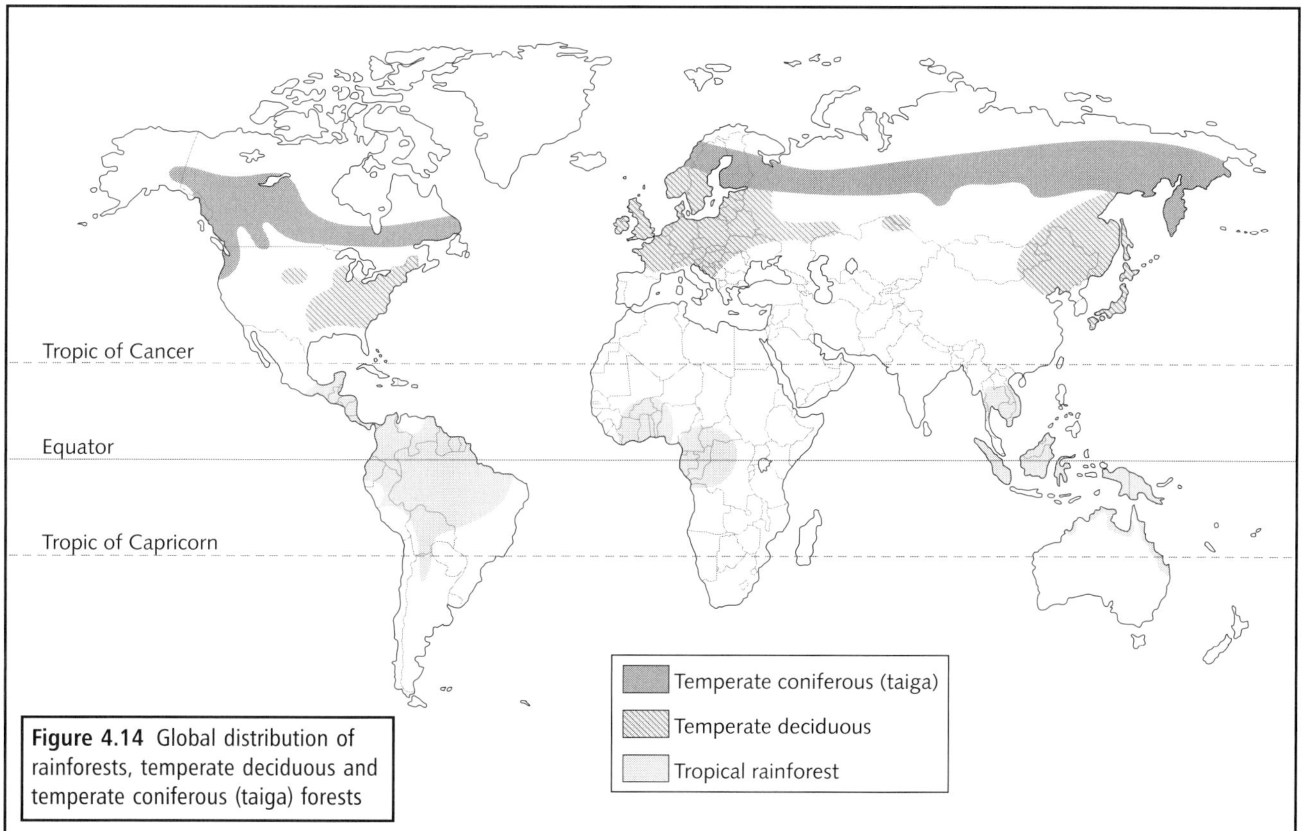

Figure 4.14 Global distribution of rainforests, temperate deciduous and temperate coniferous (taiga) forests

Check this!...

Describe the global distribution of:
a) tropical rainforests
b) temperate deciduous forests
c) temperate coniferous forests.

Key words to know

Annual temperature range
Convection

How trees have adapted to the natural environment

Back to …

The New Wider World **page 235** Figure 14.17, a photograph of a coniferous forest.

The taiga

The natural vegetation of the taiga, or coniferous forest, consists of vast, uninterrupted stands of spruce, pine and fir.

These trees have had to adapt (see Figure 4.16 opposite) to a harsh physical environment where:

- winters are long and extremely cold, often with strong winds
- precipitation falls as snow and, as groundwater is frozen, moisture is unavailable for plants
- summers are cool and the growing season is short, but there is some rain for plant growth
- soils are often thin and poor.

Back to …

The New Wider World **page 232** Figure 14.9, a photograph of a buttress root.

Key word to know

Emergent

Tropical rainforests

In tropical rainforests trees have had to adapt to constant high temperatures, heavy rainfall and a continuous growing season:

- Trees shed their leaves at any time, giving the forest an evergreen appearance.
- Vegetation grows in distinct layers. The lowest layer consists of shrubs, and above this is the under canopy, the main canopy and, rising above, the **emergents**, which can grow to 50 m in height. Trees have to grow rapidly in order to reach the sunlight.
- Tree trunks are straight and, in their lower parts, branchless in their efforts to grow tall.

Figure 4.15 Vegetation layers in the tropical rainforest

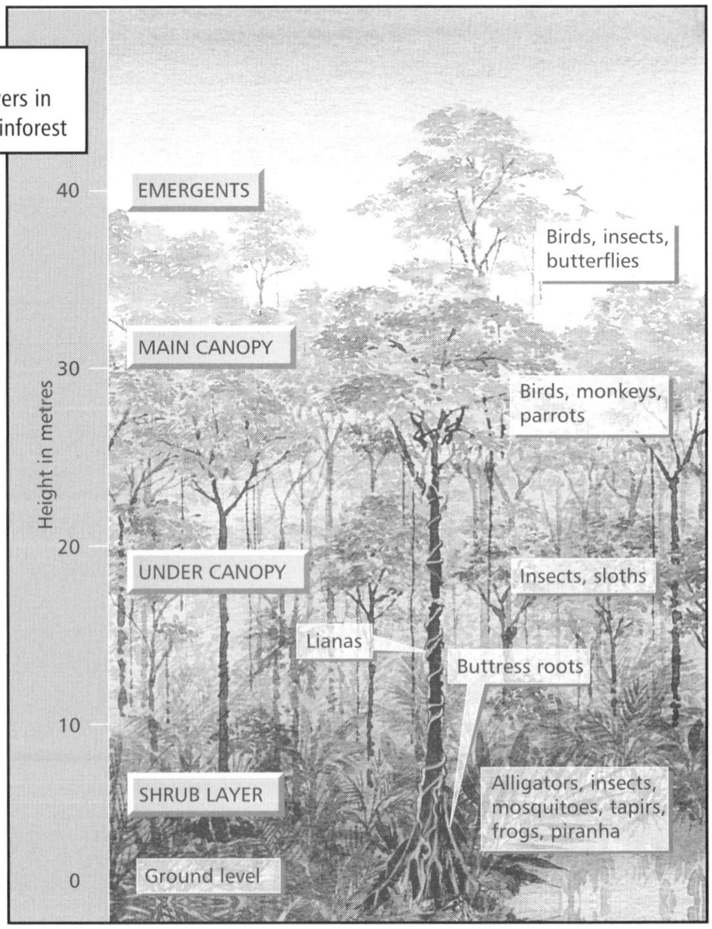

Figure 4.16 How conifers adapt to the cold climate

Back to ...

The New Wider World **page 253** Figure 15.32, a diagram of tropical red earth soil.

- Large buttress roots stand above the ground to give support to trees.
- Lianas, which are vine-like plants, use the large trees as a support in their efforts to reach the canopy and sunlight.
- As only about 1 per cent of the incoming sunlight reaches the forest floor, there is little undergrowth. Shrubs and other plants which grow here have had to adapt to the lack of light.
- Leaves have drip-tips to shed the heavy rainfall.
- Fallen leaves soon decay in the hot, wet climate.

Despite its luxuriant appearance, the rainforest is a fragile environment. This is partly because of the soil type found – tropical red earth. In the rainforest, the heavy, continuous leaf fall gives a thick litter layer which is rapidly broken down due to the hot, wet climate and the large number of soil organisms. The heavy rainfall leaches nutrients out of the soil and one of these, iron, is deposited in the lower layers, giving this soil its characteristic red colour. Under normal conditions this soil is relatively fertile but once the nutrient cycle is broken by farming or deforestation, leaching rapidly increases and the soil quickly loses its fertility.

Check this!...

1 How have trees in the tropical rainforest adapted to the natural environment?

2 How have trees in the taiga adapted to the natural environment?

Tropical rainforests and sustainable development

Rainforests are very valuable for a wide variety of reasons, including being a habitat for a huge range of animals and plants, and the important role they play in climate on local and global scales. As a result attempts are made to protect them for the future but at the same time allow people, especially indigenous tribes, to be able to make a living from them. Many governments, especially in poorer LEDCs, wish to develop parts of their rainforest in order to generate income for other areas such as education and health care. In order not to destroy the forests completely, sustainable development is seen as the way forward.

Case Study

Forestry in Malaysia

Back to ...

The New Wider World **pages 238–240** for this case study of forestry in Malaysia.

Using your case study

You need to know how and why the rainforests in Malaysia are being exploited for their timber, and the different ways in which the money earned from the timber is used. You need to be able to describe attempts to conserve the forest, such as improving the Taman Negara National Park, and know about methods of logging which are more sustainable, e.g. helilogging, and the Community Forest Development Scheme.

Update

Go to *The New Wider World Coursemates* website for a link to a summary of the Malaysian Tropical Forest Conservation Project.

Learn it!

1 List the different reasons for exploiting the rainforest.

2 Describe the clearfelling method of logging and explain why this is unsustainable.

3 Explain attempts being made to conserve some areas of forest.

4 Describe the attempts made by the Malaysian government to introduce more sustainable methods of logging.

The roles of different interest groups and the conflicts between them

In Malaysia, there are several different groups with interests in the rainforest. However, these interests are different, and are sometimes in conflict.

- **Indigenous communities** are angry that they are often not consulted when logging rights are sold to large companies – their land is destroyed and their water supplies are polluted by logging operations, affecting their food supplies and livelihood.
- **Environmental groups** are concerned about deforestation rates and its consequences. For every tree cut down for timber, five more are damaged; 60 million tonnes of exposed soil has been washed into rivers which become silted up.
- **Logging companies** clearly profit from rights to land in Malaysia and the demand for timber globally is increasing.
- The Malaysian government is in favour of logging because of the revenue it brings the country. However, it has also begun to realise that logging must be carried out in a more sustainable way as trees are such a valuable resource.

Check this!...

1 Name two groups of people against logging in Malaysia.

2 Name two groups of people in favour of logging in Malaysia.

3 Give an example of two groups of people who hold conflicting views about how the rainforest should be used.

EXAM PRACTICE

1 Describe the origins and characteristics of the four main air masses which affect the UK. (4)

2 Explain the formation of:
a) relief rainfall
b) frontal rainfall. (6)

3 Compare and contrast the weather experienced in the UK under anticyclonic conditions in summer and winter. (6)

4 Describe the differences between the West European maritime climate and the East European continental interior climate. (4)

5 Explain, with examples, how the following factors affect climate:
a) distance from the sea
b) ocean currents
c) latitude. (4)

6 Using an example you have studied, explain how sustainable development is being used to control deforestation and conserve tropical rainforests. (6)

Back to ...

The New Wider World Coursemates website to check your answers to the exam practice questions.

EXAM TIPS

Weather and climate topics can sometimes be difficult and confusing to learn and diagrams are often a helpful way of both learning the information and answering exam questions. For question 1, for example, a rough outline of the UK can be drawn with arrows to represent the direction of the main air masses. Annotations can then be added to describe the characteristics of each air mass. Annotated diagrams are also useful to show the formation of the different types of rainfall in question 2.

The New Wider World, pp128–131, 254–258, 286–289, 291, 293–295, 304, 306–309

5 Managing the environment

KEY IDEAS

1. Coasts are under threat and need to be managed
2. River floods are the result of human and physical factors
3. Fragile environments require sustainable management

1 Coasts are under threat and need to be managed

Causes of cliff recession

Parts of Britain's coastline are constantly under threat from cliff recession caused by coastal erosion. This occurs when:

- cliffs consist of resistant rock, as at Flamborough Head (Yorkshire) and Beachy Head (Sussex) – here waves erode at the cliff base, forming a wave-cut notch and causing the rock above to become unstable and, in time, to collapse
- cliffs consist of less resistant rock, such as in Holderness (Yorkshire) and at Barton-on-Sea (Hampshire); here heavy rain can cause material to move downslope (mass movement) where it is removed by waves and coastal currents
- sand and shingle, which forms a natural protection at the foot of a cliff, is removed by human activity enabling erosion by waves to accelerate, e.g. at Druridge Bay, on the Northumberland coast, sand used to be removed for the construction industry
- people have built on cliff tops, as this adds weight which can cause cliffs to collapse, e.g. at Overstrand, north Norfolk, the Overstrand Hotel was built close to a cliff edge and later collapsed when erosion caused the cliff to slump.

Effects of cliff recession

- In 1999, a section of chalk 200 m long and 15 m deep fell 180 m into the sea at Beachy Head.
- Cliffs near Barton-on-Sea have retreated by up to 60 m since 1971.
- A cliff collapse near Scarborough in 1993 destroyed a hotel.

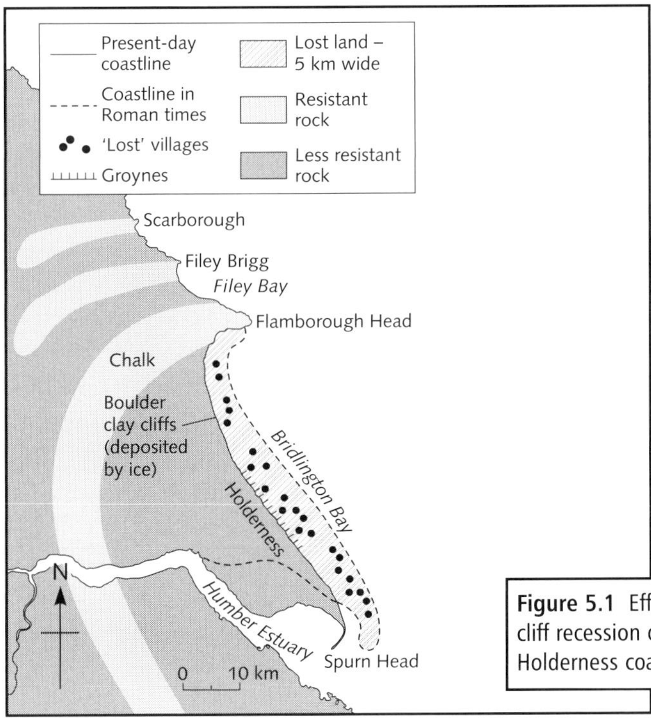

Figure 5.1 Effects of cliff recession on the Holderness coast

Back to ...

Chapter 1, page 11 in this book, Figure 1.13, which shows the formation of a wave-cut platform and notch.

The New Wider World **page 304** Figure 18.14, a photograph of a collapsing cliff at Holderness; **page 306** Figure 18.21, a photograph of slumping on the Dorset coast at Naish Farm Holiday Village, Barton-on-Sea; see also Chapter 1, pages 12–13 of this book for information on mass movement.

Key words to know

Hard engineering
Soft engineering

Back to ...

Page 13 Figure 1.17 in this book, a diagram showing the process of longshore drift; *The New Wider World* **page 302** Figure 18.9, a photograph of groynes at Worthing, West Sussex; **page 304** Figure 18.16a, a photograph showing a sea-wall and revetments at Felixstowe, Suffolk; **page 304** Figure 18.16b, a photograph of riprap at Felixstowe, Suffolk.

- Further south, in Holderness, the coastline is retreating by an average of 2 m a year. Here, it is now 3 km further west than it was in Roman times and some 50 villages mentioned in the Domesday Book of 1086 have been lost to the sea.

Management of cliff recession

- Attempts to protect the coastline involve either **hard engineering** or **soft engineering**, as outlined in Figure 5.2.

Figure 5.2 Hard and soft sea-defence engineering

Hard	• **Wooden groynes**: help reduce the force of waves and can trap material being moved along the beach by longshore drift. Groynes help widen beaches and protect cliffs.
	• Concrete **sea-walls**: may be curved at the top to divert the force of the waves back out to sea.
	• Wooden slatted **revetments**: help dissipate the force of the waves.
	• Concrete blocks called **riprap:** absorb the power of the waves.
	• Artificial offshore **breakwaters** or **reefs.**
Soft	• **Beach nourishment:** by which the Environment Agency replaces lost beach material.
	• **Cliff stabilisation:** in which pipes are inserted to remove excess water, and vegetation is planted to stabilise exposed soil.

Key words to know

Boulder clay
Fetch

Case Study Extra

Management of cliff recession on the Holderness coast, Yorkshire

The area of the Yorkshire coast south of Scarborough, known as Holderness, experiences the highest rates of cliff recession in the country: 2 m a year. Twenty-nine villages have been lost since Roman times. Agricultural land, roads and small coastal settlements are all under threat, as well as the gas terminal at Easington. Erosion rates are so great because of the geology of the area, marine and sub-aerial processes and rising sea-levels.

- The geology of the area: land is low; cliffs are made of soft glacial and alluvial deposits known as **boulder clay** which dip eastwards and lie on a layer of chalk.
- When winds are from the north-east, they travel over a large area of open sea (known as the **fetch**) and produce large, powerful waves.
- Rain saturates the soft boulder clay which becomes unstable and slumps downwards.
- Debris is removed by the powerful waves and transported south down the coast by longshore drift.
- The threat of rising sea-levels increases the likelihood of faster erosion in the future.

Those parts of the Holderness coastline which are economically valuable have been protected in different ways, although this has often created problems further down the coast:

- Mappleton village was in danger of falling into the sea and several houses had already been lost. When the B1242 was also threatened, an offshore bar of granite was built at a cost of £2 million. This slowed the path of the waves and dissipated their energy before they reached the shoreline. The road and village were saved but the bar also restricted the southward movement of material and caused greater erosion at

Cowden, where a farm belonging to Sue Earle had to be abandoned in 1997.

- At Hornsea a sea wall and wooden groynes were constructed in the 1990s to protect cliff-top residences and businesses. The groynes prevented longshore drift and beaches developed which not only benefited the tourist industry but also protected the cliffs. These defences are reinforced regularly and recently a stone gabion was added to protect a caravan park to the south of the town.

Using your case study

You can use this case study to describe the effects and explain the causes of cliff recession. You should also learn some specific details of management strategies used and make sure you can explain how they protect the coastline as well as sometimes creating problems further south.

Update

Go the *The New Wider World Coursemates* website for a link to sites showing images of the Holderness coastline and giving information on coastal defences.

Learn it!

1 Where is Holderness? Draw a sketch map of the Yorkshire coastline to show the location of Mappleton, Hornsea and Easington.

2 Describe some of the effects of cliff recession on people and the environment.

3 Explain the main causes of cliff recession in this area.

4 Explain what management strategies have been used to protect settlements from cliff recession.

Case Study

The New Forest coastline

Back to ...

The New Wider World **pages 306–309** for this case study of the various management issues along the New Forest coastline in Hampshire.

Using your case study

You can use this case study to cover many aspects of coastal management issues, including the causes of coastal erosion (physical and human), arguments for and against management, and details of the New Forest District Council's coastal management plan.

Update

Go to *The New Wider World Coursemates* website for a link giving you information on Hampshire's coastal management strategy.

Learn it!

1 Draw a large sketch map of the New Forest coastline. Divide it into three sections and add annotations to show the different problems and pressures facing:
a) Christchurch Bay
b) the western Solent
c) Southampton Water.

2 What are the main aims of the New Forest District Council's coastal management plan?

3 Describe the attempts being made to protect the coast at:
a) Barton-on-Sea
b) Hurst Spit
c) low-lying areas near Lymington
d) wildlife habitats.

Advantages and disadvantages of coastal management techniques and conflicts of interest

It is becoming increasingly expensive to provide new defences and maintain existing ones (a £1.3 million scheme at Barton-on-Sea was destroyed in four years), while the construction of sea defences in one place often seems to increase the rate of erosion elsewhere. People who live in areas at risk, hotel and restaurant owners and shopkeepers, and also holidaymakers and day trippers who regularly visit resorts such as Barton-on-Sea, are often in favour of sea defences because they protect

Back to ...

The earlier Case Study Extra on Holderness (pages 62–63) for some examples of the advantages and disadvantages of coastal defences.

people's livelihoods and the areas they enjoy. Often, however, taxpayers in areas further inland, and environmentalists, object especially to the more obtrusive hard engineering defences which completely alter the natural landscape.

It is now therefore accepted that decisions have to be made between defending the coast at all costs or allowing nature to take its course:

- Should we allow cliffs to be eroded, spits breached and low-lying areas flooded?
- Should natural landscapes and wildlife habitats be protected or should they be developed for people who want to live and/or work here, and for people who wish to visit the area?

Check this!...

1. List, with examples, some of the causes of cliff recession.
2. Describe some effects of cliff recession.
3. Explain how hard engineering techniques can be used to manage cliff recession.
4. Describe some of the conflicting opinions held by different people about coastal defences.

2 River floods are the result of human and physical factors

Rivers provide attractive sites for settlement and economic development. They provide:

- a water supply for domestic, industrial and agricultural use
- a source of power, food and recreation
- a means of transport.

However, under certain conditions rivers can flood and cause death and widespread damage. The effects of flooding can be equally severe in MEDCs and LEDCs.

Causes of river floods

Causes of river floods can be physical or human. Figures 5.3–5.5 summarise these causes in relation to the Lynmouth flood of 1952 and the floods in Bangladesh in 1998.

Figure 5.3 Drainage basin of the East and West Lyn rivers, 1952

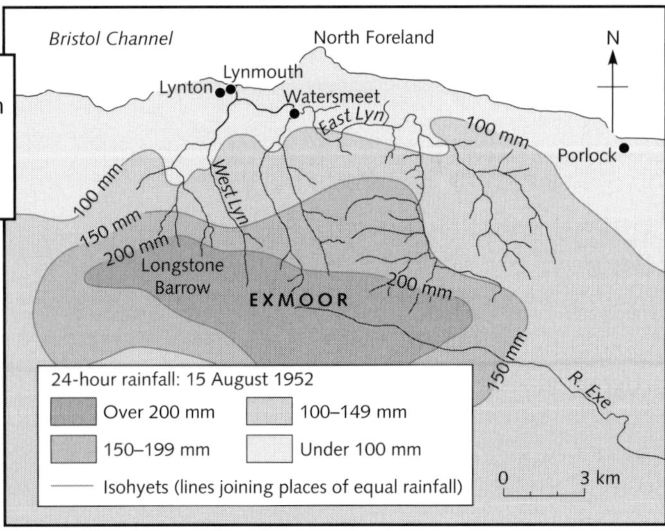

Physical causes of flooding

- Impermeable rock on Exmoor caused surface runoff.
- Very wet August meant the ground was totally saturated.
- Heavy thunderstorms and frontal rain, with over 200 mm in 14 hours.
- Small catchment basin with narrow, steep-sided valleys.

Figure 5.4 Major rivers in Bangladesh

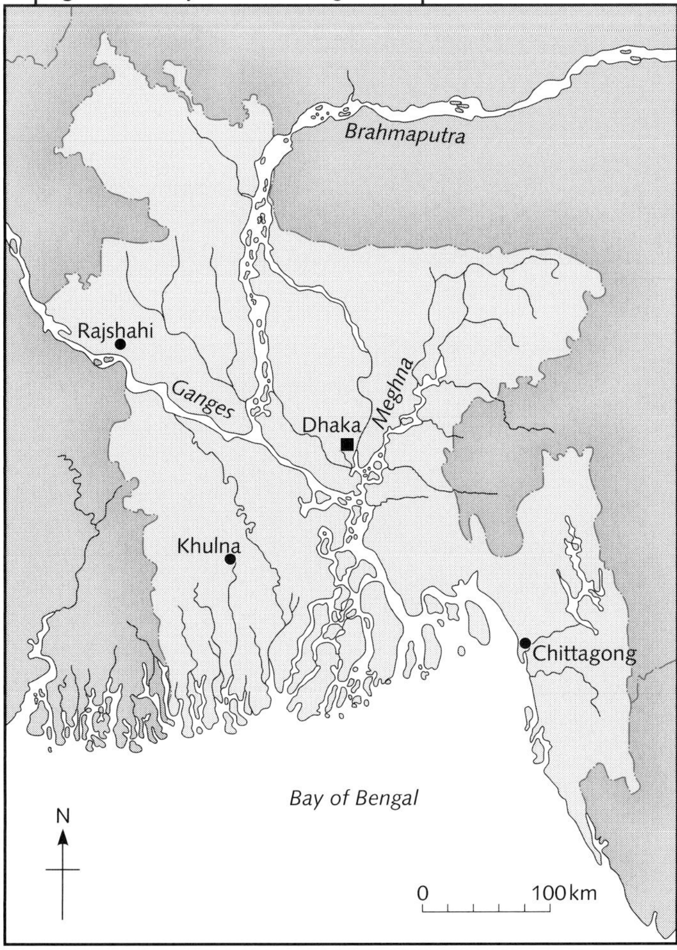

Physical causes of flooding

- Much of Bangladesh consists of the floodplain of the Ganges and Brahmaputra rivers which naturally flood annually.
- Over half the country lies below 6 m above sea-level.
- Bangladesh has a monsoon climate with most places receiving heavy rain – 1800–2600 mm a year. 80% of this is concentrated between June and September.
- The period of heavy rain combines with a period of high temperatures which melt ice and snow in the Himalayas adding to the river discharge.
- The monthly high spring tides and the effect of tropical storms can prevent floodwater escaping into the sea.
- Silt is brought down by the rivers and deposited within their channels. This results in the heightening of the river beds, increasing the risk of flooding.

Key word to know

Deforestation

Figure 5.5 Human causes of flooding

Lynmouth	Bangladesh
• River Lyn had been diverted and its channel made narrower due to the building of tourist accommodation and amenities. • No recording of river levels and no flood early warning system. • Narrow bridges over the river trapped trees and boulders.	• Global warming is causing glaciers in the Himalayas to melt (increasing runoff) and sea-level in the Bay of Bengal to rise. • Building on the floodplain to house the country's growing population has increased the possibility of loss of life and damage. • Cutting down trees in the upper drainage basin (e.g. in Nepal) – **deforestation** – increases the rate and amount of runoff.

Check this!...

1 Explain why rivers are attractive sites for settlement and economic development.

2 Using examples, describe some physical causes of flooding.

3 Using examples, describe some human causes of flooding.

Figure 5.6 Effects of the Lynmouth flood, 1952

Effects of river floods

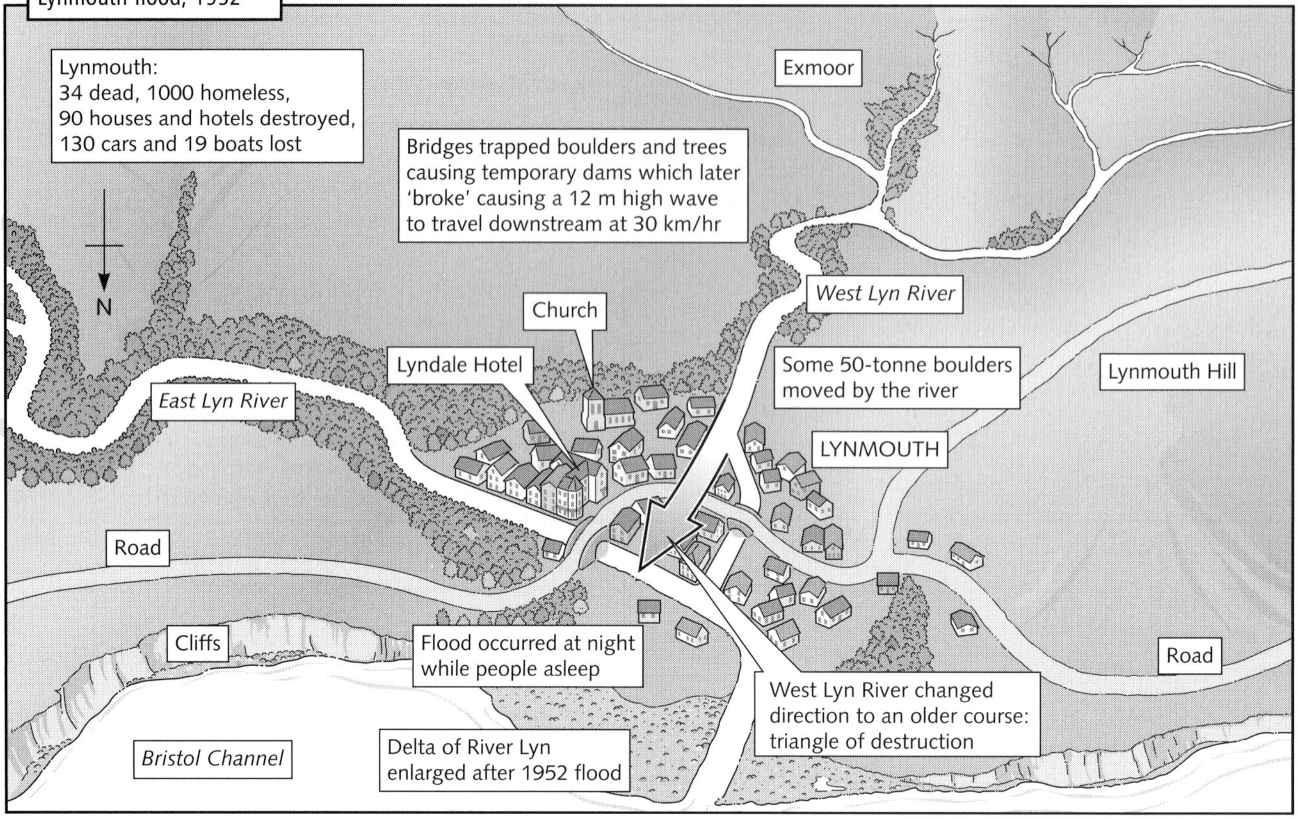

Back to ...

The New Wider World **pages 286–289** for case studies of flooding in Lynmouth in 1952 and Bangladesh in 1998.

Key words to know

Hard engineering
Levée

In Bangladesh in 1998, 68 per cent of the country was flooded, some places for more than 70 days. The effects of the floods on the people were even more devastating:

- Buildings were almost completely submerged.
- Railways, roads and bridges were swept away.
- There was no electricity for several weeks.
- A lack of safe drinking water led to dysentery, diarrhoea and the threat of a cholera outbreak.
- Parts of Dhaka, including the international airport, were under 2 m of water.
- Over 1000 people were killed, 7 million homes were destroyed and more than 25 million people left homeless.

Check this!...

1 Using an example from an LEDC, describe some physical causes of floods.

2 Using an example from an MEDC, explain the effects of flooding on:
a) the environment
b) people.

Back to ...

Chapter 1 of this book, page 5 Figure 1.6 showing the formation of levées.

Management of river floods

Hard engineering techniques

Many rivers, such as the Mississippi in the USA, have built up their river beds so that they flow above the level of their floodplains. Such rivers can only be prevented from flooding by **hard engineering** techniques such as building dams, diversion channels and artificial embankments or **levées.**

Case Study

Hard engineering – the Three Gorges Dam on the Yangtze River

Back to …

The New Wider World **pages 293–295** for this example of flood control.

Using your case study

You need to know about the causes and effects of flooding on the Yangtze in order to understand why the Chinese government decided to build the Three Gorges Dam. You should learn some specific details about the project and why it is a multipurpose scheme. Make sure you can describe what effects the flooding of land behind the dam will have on both the people and the environment. Learn some specific advantages and disadvantages of the project and consider different groups of people and their opinions, for example:

- the villagers forced to move
- environmentalists concerned about wildlife
- people who will be protected from flooding and transport companies who will benefit from an easier shipping route.

Update

Go to *The New Wider World Coursemates* website for a link to a site giving information on why the Chinese government is building the dam, and another which presents the arguments against its construction.

Learn it!

1 Where is the Yangtze? Draw a sketch map to show the location of the Three Gorges Dam Project.

2 List the causes and effects of flooding on the Yangtze.

3 Describe the Three Gorges Dam Project and explain how it is a multipurpose scheme.

4 Who would be in favour of the Three Gorges Dam Project, and why?

5 Who would be against the Three Gorges Dam Project, and why?

Soft engineering techniques

After the Lynmouth flood of 1952, the village was rebuilt to try to ensure the safety of its inhabitants rather than to try to recapture all of its former character.

Figure 5.7 Management of the River Lyn in the 1990s

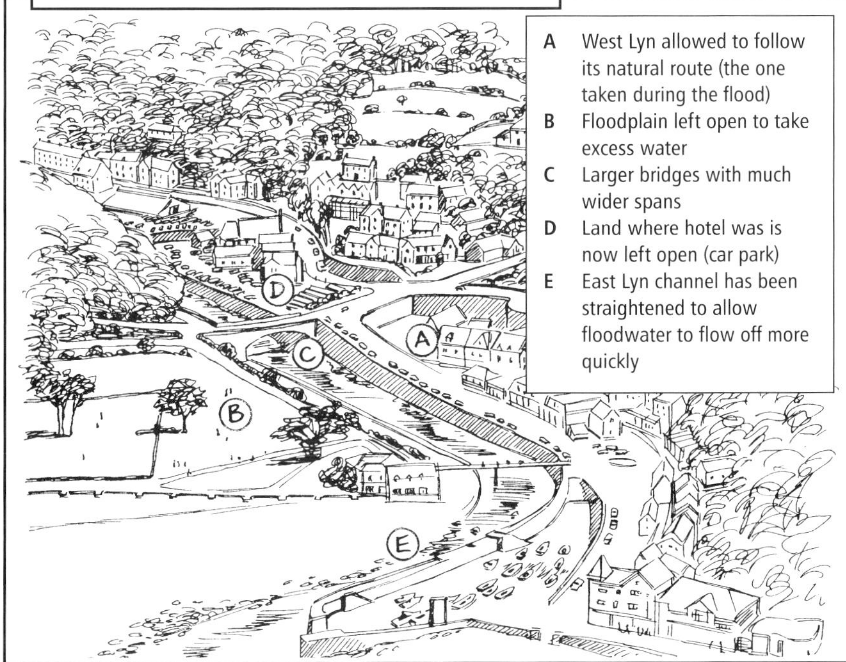

A West Lyn allowed to follow its natural route (the one taken during the flood)
B Floodplain left open to take excess water
C Larger bridges with much wider spans
D Land where hotel was is now left open (car park)
E East Lyn channel has been straightened to allow floodwater to flow off more quickly

Key word to know

Soft engineering

Leaving land open, e.g. the car park, and not allowing parts of the floodplain to be built on so that it can absorb excess water, are both examples of **soft engineering** techniques.

Advantages and disadvantages of flood management techniques, and conflicts of interest

The problem with hard engineering techniques such as levées is that, during a serious flood, they may break, or may not have been built high enough. Large areas of land are flooded and numerous lives are put at risk. Following the Mississippi floods of 1993, scientists and engineers began asking whether the dams, diversion channels and levées had actually aggravated that and other floods. There are two conflicting schools of thought:

- **Against management:** accepting that floods are part of a river's natural cycle and the drainage basin's ecosystem – flooding should therefore be allowed as a natural event. Conservationists are often against hard engineering schemes because they completely alter natural ecosystems and habitats.

Figure 5.8 Arguments for and against controlling rivers

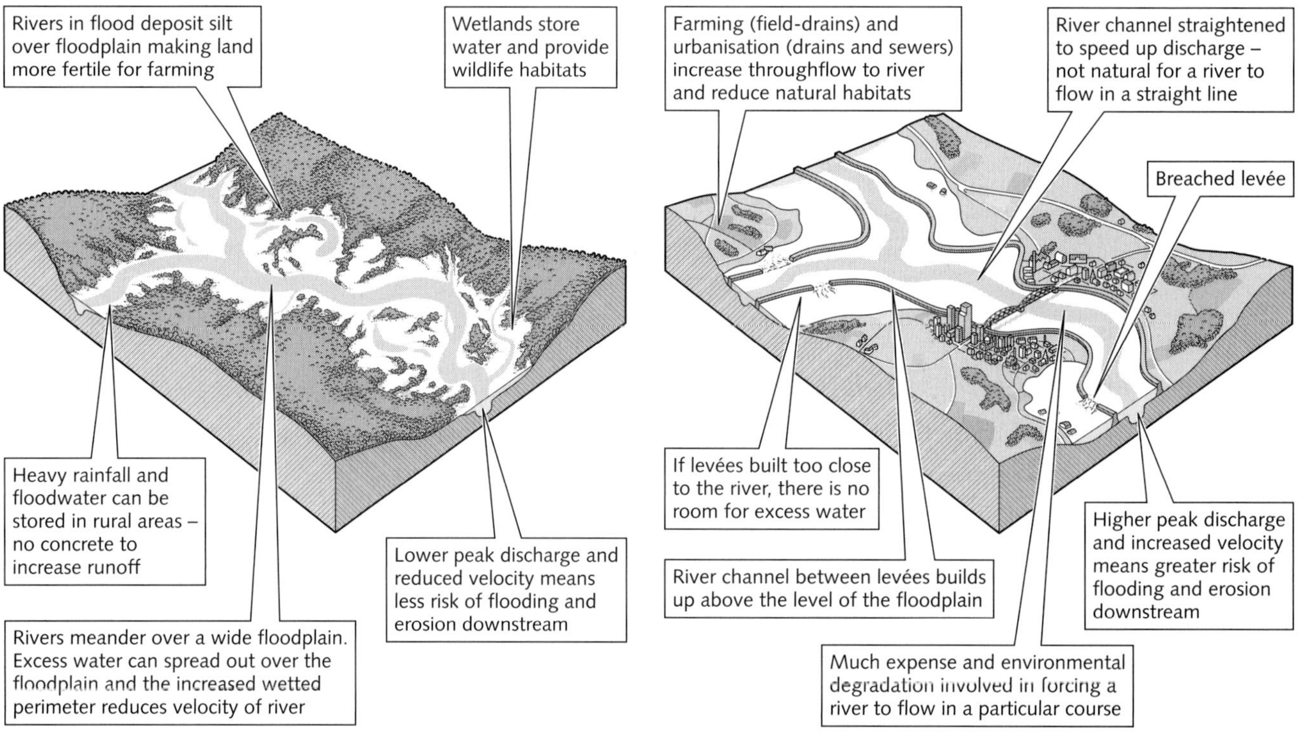

- **For management:** better flood defences should be developed in order to more effectively control rivers, because they are potentially so useful. People who live and work in towns and cities built on floodplains are in favour of river management as this is the only way to protect their homes and livelihoods.

Check this!...

1 Describe some hard engineering techniques used to control rivers.

2 What soft engineering techniques were used after the Lynmouth floods?

3 List some of the arguments for and against controlling rivers.

3 Fragile environments require sustainable management

Many natural environments, such as the rainforests previously studied in Chapter 4, are very fragile – in other words they are easily damaged by human activities. At the same time, they may also be very valuable for people in terms of the resources they provide and the populations they support. Sustainable management techniques are needed in order for these environments to be preserved for the future whilst still being used for the current generation to make a living and for countries to develop economically.

Case Study

LEDC example – desertification in the Sahel

Back to ...

The New Wider World **pages 256–258** for this case study of the Sahel and how human activities such as farming combine with physical conditions to cause damage; also **page 254** for more detail on soil erosion, and **page 255** for ways in which soil can be managed.

Using your case study

You need to know where the Sahel is and which countries it covers. You should learn a definition of desertification; its causes – physical and human; and effects on the natural environment. You also need to know about more sustainable practices for managing soil.

Update

Go to *The New Wider World Coursemates* website for a link giving information on the countries in the Sahel, and projects to improve the environment and quality of life for the people who live there.

Learn it!

1 Draw a sketch map to show the location of the Sahel. Label the countries it covers.

2 What is desertification?

3 Explain how the following lead to desertification:
a) climatic change
b) overgrazing
c) population growth.

4 Explain the effects of desertification on:
a) soil
b) people.

5 Explain the techniques which can be used to manage soil and prevent soil erosion.

Check this!...

1 Why are some natural environments 'fragile'?

2 What are sustainable management techniques? Why are they needed in fragile environments?

Case Study

MEDC example – the exploitation of oil in Alaska

Back to …

The New Wider World **pages 128–131** for this case study on the potential damage of resource exploitation.

Using your case study

You need to be able to explain why Alaska is a fragile environment and why it is being used for oil exploitation. You should learn how the activities associated with oil exploitation are affecting the natural vegetation, wildlife and local people. You need to be able to describe attempted solutions to these problems. You should also learn specific detail about the *Exxon Valdez* oil spill – what happened, what damage was caused to the natural environment and what was done to clean up the pollution. Find out which groups of people are in favour of oil exploration and which groups are against it, and make sure you can explain why.

Update

Go to *The New Wider World Coursemates* website for a link to a site giving a Powerpoint presentation on the development of oil in Alaska.

Learn it!

1 Where is Alaska? Draw a sketch map to show its location and add the route of the Alaska pipeline.

2 List some of the physical problems which were encountered during construction of the pipeline and explain how these were overcome.

3 Describe the environmental concerns about the pipeline.

4 Describe the causes of the *Exxon Valdez* disaster.

5 Explain how the environment was affected and what attempts were made to clean up the oil slick.

6 Who is in favour of new oil exploration in Alaska, and why? Who is against it, and why?

EXAM PRACTICE

1 Many coasts are threatened by cliff recession. Give three reasons why this happens. (3)

2 Referring to an example you have studied:
   a) describe the effects of cliff recession on people and the environment
   b) explain the management techniques used to protect the area from cliff recession. (8)

3 Choose an example of a river flood.
   a) Describe the effects of the flood on the people and the environment.
   b) Explain what happened after the flood to protect the area in the future. (8)

4 Choose a fragile environment which has been damaged by agriculture. Describe how the damage was caused and explain what management techniques have been introduced to protect the area in the future. (6)

Back to …

The New Wider World Coursemates website to check your answers to the exam practice questions.

EXAM TIPS

'Describe' and 'explain' are two of the most common command words, yet students frequently misinterpret them in an exam question. When you are asked to describe the effects, for example of cliff recession or a river flood, you must do this by using specific detail which relates to your chosen event. All floods cover the land in water and damage homes, but the Lynmouth flood destroyed the Lynmouth hotel and 90 other houses. Often you are asked to explain, e.g. how management techniques prevent coastal erosion. In this case more than just a description of a groyne, for example, is needed – you must add that the groyne prevents longshore drift, leading to the creation of a beach which protects the cliffs from the erosive power of the waves.

The New Wider World, pp216–217, 262–274, 312–313

6 Managing hazards

1 Some places are more hazardous than others

The global distribution of tropical storms

Tropical storms are areas of intensive low pressure known locally as **hurricanes, cyclones** or **typhoons**. Tropical storms develop:

- over warm tropical oceans, where sea temperatures exceed 27°C over a vast area, and where there is a considerable depth of warm water
- in late summer and early autumn, when sea temperatures are at their highest level
- in the trade wind belt between latitudes 5 and 20 degrees north and south of the Equator.

KEY IDEAS

1. Some places are more hazardous than others
2. Hazards have an impact on people and the environment
3. People can prepare for hazards, and they respond to events in different ways

Figure 6.1 Location and frequency of tropical storms

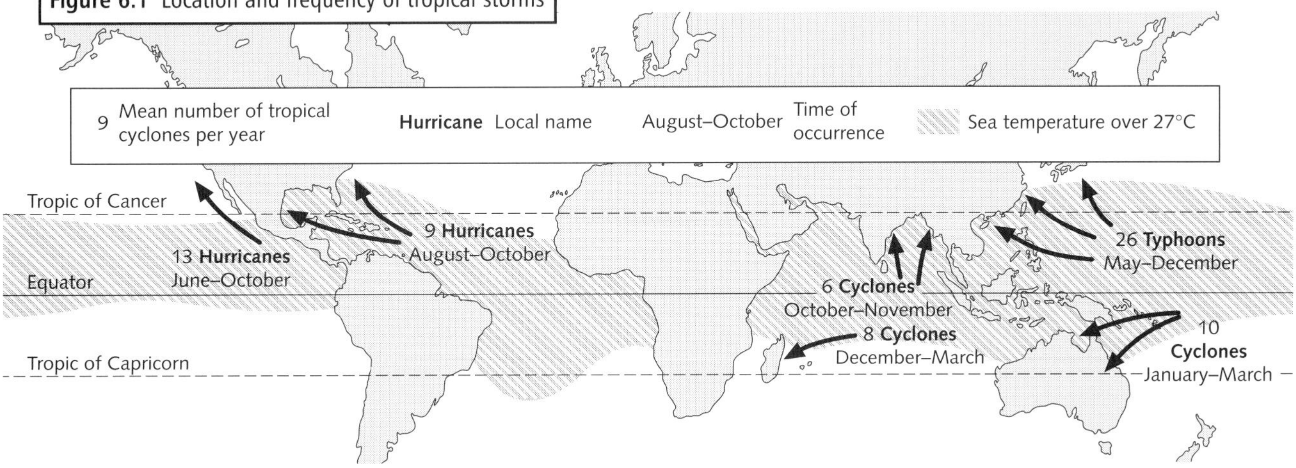

A strong, vertical movement of air draws water vapour with it from the ocean below. As the air rises, in a spiral movement, it cools and condenses – a process that releases enormous amounts of heat energy. This heat energy powers the storm and allows it to move. In time, an

Key words to know

Hurricane
Cyclone
Typhoon

Figure 6.2 The features of a tropical storm

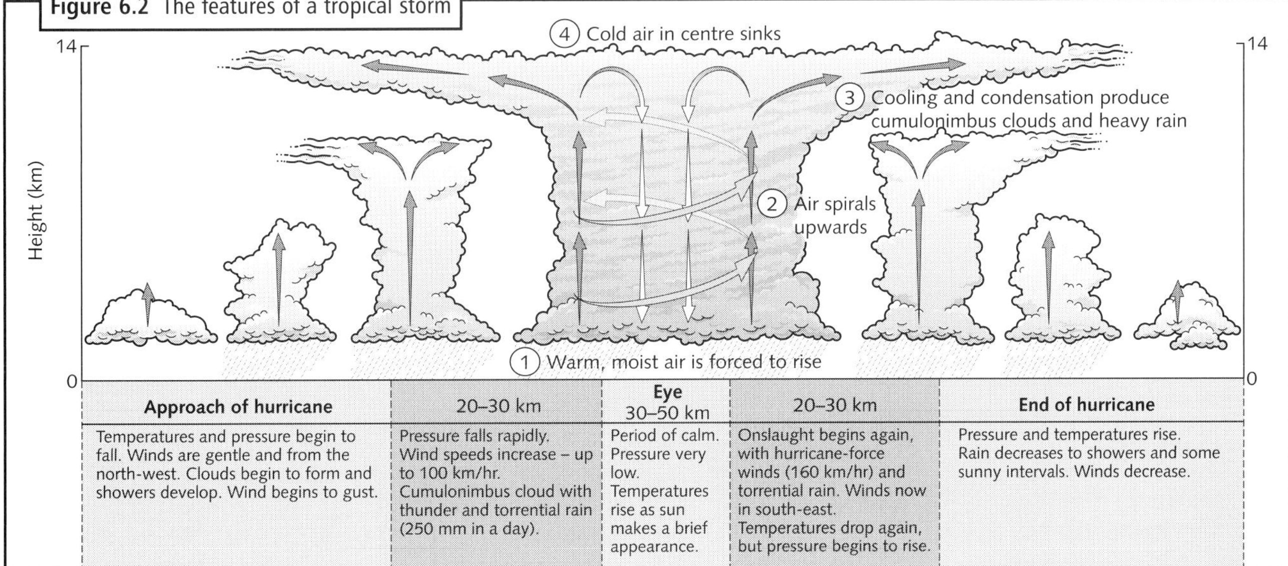

Check this!...

1 Describe the location of tropical storms.
2 List the conditions under which tropical storms develop.

area of colder air sinks downwards through the centre of the hurricane to form a central eye. Once the storm reaches land, and its source of energy and moisture is removed, it rapidly decreases in strength. Its average lifespan is 7–14 days. Figure 6.2 shows the characteristic pattern of weather associated with a tropical storm.

The global distribution of volcanic and earthquake activity

Figures 6.3 and 6.4 show the distribution of earthquakes and volcanoes and the locations of some of the more recent events.

Figure 6.3 The distribution of earthquakes

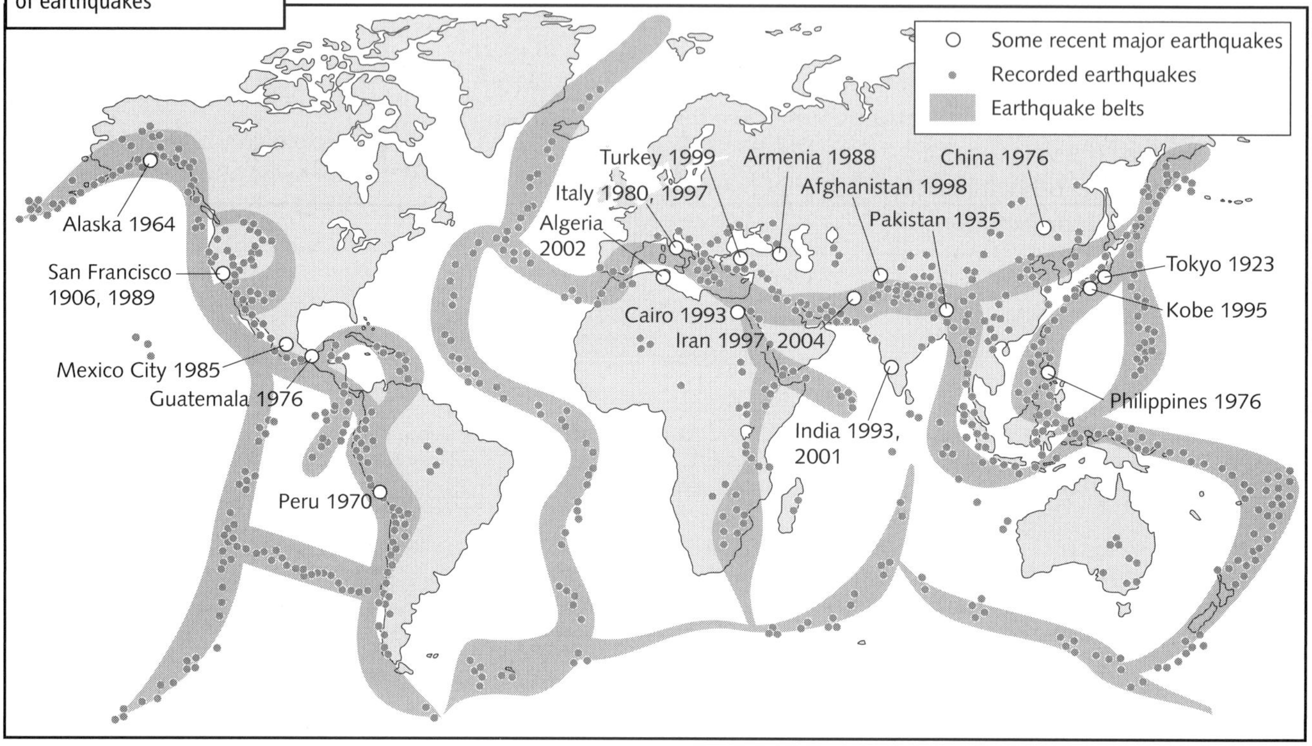

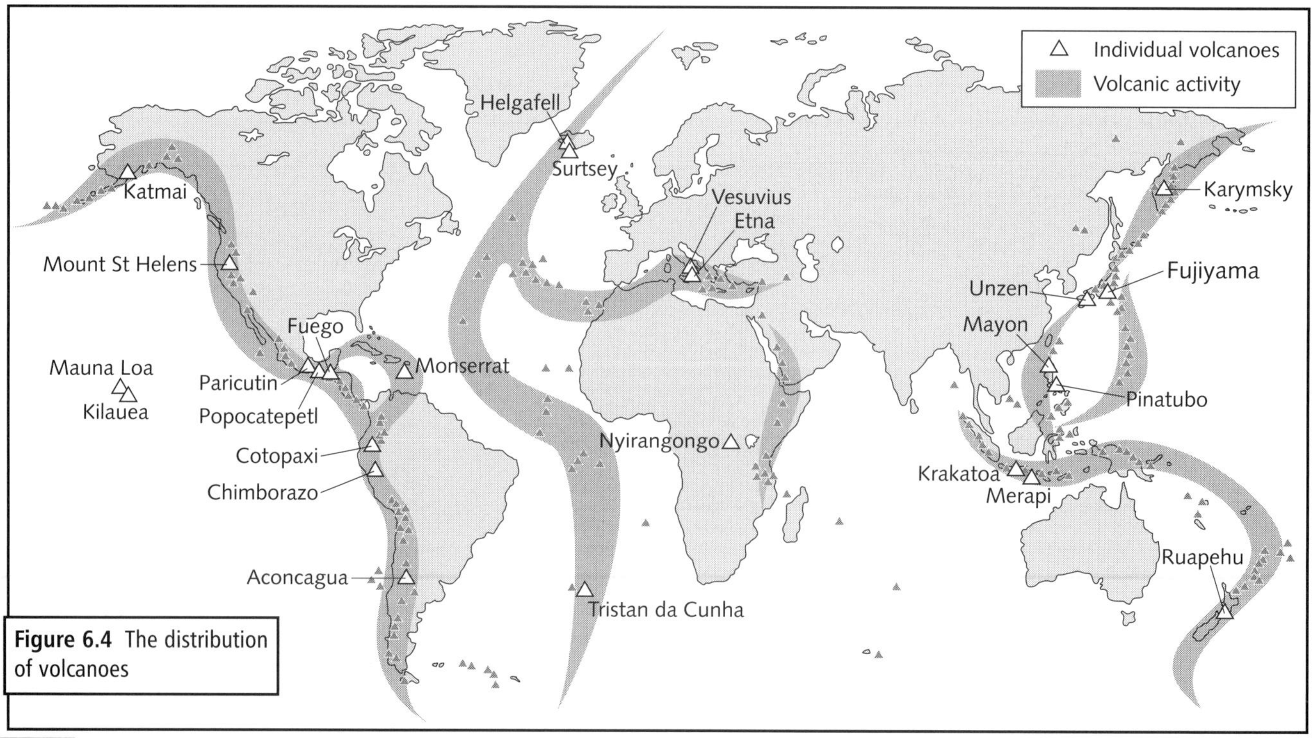

Figure 6.4 The distribution of volcanoes

There are well-defined patterns of earthquakes and volcanoes occurring in long narrow belts, e.g.

- around the Pacific Ocean, known as the 'Pacific Ring of Fire'
- down the length of the mid-Atlantic Ocean
- an earthquake belt across southern Europe and Asia
- areas of volcanic activity in southern Europe, the Caribbean, east Africa and the mid-Pacific Ocean.

Plate boundaries – characteristic features and effects of movement

Figure 6.5 Plate boundaries and zones of activity

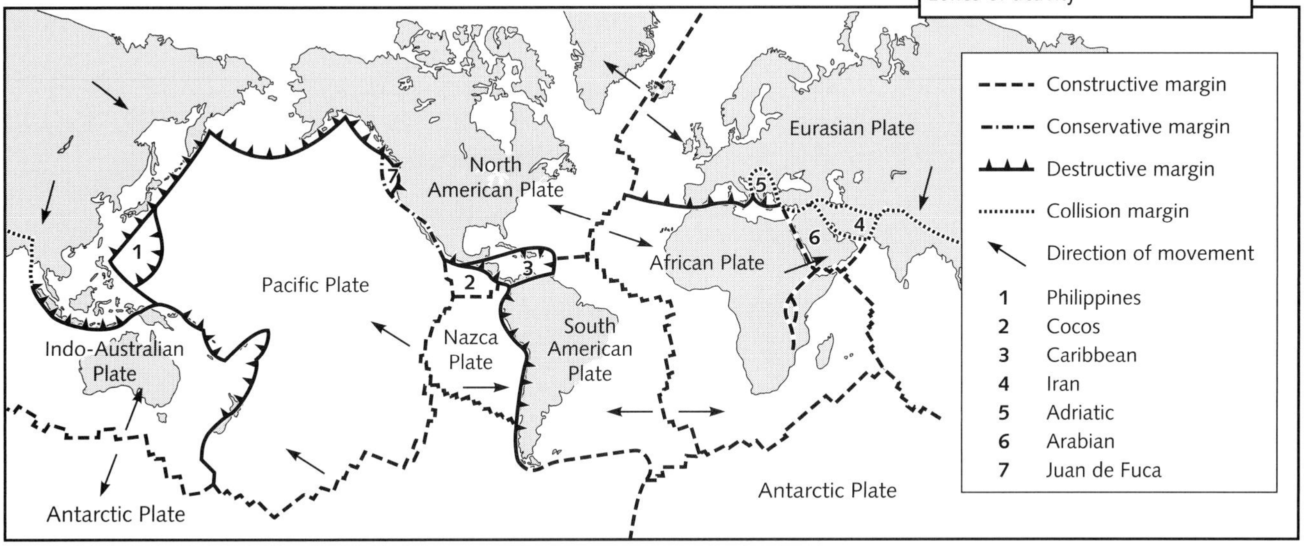

The **plates** which make up the Earth's **crust** float on the **mantle** (area underneath the crust where temperatures are so high that rock exists in a semi-molten, or liquid, state). Heat from within the mantle creates **convection currents** which cause the plates to move, perhaps by a few centimetres a year.

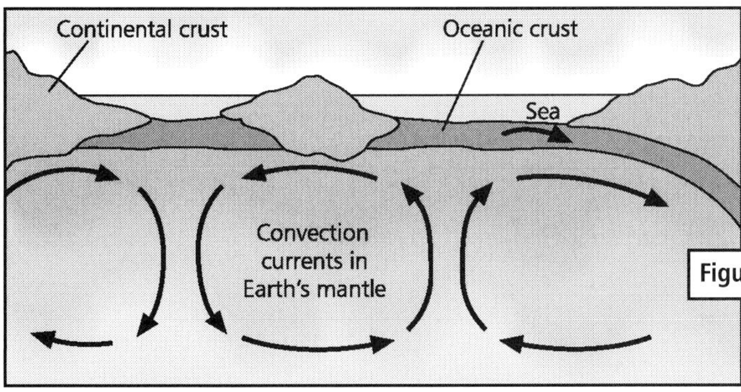

Figure 6.6 How plates move

Plates may either move away from, towards, or sideways past neighbouring plates, as the arrows on Figure 6.5 show. Plates meet at **plate boundaries** (or **margins**) and it is at these boundaries that most of the world's earthquakes and volcanoes occur and where high mountain ranges are located.

Plates consist of two types of crust: continental crust and oceanic crust.

- **Continental crust** is older, lighter, cannot sink and is permanent.
- **Oceanic crust** is younger, heavier, can sink and is constantly being destroyed and replaced. These differences in the crust account for the different ways in which plates move.

Key words to know

Plate
Crust
Mantle
Convection current
Plate boundary (margin)
Continental crust
Oceanic crust

Figure 6.7 Types of plate margin

(a) **Divergent (constructive) margin**

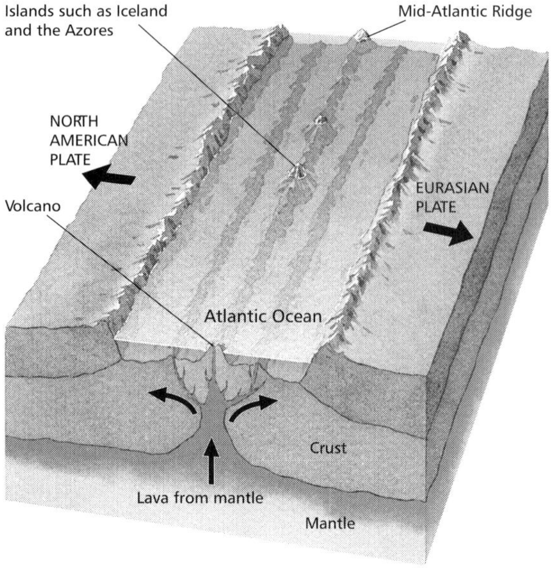

Two plates move away from each other. Molten rock, or **magma**, rises to fill any possible gap and forms new oceanic crust, often along mid-ocean ridges with volcanoes. When this happens repeatedly, new islands may be formed, e.g. Surtsey, Iceland, which emerged in November 1963 after submarine explosions in the Atlantic Ocean. Gentle volcanic and earthquake activity

(b) **Convergent (destructive) margin**

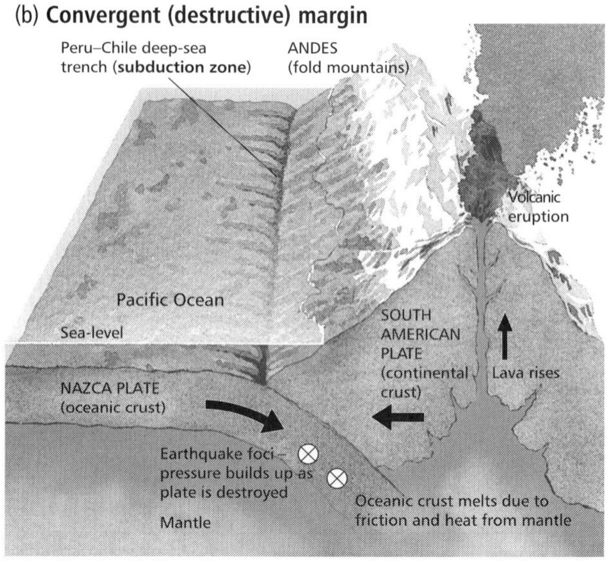

An oceanic plate, e.g. the Nazca plate, moves towards a continental plate, e.g. the South American plate. When they meet, the heavier oceanic plate is forced downwards to form a **subduction zone** (area where an oceanic plate slides under a continental plate and the oceanic plate melts due to intense friction and heat). A deep-sea trench is also formed. As the oceanic plate is forced downwards there is an increase in pressure which can trigger earthquakes. As the oceanic plate melts due to the increasing temperature in the mantle, the newly formed magma is lighter and may rise to the surface to form volcanoes (e.g. Cotopaxi) and fold mountains (e.g. the Andes).

(c) **Conservative margin**

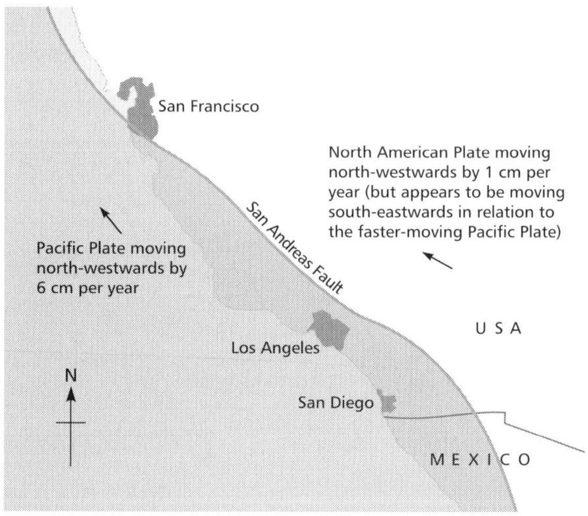

Two plates slide past each other. No new landforms are created and there is no volcanic activity. However, earthquakes can occur if the two plates 'stick'. This happens along the San Andreas Fault which marks the junction of the Pacific and North American plates. The North American plate moves more slowly than, and at a slight angle into, the Pacific plate. Instead of slipping evenly past each other, the plates stick until sufficient pressure builds up and one plate is jerked forward sending shockwaves to the surface. These shockwaves cause earthquakes, e.g. San Francisco in 1906 and 1989.

Check this!...

1 Explain the difference between oceanic and continental crust.
   a) Describe what happens at divergent, convergent and conservative margins.
   b) Give an example of each type of margin and any associated features.

2 With the aid of a labelled diagram explain why:
   a) volcanoes occur at divergent plate margins
   b) volcanoes and earthquakes occur at convergent plate margins
   c) earthquakes occur at conservative plate margins.

Back to ...

The New Wider World **pages 264–265** for more information on the types of plate movement and processes of tectonic activity.

Key words to know

Divergent (constructive) margin
Magma
Convergent (destructive) margin
Subduction zone
Conservative margin

2 Hazards have an impact on people and the environment

Impact of tropical storms

Hazard	Impact on people	Impact on the environment
Winds – often exceed 160 km/h	• In LEDCs whole villages destroyed • In MEDCs houses and coastal developments severely damaged • Telephones and power supplies disrupted • Export crops destroyed	• Trees uprooted
Flooding – caused by torrential rain	• Loss of life • Loss of or damage to property and possessions • Pollution of drinking water	• Outbreak of diseases such as cholera • Farmland destroyed
Storm surges – up to 5 m in height	• Floods in low-lying coastal areas causing loss of life	• Resulting floods block escape and relief roads
Landslides	• Heavy rainfall washes away buildings erected on steep, unstable slopes	• Resulting floods block escape and relief roads • Trees damaged and farmland destroyed by landslides

Figure 6.8 The impact of tropical storms on people and the environment

Case Study

Tropical storms – in an LEDC (Hurricane Mitch) and in an MEDC (Hurricane Andrew)

Back to ...

The New Wider World **page 217** for this case study on Hurricanes Mitch and Andrew.

Using your case study

You can use Hurricane Mitch as an example of how devastating a hurricane can be in an LEDC such as Honduras, and Hurricane Andrew to describe how impacts of a tropical storm are different in an MEDC. In each case you need to learn specific details about the effects on people (e.g. lives lost, numbers made homeless), the economy (e.g. loss of income for farmers) and the environment (e.g. farmland destroyed, floods and outbreaks of diseases). You should also consider which effects were primary (e.g. crops flattened in high winds) and which were secondary (e.g. shortage of food resulting from the destruction of crops) as well as those which were short-term (e.g. power failures) and long-term (e.g. loss of export sales because of damaged crops). You should also be able to explain why the effects were so devastating in Honduras, considering the lack of accurate prediction and early warning, the limited emergency services and poor construction of buildings. By comparison, while it did a great deal of damage in the USA, the effects of Hurricane Andrew were much less harmful to the people and the economy of the USA. This is largely a result of the high level of development in the USA (an MEDC) compared with that of Honduras (an LEDC).

Update

There is plenty of information on the internet about Hurricane Mitch. Go to *The New Wider World Coursemates* website for a link to a search engine through which you can find newspaper reports and satellite information on the event. Another link takes you to a site where you can find an account of the effects of Hurricane Andrew in 2002, as well as details of how people and the authorities have prepared for hurricanes since then.

Learn it!

1 Draw a sketch map to show the paths of Hurricanes Mitch and Andrew.

2 Describe some of the effects of each hurricane on:
a) the people
b) the economy
c) the environment.

3 Explain why the effects of Hurricane Andrew were not as devastating as those of Hurricane Mitch.

Why do people continue to live in areas at risk from tropical storms?

Despite the risks, large numbers of people live in coastal regions where tropical storms are frequent. Compare Figure 6.9 below (which shows world population distribution) with Figure 6.1 on page 71 of this book which shows the distribution of tropical storms.

Figure 6.9 World population distribution

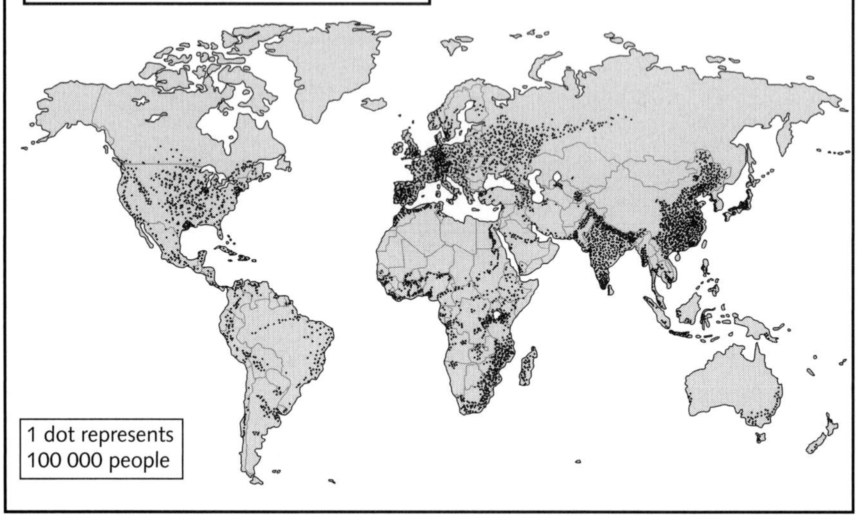

There are a number of reasons which help to explain this:

- People live and work in these areas because they must grow their main food crop here and useful land is limited, e.g. subsistence rice farmers in Bangladesh.
- People feel that the risk is worth taking because they have a good quality of life and live in pleasant surroundings, e.g. Florida.
- People in LEDCs have nowhere else to go and cannot afford to move, so they remain in the area and try to rebuild their homes after a tropical storm, e.g. Honduras.
- MEDCs people may feel they are safer and protected from the effects by early warning systems, efficient emergency services and hazard-proof buildings, e.g. USA.
- Their friends and family may all live in the area and they do not wish to move.

Check this!...

1 Why do people live in areas at risk from tropical storms?

2 How are the reasons for living in these areas different in MEDCs and LEDCs?

3 People can prepare for hazards, and they respond to events in different ways

Preparing for earthquakes and volcanic eruptions

The two ways of preparing for earthquakes and volcanic eruptions are:

- predicting when they will happen
- preparing buildings, people and emergency services.

	Volcanic eruptions	Earthquakes
Prediction	It is easier to predict volcanic eruptions than earthquakes because: • Tremors increase within the volcano. • As magma begins to rise, so do ground temperatures. These can be detected by satellites using heat-seeking cameras (new technology). • The rising magma causes the volcano to swell and bulge. This can be measured by **tiltmeters** (instruments which measure slope angles) and satellite global positioning systems. • Immediately before an eruption, the volcano emits an increasing amount of gas and steam. • At Merapi, Indonesia, each month a team visits the summit to note any changes in pressure and temperature. Hopefully, this will enable scientists to give villagers sufficient time to seek safety before an eruption occurs.	• Install sensitive instruments that can measure an increase in earth tremors **(seismometer)**, pressure, and any release of radon gas. • Map **epicentres** (the point where the earthquake begins) and frequencies of previous eruptions to see if there is a location and/or time pattern (this can only give possible timings of an event and not a precise location). • Observe unusual animal behaviour – dogs howling, mice fleeing houses (less scientific but has proved useful). • Before the Kobe earthquake in 1995, seismologists had monitored slight movements where the Philippine plate is being forced under the Eurasian plate. However, as with all earthquakes, it is very difficult to predict exactly when, and even if, a major earthquake will follow smaller earth movements.
Preparation	• Setting up monitoring and warning systems using new technology. • Preparing evacuation and post-eruption plans. • Training emergency services such as police, fire and ambulance crews. • On Merapi, dams have been built across valleys to hold back **lahars** (mudflows). The dams trap the mud, which can be spread over fields, and slowly release the water. Over 70 dams have been built to protect villages, roads, a major canal system and tourist sites. • Also on Merapi, a task force of local people has been specifically trained to give emergency treatment to the injured and to organise transport to evacuation camps and temporary accommodation.	• This includes constructing buildings and roads to withstand earthquakes (e.g. San Francisco; and see Figure 6.11). • Training emergency services and having them available, e.g. helicopters, ambulances and fire engines. • Setting up a warning and information system for use on TV and radio (earthquake preparation is part of the Japanese school curriculum). • Although the people of Kobe knew what to do in an earthquake, many older, traditional houses could not withstand the tremors and were damaged or collapsed.

Figure 6.10 Ways of preparing for earthquakes and volcanic activity

Building design

As technology has improved, together with our understanding of earthquakes and their impacts, new buildings have been constructed which are said to be 'earthquake proof (Figure 6.11). This means they are strong enough to withstand the force of an earthquake without collapsing.

Key words to know

Tiltmeter
Lahar
Seismometer
Epicentre

Back to ...

The New Wider World **pages 266–273** for the MEDC and LEDC case studies on the causes and effects of volcanic eruptions and earthquakes.

Figure 6.11 How buildings are designed to withstand earthquakes

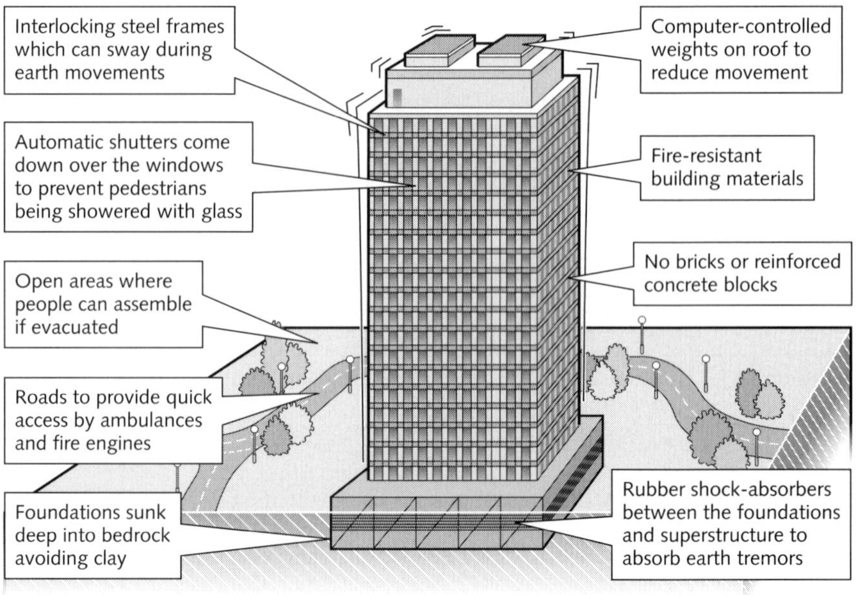

Responding to earthquakes and volcanic activity

In MEDCs human responses to hazards are usually much quicker and more efficient in countries such as the USA and Japan. This means that the effects of earthquakes and volcanic eruptions are usually much less than in LEDCs, such as Indonesia and Afghanistan, where people often have to rely upon, and wait for, international aid. The aftermath of volcanoes and earthquakes can be managed by organising:

- transport, accommodation and food for those who need to be moved
- emergency services to provide water, food and power
- post-eruption plans to include repairing communications and buildings.

Case Study

An earthquake in an MEDC – Kobe, Japan

Back to ...

The New Wider World **pages 270–271** for this case study of an earthquake in an MEDC.

Using your case study

You can use this case study to show how an MEDC such as Japan is much more able to recover from a major earthquake than an LEDC. It is also a good example to use when discussing the **primary effects** and **secondary effects** of and responses to an earthquake. (Primary effects are the immediate impacts such as damaged buildings and burst water pipes. Secondary effects include further damage after the event itself, e.g. the outbreak of fires from burst gas pipes, and unsafe buildings which later have to be demolished.) You can also use it to compare the effects of and responses to earthquakes in an MEDC with those in an LEDC such as Afghanistan.

Key words to know

Primary effects
Secondary effects

Update

Go to *The New Wider World Coursemates* website for a link to the National Earthquake Information Centre which gives up-to-date information on earthquakes; another link gives specific information on Kobe.

Learn it!

1 Where is Kobe?

2 What caused the earthquake in 1995?

3 What were the primary and secondary effects?

4 a) What happened in the months after the earthquake?
b) How long did it take Kobe to recover from the earthquake?
c) What new precautions were taken after the earthquake?

Back to ...

The New Wider World **pages 272–273** for a case study of an earthquake in an LEDC – Afghanistan.

Case Study

A volcanic eruption in an LEDC – Merapi, Indonesia

Back to ...

The New Wider World **pages 268–269** for this case study of the different effects of a volcanic eruption in an LEDC.

Using your case study

You can use this case study to describe the effects of living near a volcano on people in small villages in an LEDC, explain why they still live there, and give examples of ways in which people in Indonesia are both trying to predict and prepare for eruptions. You might need to use it in a question which asks you to compare the effects of volcanoes on people in an MEDC, e.g. Mount St Helens, USA, with effects on people in an LEDC.

Update

Go to *The New Wider World Coursemates* website for a link to Volcano World which gives up-to-date information on all volcanoes.

Learn it!

1 Where is Indonesia? Draw a sketch map to show the location of Merapi.

2 What were the effects of the eruption of Merapi in 1994 on:
a) the people who live and farm near the volcano
b) the environment?

3 Why do people keep returning to their homes after each eruption?

4 How do people in places like Merapi prepare for an eruption?

5 Describe the short-term responses and the long-term effects of the 1994 Merapi eruption.

Back to ...

The New Wider World **pages 266–267** for a case study of a volcanic eruption in an MEDC – Mount St Helens, USA.

Check this!...

1 What can be done to predict and prepare for earthquakes and volcanoes?

2 How do people cope in the aftermath of an earthquake or volcanic eruption?

3 What differences can you identify between the ways in which people in MEDCs and LEDCs cope with volcanoes and earthquakes?

Sources of aid

When an earthquake or a volcanic eruption occurs in an LEDC the country often relies on **aid** – the giving of resources by one country, or by an organisation (known as the **donor)** to another country (the **recipient**). Aid may come from several sources, including governments, NGOs (non-governmental organisations) such as ActionAid, and charities such as Disaster Relief. The resources may be in the form of:

- money
- food or machinery such as earth-moving equipment
- people who have skills and knowledge, e.g. nurses.

This aid is short-term, immediate help providing food, clothes, medical supplies and shelter and is given to places and people directly in need. This was particularly important in the Afghanistan earthquake on 4 February 1998, as the timeline in Figure 6.12 shows.

Figure 6.12 Effects of the earthquake in Afghanistan in 1998

4/2/1998	Earthquake reading 6.1 on the Richter scale occurs in remote northern Afghanistan. News takes 3 days to reach the capital, Kabul.
8/2/1998	Relief teams from Médecins sans Frontières and the Red Cross travel to the area by donkey and horse. Landslides triggered by the earthquake have made roads unsuitable for motor vehicles.
9/2/1998	Urgent food and medical supplies have still not reached the area due to poor weather which prevents helicopters from flying; snow and landslides block roads; there is a local civil war involving the Taliban.
10/2/1998	Aid flights still held back by bad weather. Reports say that survivors are living without shelter in sub-zero temperatures. Hundreds of villagers start to leave the area in search of food and shelter.
16/2/1998	12 days after the earthquake helicopters are finally able to drop supplies to 3 isolated villages. 488 blankets, 220 tents, 800 quilts, 1500 tonnes of food and 1.7 tonnes of medical kits are received.

Key words to know

Aid
Donor
Recipient
Human Development Index

In Afghanistan, a local agency, the Afghan Red Crescent Society, provided emergency medical teams but much aid was also needed from outside agencies. This is because Afghanistan is a poor country and unable to cope with a major earthquake for several reasons:

- According to the United Nations' **Human Development Index** (a measurement of quality of life based on data for health, education and standard of living), in the late 1990s Afghanistan was ranked 171 out of 173 countries. Since then the country has experienced several years of drought, a long-standing civil war culminating in the intervention of the USA after 11 September 2001, and several major earthquakes including the one of 1998.
- Afghanistan does not have the money, the infrastructure or the technology to predict, plan for or cope with major earthquakes, e.g. there is a lack of helicopters to take in emergency supplies and bring out the injured.
- Houses are often poorly built and even in the capital are unlikely to be reinforced to withstand earthquakes.
- Roads are poor – often only rough tracks in rural areas and through mountains – making access very difficult for any emergency vehicles which are available.
- Mountainous terrain and a severe climate (long, cold winters and heavy snowfall) disrupt transport and hinder the arrival of emergency aid.
- Many remote areas are without telephones or electricity which increases the difficulty of communicating with the outside world.

Check this!...

1 What different types of aid are needed in an LEDC after an earthquake or volcanic eruption?

2 Describe some of the difficulties faced by relief operations in Afghanistan after the 1998 earthquake.

3 Explain why aid in a very poor country such as Afghanistan may not always be successful.

EXAM PRACTICE

1 Describe the location of tropical storms in relation to population distribution. (4)

2 Describe the effects of tropical storms on people and the environment. Refer to specific examples. (4)

3 Explain how the effects of tropical storms are different in MEDCs and LEDCs. (4)

4 Referring to an example of an earthquake you have studied:

a) describe the needs of the people immediately after the earthquake

b) explain the long-term problems created by the earthquake

c) describe attempts made to reduce damage in future earthquakes. (8)

5 With reference to examples, explain why people live in areas where there are volcanic eruptions. (5)

EXAM TIPS

Many candidates do not achieve above 3 or 4 marks in an 8 mark question because they do not address all the different aspects asked for and/or they have not learned enough specific detail of a named event. In question 4 above, to achieve Level 2 (4–6 marks) you must include specific detail and for 6 marks this must cover short-term needs, long-term problems and attempts made to reduce further damage. For Level 3 (7–8) marks, you need specific detail and explanations of the long-term problems – this means stating what the problems were and also explaining why they occurred.

Back to ...

The New Wider World Coursemates website to check your answers to the exam practice questions.

7 Managing tourism

The New Wider World, pp92, 160–169, 172–175

KEY IDEAS

1. The global tourist industry has grown rapidly. Different types of tourists can be identified
2. The rapid growth of tourism has had an impact on people and their environments
3. The impacts of tourism have led to the need for management

Key words to know

Mass tourism
Primary
Secondary
Tertiary
Multiplier effect

Figure 7.1 International tourist arrivals by region

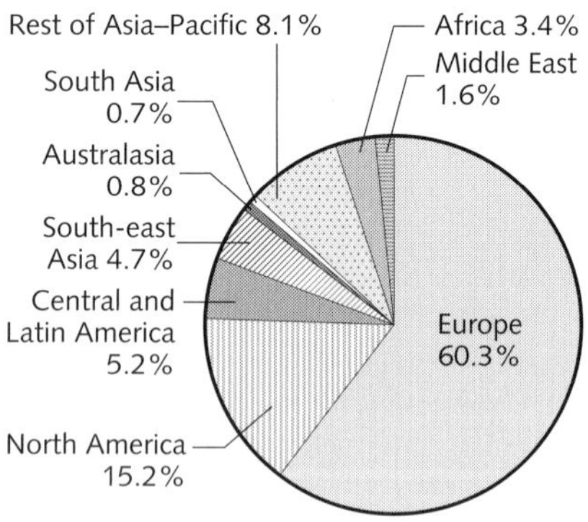

1 The global tourist industry has grown rapidly. Different types of tourists can be identified

Tourism has become the world's fastest growing and largest industry. It is an important factor in the economy of most developed countries and is seen by many developing countries as the one possible way to obtain income, create jobs and to improve their standard of living. It has grown rapidly in the last 50 years:

- in 1950, 25 million 'international' arrivals were recorded worldwide
- this figure had risen to 225 million by 1975 and 700 million by 2000
- in addition there are many more domestic tourists.

As tourism has grown, travel for a privileged few has been replaced by **mass tourism** as large numbers of holidaymakers have been able to travel further afield.

The impact of tourism on primary, secondary and tertiary industry

Tourism has had an impact on jobs in different economic sectors:

- creating a market for local produce/crafts and so increasing demand for jobs in the **primary** sector
- growth in the building industry and associated **secondary** activities as the demand for hotels increases
- need for more people to be employed as hotel receptionists, waiters and other jobs in the **tertiary** sector.

This means that tourism can have different impacts in countries at different stages of development.

Figure 7.1 shows that the more economically developed countries (MEDCs) receive just over 75 per cent of all international tourist arrivals. However, their share has fallen from 82 per cent in 1980 as destinations in less economically developed countries (LEDCs) in Africa, South-east Asia and the Pacific and the Middle East have become more popular and more accessible.

As the growth of tourism creates jobs in the tertiary sector it also encourages the growth of jobs in the secondary and primary sectors – this is known as the **multiplier effect**. For example, when a tourist spends £500 in a hotel, some of that money is used directly in the hotel, to pay the waiters and chambermaids, and some is used to pay people who provide the hotel with other services – the local farmer who sells his produce, or the laundry that washes the linen. Both the farmer and the laundry staff may spend some of their earnings in local bars and shops, creating more demand for goods and employment.

Since the early 1980s, European tourists have become increasingly less satisfied with package tours to the Mediterranean. Like tourists from North America and Japan, they have sought holidays in places farther afield where the environment and culture is very different from their own. The chief beneficiaries of this change in holiday fashion and demand have been several developing countries located within, or near to, the Tropics – places such as Kenya, Egypt, Sri Lanka, Thailand, Malaysia and the West Indies.

The attraction of earning money from tourism is considerable to LEDCs, many of which see it as the only possible way to raise their standard of living. However, only a limited number of LEDCs have the potential to develop a successful tourist industry and even then the damage to their culture and environment can, at times, outweigh the benefits.

Back to ...

Chapter 3 page 34 of this book for definitions of primary, secondary and tertiary activities and an explanation of how employment structure changes with development.

Figure 7.2 Tourism in developing countries

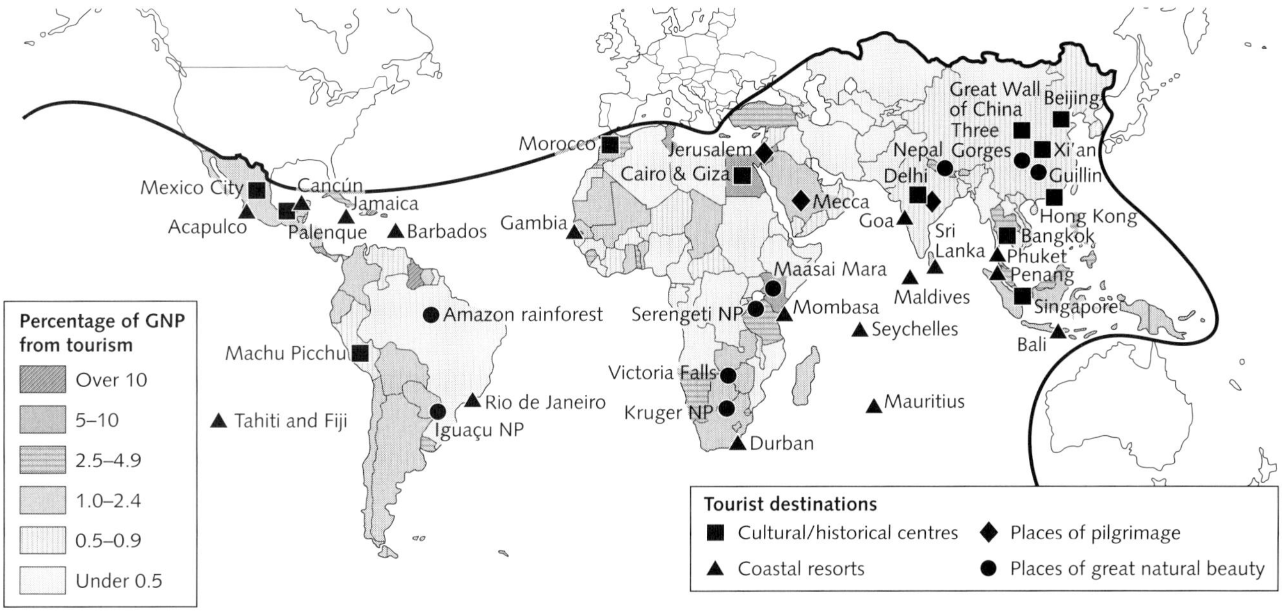

Check this!...

1 Describe how the global tourist industry has grown rapidly.

2 What is the multiplier effect?

3 Describe how tourism has become more important in LEDCs.

Causes of the rapid growth in tourism

The causes of the rapid growth in tourism can be classified into groups.

- **Social**
  - An increase in mobility as greater car ownership has given people more freedom to choose where and when they go for the day or for a longer period.
  - As more roads have been built, especially motorways and urban by-passes, accessibility has improved. They have reduced driving times and encouraged more people to travel more frequently.
  - Changes in lifestyle, such as a shorter working week, flexi-time and an increase in the number of home workers, give people greater freedom of choice about when they travel.
  - There is a greater awareness of places due to coverage by the media and TV – holiday programmes, magazines and brochures promote new and different places and activities.
  - In MEDCs there is an ageing population, and retired people have more free time to travel.

Figure 7.3 Number of holidays taken by UK residents in a year

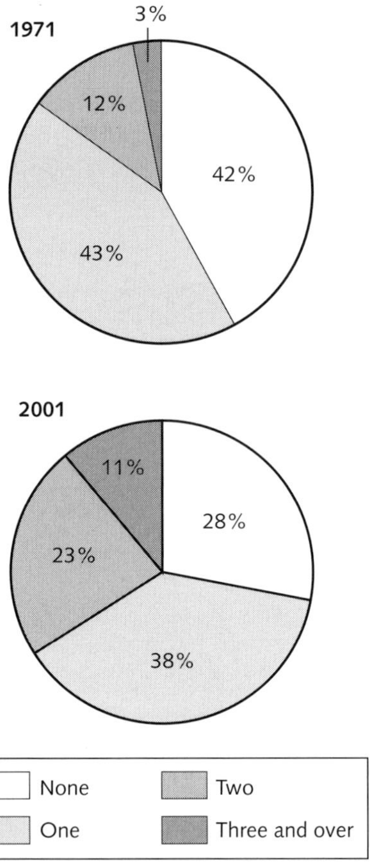

- **Economic**
  - There is an increase in **affluence** (wealth) as salaries have increased and people have more **disposable income** (money left to spend after the necessities have been paid for).
  - People receive holiday pay which means they can take more than one holiday a year.
  - The organisation of mass tourism by transnational companies such as Thomas Cook, has lowered prices.
- **Technology**
  - Improvements in transport, e.g. the introduction of larger jet planes, have enabled more people to travel greater distances.
  - Improved and enlarged airports, and reduced air fares with the introduction of low-cost 'no frills' airlines such as Easyjet, have increased the flow of tourists.
  - Computerised reservation systems enable travel agents to deal with more holidays and people are able to book their own holidays on the internet and by teletext.
  - Global distribution systems such as Galileo and Worldspan have made it possible for companies such as Thompson to operate globally.
- **Product development and changing customer needs**
  - One of the earliest products to be developed were the Butlin's holiday camps in the 1950s.
  - A more recent development has been the growth in theme parks.
  - Another important product was the development of the package holiday – a tour company providing travel, accommodation and sometimes activities.

Key words to know

Affluence
Disposable income
Active
Passive
Cultural
Ecotourism (green tourism)

Tourists can be classified

Tourists can be classified according to:

- the nature of the activity which may be **active** (taking part in an activity such as skiing) or **passive** (relaxation, sunbathing)
- their locational preference: mountain, coastal
- the duration of their trip: weekend break, summer holiday
- the distance travelled: regional, national, international.

Recent years have seen growth in some areas:

- **cultural** holidays and breaks (visits to cities in different countries and places of historical or religious activities)
- introduction of **ecotourism**, sometimes known as **green tourism**.

Ecotourism is a sustainable form of tourism that is more appropriate to developing countries than the mass tourism associated with places such as Florida and the Spanish costas in developed countries. It includes:

- visiting places in order to appreciate their scenery and wildlife and to understand their culture
- creating economic opportunities (jobs) in areas while at the same time protecting natural resources (scenery and wildlife) and the local way of life (culture).

Back to ...

The New Wider World **page 161** for more detailed information on the growth and development of tourism in the UK.

Check this!...

1 Explain the causes of the rapid growth in tourism.

2 Describe the different ways in which tourists can be classified.

2 The rapid growth of tourism has had an impact on people and their environments

Tourist destinations have different physical and human attractions which have led to the growth of tourism and its associated economic, social and environmental impacts.

Physical attractions are often linked to the climate. For example, in the Mediterranean summers are hot, sunny and dry and even in winter it is usually warm enough for people to sit outside. Long, sandy beaches and warm seas are other physical attractions of the Mediterranean. Where a location has several physical attractions, tourist resorts develop with a wide range of human attractions including a range of accommodation (hotels, timeshare apartments, campsites); shops, restaurants and cafés; activities such as water sports and golf courses. These attractions lead to an increase in the number of visitors and a range of impacts which can be both positive and negative and affect different groups of people in different ways.

- **Economic impacts**
  - Tourism creates local employment in construction, hotels, cafés and shops but may lead to a decline in fishing and farming.
  - The income of local people is improved as more jobs are created. However, these may only be seasonal or part-time.
- **Social impacts**
  - Local people benefit from improved infrastructure and services, but they may also suffer problems of congestion in town centres.
  - Crime and vandalism may increase.
- **Environmental impacts**
  - Farmland is built over and wildlife frightened away.
  - Mountain views become hidden by hotels, litter is left on beaches and the sea becomes polluted.

Case Study

Tourism in a coastal area in an LEDC – West Indies

Back to ...

The New Wider World **page 169** for this case study on tourism in the Caribbean.

Using your case study

You can use this example to show why tourists are attracted to the West Indies and the associated costs (disadvantages) and benefits (advantages) of tourism in an LEDC.

Update

Go to *The New Wider World Coursemates* website for a link to find out about Antigua, one of the first islands in the West Indies to promote tourism.

Learn it!

1. Where are the West Indies and what are its physical attractions to tourists?
2. What are the social, economic and environmental costs of tourism in the West Indies?
3. What are the benefits that tourism brings to the West Indies?
4. Explain who might be in favour of tourism in the West Indies and who might be against it.

Case Study

Tourism in a mountain area in an MEDC – Courmayeur, (Italy)

Back to ...

The New Wider World **pages 166–167** for this case study of a popular ski resort in Italy.

Using your case study

You can use this case study to show how recreational activities such as skiing can have both benefits and disadvantages for the physical environment and the local people. Depending on the exam question you may need to categorise the impacts, for example into social, environmental and economic.

Update

Go to *The New Wider World Coursemates* website for a link to a site giving information on why Courmayeur is an attraction for skiers.

Learn it!

1 Where is Courmayeur? Draw a sketch map to show its location.

2 Describe the physical attractions of Courmayeur and its facilities for tourists.

3 Explain how tourism can bring both benefits and problems for:
a) the people
b) the economy
c) the environment.

Check this!...

List some physical and human attractions of:
a) coastal resorts
b) mountain destinations.

Back to ...

The New Wider World **pages 172–175** for an alternative study of the effects of tourism in a mountain area – the Lake District, UK.

3 The impacts of tourism have led to the need for management

Conservation of fragile environments and sustainable tourism

As tourism can damage fragile environments in the same way as other human activities, there is a need for a more sustainable approach to the way in which holidays are developed. This will help to preserve the natural beaches and mountains which attract the tourists in the first place.

Case Study Extra

Issues of tourism in an LEDC – Kenya

Kenya has experienced a large increase in tourism, both for safari and beach holidays, although this has brought about both benefits and problems.

Back to ...

The New Wider World **pages 170–171** for a case study on the development of tourism in Kenya, an LEDC.

In 1996 the Ecotourism Society of Kenya was founded to 'promote tourism practices that will conserve Kenya's natural environment and improve the livelihoods of associated communities'. This organisation has developed an 'Ecorating' system for scoring hotels and lodges according to the extent to which they conserve the environment whilst offering tourist facilities. There are three levels – bronze, silver and gold – and so far 20 lodges have achieved bronze rating. One of the criteria is how energy-efficient the development is. This is especially important in remote locations not serviced by the national grid, in order to avoid over-consumption of wood for fuel and heating. The Ecotourism Society has also developed a Safari Code with a wide range of regulations for tour operators and visitors to adhere to, including:

- keep to the designated roads in parks and reserves
- keep to the minimum recommended distances from animals
- keep to the speed limits
- take all litter away with you.

Whilst most tour operators and visitors keep to the guidelines set out, not all are aware of them. Whilst local tribes, such as the Maasai, may benefit from being tour guides and allowing tourists to experience their culture, some people think they are being exploited, for example when they perform traditional dances especially for tourists. Much work continues in Kenya to improve tourism so that the environment may be sustained and local cultures preserved. Recently Wangari Maalhai, a well-known Kenyan conservationist, was awarded the Nobel Peace Prize for her commitment to the conservation of forests and wildlife in Kenya, and much of her work has been centred around tourism.

Using your case study

You can use this case study to show how tourism can bring both benefits and problems to an LEDC such as Kenya. You also need to be able to describe ways in which these problems can be resolved through conservation and sustainable development. You should be able to explain how different groups of people may have different, and sometimes conflicting, attitudes to tourism, including tour operators, local communities, the tourists and the Kenyan government.

Update

Go to *The New Wider World Coursemates* website for a link to the official tourism website for the Kenyan Government; another link giving information on how Kenya's National Parks are being affected by tourism; and another to the Ecotourism Society of Kenya where you can find more detailed information on their eco-rating scores and safari codes.

Learn it!

1 Where is Kenya and what are its attractions for tourists?

2 What can the money earned from tourism be used for?

3 Describe the impacts tourism has on:
a) the environment
b) the wildlife
c) the people.

Case Study

Issues of tourism in an MEDC – the Costa del Sol

Back to ...

The New Wider World **pages 164–165** for this case study on the development and consequences of tourism in an MEDC.

Using your case study

You can use the example of the Costa del Sol to show how and why tourism developed here, how it affected the environment and how the Spanish government has attempted to make tourism more sustainable.

The main issues which need to be addressed in the Costa del Sol are water conservation, sewerage, landscape and wildlife conservation. Many companies and local authorities in Spain now follow EU guidelines on sustainable tourism. Money is also available from the EU for footpath improvements and replanting bushes along coastal paths. The Sol Melia hotel chain promotes sustainable tourism by establishing guidelines for environmental management which must be adhered to. Locally, authorities make improvements to maintain the environment so that it will continue to attract tourists. For example, beaches in Torremolinos are regenerated with sand and nature parks have been established, for example at Doñana.

Case study links

See *The New Wider World* pages 174–175 for information on the problems created by tourism in the Lake District National Park and some possible solutions.

Update

Go to *The New Wider World Coursemates* website for a link giving you information on the main holiday resorts in the Costa del Sol.

Learn it!

1 Where is the Costa del Sol and what are its attractions for tourism?

2 How did the growth of tourism have negative effects on the environment?

3 How did the Spanish government respond to the problems caused by mass tourism?

4 Describe some of the attempts made to make tourism more sustainable in the Costa del Sol.

Check this!...

1 Giving examples, list some problems caused by tourism.

2 How can tourism be made more sustainable?

3 Compare the ways in which tourism is managed in the Costa del Sol and Kenya. What are the similarities and differences?

EXAM PRACTICE

1 Explain the difference between active and passive tourism. (4)

2 Explain the causes of the rapid growth in tourism. (5)

3 With reference to a fragile environment:
a) explain the problems created by tourism
b) describe attempts made to manage these problems. (8)

4 With reference to a named mountain area:
a) describe the physical and human attractions of the area
b) explain how the growth of tourism created both social and environmental problems. (8)

Back to ...

The New Wider World Coursemates website to check your answers to the exam practice questions.

EXAM TIPS

There are many different aspects to tourism case studies and not all of them will be required in any one question. You must therefore read the question carefully and decide which parts of the case study you have learned are relevant. Make sure your revision covers physical and human attractions, economic, social and environmental impacts (positive and negative), how different groups of people are affected as well as ways in which fragile environments can be preserved through a more sustainable approach to tourism.

8 Managing urban areas

KEY IDEAS

1. Urban areas in MEDCs are subject to constant change in their land use
2. Urban areas in LEDCs are subject to very rapid growth
3. Large urban areas face many challenges

1 Urban areas in MEDCs are subject to constant change in their land use

Note: For this Key Idea the Edexcel A specification states that you should study 'one named area in an MEDC…'. Whilst there are general similarities in MEDC cities it is important that these are supported by specific named areas from the chosen city. In this book, examples have been quoted from Newcastle upon Tyne, although it is possible to substitute these with other locations if you have studied a different city.

Inner city decline, redevelopment, renewal and brownfield potential

The Industrial Revolution of the nineteenth century led to the growth of towns in the UK. The rapid influx of workers into these towns, including Newcastle upon Tyne, meant a big and immediate demand for cheap housing and so builders constructed as many houses as possible in a small area, resulting in **high-density housing** with an overcrowded population. The houses were built in long, straight, narrow rows, or terraces. Few amenities were provided either in the house (e.g. no indoor toilet, bathroom, sewerage or electricity) or around it (e.g. no open space or gardens). The original terraces in the Byker area of East Newcastle, overlooking the River Tyne, were built like this but were demolished in the 1960s.

Key words to know

High-density housing

Back to …

The New Wider World **pages 44 and 45** for a photograph of typical nineteenth-century housing (Figure 3.25) and an aerial view of land use in the traditional inner city (Figure 3.27).

Figure 8.1 Land use and census data for an old inner city area, e.g. Benwell, Newcastle upon Tyne

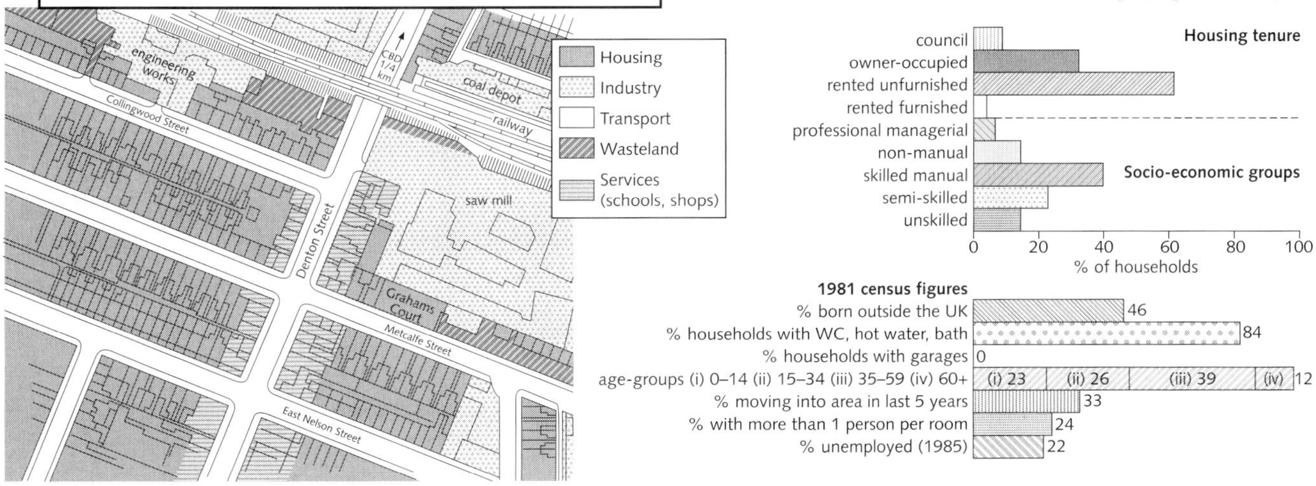

Causes of inner city decline

Many of the initial advantages of living in these areas soon became disadvantages. The dampness of the houses, lack of sanitation, closeness of the people and smoke from the nearby factories all combined to ruin people's lives and reduce their life expectancy. Two main processes led to the decline of inner city areas:

- **Deindustrialisation**: the early industries which attracted workers to cities, such as shipbuilding and glassmaking in Newcastle upon

Tyne, later faced competition from newer, overseas locations and many closed down, leaving derelict buildings and an unemployed workforce, e.g. in Walker. Later, other industries moved to newer locations on the edge of cities where more space was available. In Newcastle upon Tyne the Sage company has recently moved to a new development within the green belt called the Newcastle Great Park.

- **Decentralisation:** as some industries moved to out-of-town locations, other tertiary activities such as shops and offices began to follow as retail parks (Kingston Park) and industrial estates (Newcastle Airport Industrial Estate) grew up on the rural–urban fringe.

Key words to know

Deindustrialisation
Decentralisation
Urban renewal
Slum clearance
Urban redevelopment

Check this!...

1 Why was there growth of inner city areas in the nineteenth century?

2 Describe the houses built at that time.

3 What caused the decline of inner city areas?

Redevelopment, renewal and brownfield potential

Over the last 40 years, inner city areas have undergone great change as a result of **urban renewal** (the improvement of old houses and the addition of amenities in an attempt to bring new life to old inner city areas). In the 1960s many inner city areas underwent **slum clearance** in which large areas were bulldozed, and **urban redevelopment** (the total clearance of parts of old inner city areas and starting afresh with new houses) as high-rise flats were built to replace the old housing. In other places, new housing estates were built at a slightly lower density than the old terraces, e.g. the Byker Wall.

Case Study Extra

The Byker Wall, Newcastle upon Tyne

The Byker redevelopment scheme showed a greater awareness of the people who would be rehoused there. It was planned in conjunction with the residents and involved the demolition of the old Victorian terraces and the building of the Byker Wall. This was a continuous row of flats and maisonettes built of brightly coloured bricks.

The north side of the development:

- faces the Tyne and Wear Metro line and acts as a noise barrier
- uses five different colours to highlight vehicle and pedestrian access as well as to disguise the brickwork
- has only kitchen and bathroom windows (double-glazed) facing north which means that the other windows avoid both the noise and the coldest winds.

The south side of the development has:

- all the living rooms, bedrooms and dining rooms
- the balconies and access decks
- a bright and more varied colour scheme which breaks up the overall scale of the block
- ground floor flats with small front gardens
- access decks with brightly coloured timber and low roofs made from translucent corrugated material, which makes the decks light, airy and sheltered.

Most dwellings in the Wall are maisonettes, but there are also a few one- or two- person dwellings. Families with children were placed on ground floors; single people and childless couples had the higher dwellings.

In addition to the Wall there is also a low-rise development which is pedestrianised, with houses and small gardens, including trees to improve the environment. Different colours were allotted to houses to create sub-neighbourhoods and there were only limited parking spaces and garages as few of the original residents had cars. Local 'greens' for public use were incorporated into the development with small sitting, picnic and play areas. These are maintained by local residents and consequently vandalism has been reduced.

Using your case study

You can use the case study of Byker to explain how attempts were made to redevelop old terraced housing into a more pleasant environment. You should be able to describe in detail the characteristics of the Byker Wall and the associated low-rise developments.

Update

Go to *The New Wider World Coursemates* website for a link that gives more information and photographs of the Byker Wall.

Learn it!

1 Why was the Byker Wall scheme different from some earlier redevelopment projects?

2 Describe the features of the north side of the Wall.

3 Describe the features of the south side of the Wall.

4 Describe the low-rise redevelopment which was also part of the scheme.

Not all redevelopment projects were as successful as the Byker Wall. Although new high-rise buildings included modern amenities, apartments had to be reached by lifts which led to narrow, dark corridors. Also, despite the areas of greenery between the flats, there was still a very high housing density, for example Rye Hill, Newcastle upon Tyne. Little employment was available in these areas and people often had to travel to other parts of the city in order to find work.

Back to ...

The New Wider World **page 44** Figure 3.26, a photograph of high-rise residential redevelopment.

Figure 8.2 Land use and census data for a redeveloped inner city area

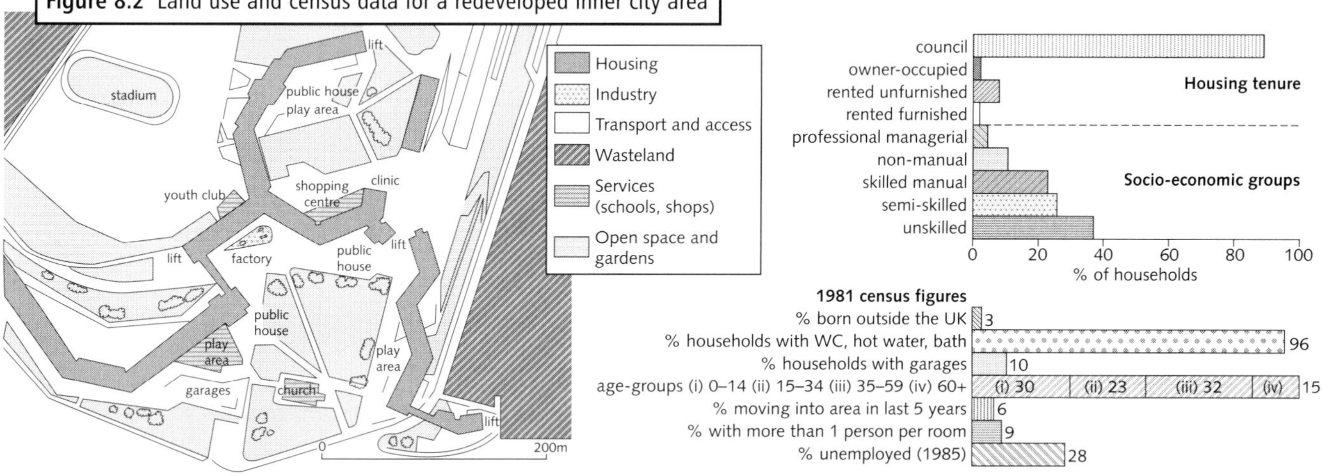

As many inner city areas still experienced cramped housing conditions and higher than average poverty, crime and unemployment rates, some of these high-rise flats have since been pulled down.

Later urban renewal was concentrated on improving existing areas. During the 1980s the government set up the **Urban Development Corporations (UDCs)** in an attempt to **regenerate** those inner city areas that had large amounts of derelict and unused land and buildings. UDCs had four main tasks and operated until 1998 in England:

- to acquire, reclaim and secure the development of derelict and unused land **(brownfield sites)**
- to provide land for industry, commerce, housing and leisure
- to build roads and improve the quality of the environment
- to encourage private sector investment to protect existing jobs and create new ones.

Key words to know

Urban Development Corporation (UDC)
Urban regeneration
Brownfield site

Case Study Extra

Tyne and Wear Development Corporation

The Tyne and Wear Development Corporation (TWDC) was set up in 1987 to bring land and buildings back into effective use in a designated area and encourage the development of new industry and commerce. It covered a stretch of land 42 km along the River Tyne in Newcastle, North Shields, South Shields and Gateshead. One-third of the land was derelict, polluted or under-used. The work of the TWDC involved the development of a series of **flagship schemes** (large, innovative developments) based around four themes:

- creating new businesses, e.g. Newcastle Business Park
- increasing employment and access to jobs
- reviving the riverside
- improving the environment.

Key words to know

Flagship scheme

One of the largest new residential areas was the Royal Quays regeneration project, in which £26 million was invested in providing social housing to meet the needs of local people. There was also a training and recruitment scheme which placed 2000 local people.

One of the more recent flagship projects, finished after the TWDC's era, has been the Millennium Bridge, which improves pedestrian access between the Newcastle and Gateshead quayside areas. The bridge cost £22 million and was built locally by AMEC of Wallsend. This project is an example of how successfully the TWDC encouraged private investment into the area which has led to companies such as AMEC spending £170 million on a series of office, leisure and retail developments.

Using your case study

You can use this example to describe the types of regeneration encouraged by development corporations. You need to know specific details of schemes such as names, dates, size and cost.

Case study links

See also *The New Wider World* pages 60–61 for information on the work of the London Development Corporation; and page 143 for the work of the Trafford Park Development Corporation (Manchester).

Update

Go to *The New Wider World Coursemates* website for a link to a site showing images of the developments along the Newcastle and Gateshead quayside area.

Learn it!

1 Why was the Tyne and Wear Development Corporation set up?

2 How did the TWDC encourage the regeneration of the riverside area?

3 Describe one of the flagship projects encouraged by the TWDC.

4 Why might there be conflicting opinions about the changes on Newcastle's Quayside area?

Brownfield potential

As in the example of the TWDC, the use of brownfield sites to manage the problems of constant change in urban areas has become more common in UK towns and cities as pressures on the countryside have increased. In 1998 the government announced that 50 per cent of new houses built would be on brownfield sites such as the Newcastle and Gateshead Quayside area. The Council for the Protection of Rural England and Friends of the Earth support the development of brownfield sites because:

- there are already 0.75 million unoccupied houses in cities that could be upgraded
- a further 1.3 million could be created by either subdividing larger houses or using empty space above shops and offices

- 1.3 million homes could be built on vacant and derelict land and another 0.3 million by re-using old industrial and commercial premises
- urban living reduces the need to use the car and maintains services, especially retailing, in the city centre
- the government assumes that 80 per cent of the demand for new houses will come from single-parent families who prefer – or need – to live in cities.

Check this!...

1 Explain the meaning of the terms *urban renewal* (or *regeneration*) and *urban redevelopment*.

2 Why did the construction of high-rise flats not always solve the problems of the old terraces they replaced?

3 Describe the part played by the Urban Development Corporations in urban renewal.

4 List the arguments for the development of brownfield sites.

Outer urban sprawl, change at the city edge, threats to the green belts and greenfield sites

Urban sprawl (the growth and spread of towns and cities outwards into the countryside) was the result of the process of **suburbanisation** – the outward development of towns and cities during the inter-war period (1920s and 1930s) when:

- public transport improved, enabling people to live away from their place of work
- the private car became more popular.

This led to the growth of numerous private, car-dependent suburbs such as Denton to the west of Newcastle upon Tyne. Many inter-war houses were semi-detached, characterised by their bay windows, garages and front and back gardens. Estates often contained small shopping parades which local residents visited several times a week, saving time in travelling and reducing transport costs.

After the 1960s suburbanisation and urban sprawl continued, with land on the rural–urban fringe being used for:

- private estates such as Chapel Park and Chapel House in Newcastle upon Tyne
- outer-city council estates such as Newbiggin Hall
- new industrial/trading estates such as the Newburn Industrial Estate.

Most of the new private estates had low-density, high-quality housing. Properties were detached, incorporating modern amenities indoors (central heating, double glazing, bathroom and kitchen) and outside (large gardens, double garage). They were built either in a cul-de-sac or along winding roads that were usually tree-lined and relatively traffic-free. Estates also included small open spaces.

Outer city council estates were created mainly during the 1950s and 1960s when local councils cleared the worst of the slums and poor-quality housing from the inner city areas. Many of the evicted residents were re-housed on what were then greenfield edge-of-city sites. A **greenfield site** is one that has not yet been built on.

Key words to know

Urban sprawl
Suburbanisation
Greenfield site

Back to ...

The New Wider World **page 46** for a photograph of typical inter-war housing (Figure 3.29) and a suburban shopping parade (Figure 3.30).

The New Wider World **page 47** Figure 3.31, a photograph of a modern estate on the rural–urban fringe.

Figure 8.3 Land use and census data for suburbia

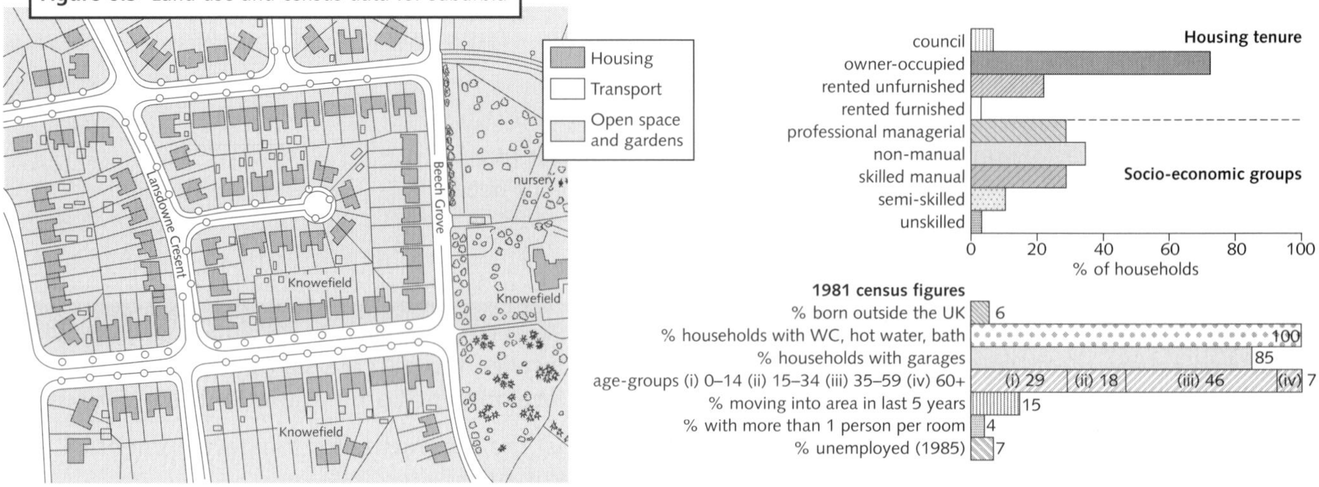

Back to ...

The New Wider World **page 47** Figure 3.32, a photograph of an outer city council estate.

Accommodation on these outer city council estates usually consisted of a mixture of high-rise tower blocks, low-rise flats and single-storey terraces. Although density was higher than on the private estates, it was lower than in the inner city areas. While many homes were small and most lacked gardens and garages, they did have indoor amenities including modern kitchens and bathrooms.

Figure 8.4 Land use and census data for an outer city council estate

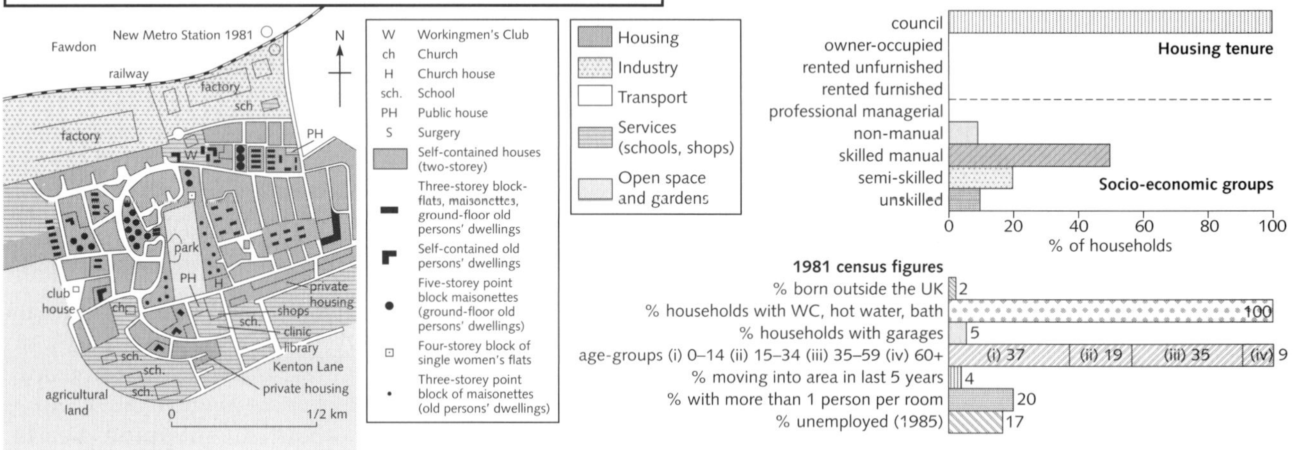

Threats to green belts and the countryside

By the end of the twentieth century an increasing number of land users saw the rural–urban fringe as the ideal location for future development because it has:

- less congestion and easier access, especially to other urban areas
- a more attractive and less polluted environment with plenty of open space
- cheaper land.

This has led to competition for land and conflict between those who wish to see the economic development and extension of the urban area and those who wish to protect the rural environment that surrounds it (see Figure 8.5).

Green belts and greenfield sites around many towns and cities are being built on because developers claim that:

- most British people want to own their own home, complete with garden, set in a rural or semi-rural location
- people are generally healthier and have a better quality of life in rural areas

- at present, for every three people moving into cities (almost 160 000 a year), five move out into the countryside (250 000 a year) – a net loss to urban areas of 90 000 a year
- greenfield sites are cheaper to build on than brownfield sites as they are likely to have lower land values and are less likely to be in need of cleaning-up operations.

Figure 8.5 Competition for land at the rural–urban fringe

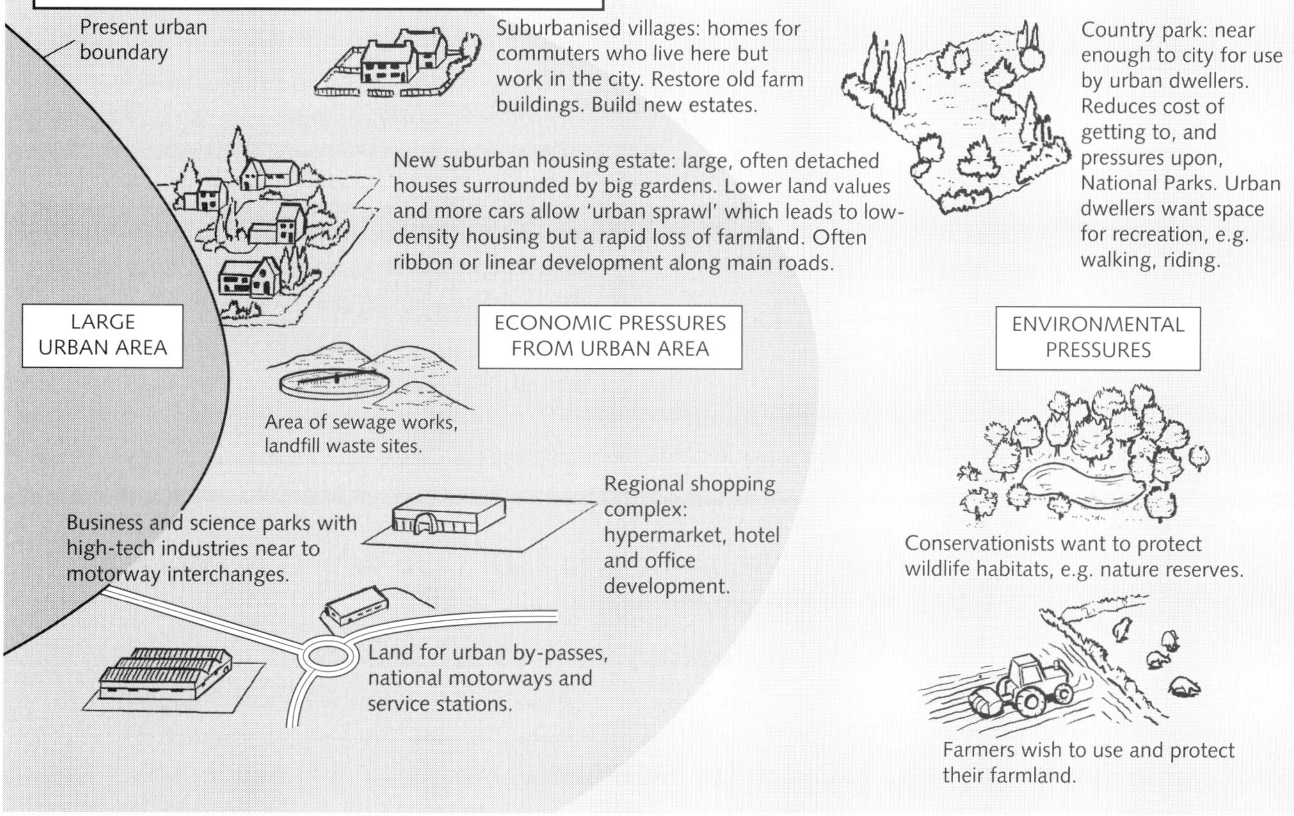

Case Study Extra

Newcastle upon Tyne's green belt

A **green belt** is an area of land around a town or city where building is restricted and the character of the countryside preserved. The purpose of a green belt is to restrict the outward spread of towns and cities and to preserve areas of countryside for farming and recreational uses. There are many pressures on local authorities to release areas of green belt land for construction. One example of this is the 600 hectare Newcastle Great Park site, 5 km to the north-west of the city centre and within the green belt surrounding Newcastle upon Tyne. This £800 million mixed use scheme will play an important part in the economic revival of the North East. The development, located close to the A1 London–Edinburgh route and Newcastle Airport, includes:

- a new business park, which will create 10,000 jobs
- the £60 million headquarters of the Sage company
- a large residential development which, when complete, will provide 2500 new homes ranging in price from £150 000 to £500 000.

The development takes into consideration the fact that this is a greenfield site by including 200 hectares of landscaped open spaces and attempts are being made to create a sustainable urban neighbourhood with a small town centre, local primary schools and access for all, including footpaths, cycle routes and bridleways.

Key words to know

Green belt

Using your case study

You can use this as an example of an occasion where a local council has allowed the development of an area of green belt land. You need to be able to describe the scheme in detail.

Update

Go to *The New Wider World Coursemates* website for a link to find a 1:200 000 map of Newcastle. This will allow you to see some of the existing land uses in the rural–urban fringe area surrounding the city, such as the airport and industrial estates. Other links give more detail of this particular development, and explain the approach taken by Newcastle City Council.

Learn it!

1 What is a green belt?

2 Why do councils sometimes release green belt land for development?

3 Describe the location and features of the Great Park development.

Check this!...

1 Explain urban sprawl and its causes.

2 List the different uses of the rural–urban fringe.

3 Describe the nature of:
  a) private estates
  b) council estates
  which were built in the rural–urban fringe.

4 Why is there often conflict about land use at the rural–urban fringe?

5 List the arguments in support of developing greenfield sites.

2 Urban areas in LEDCs are subject to very rapid growth

The global pattern of urbanisation

In 1800 only 3 per cent of the world's population lived in urban areas. By 1950 this figure had risen to 29 per cent and it is predicted to exceed 50 per cent by 2006. Although most developed countries have experienced urbanisation since the early 1800s, the process has only gathered pace in developing countries since the 1950s.

Figure 8.6 Percentage of population living in urban areas

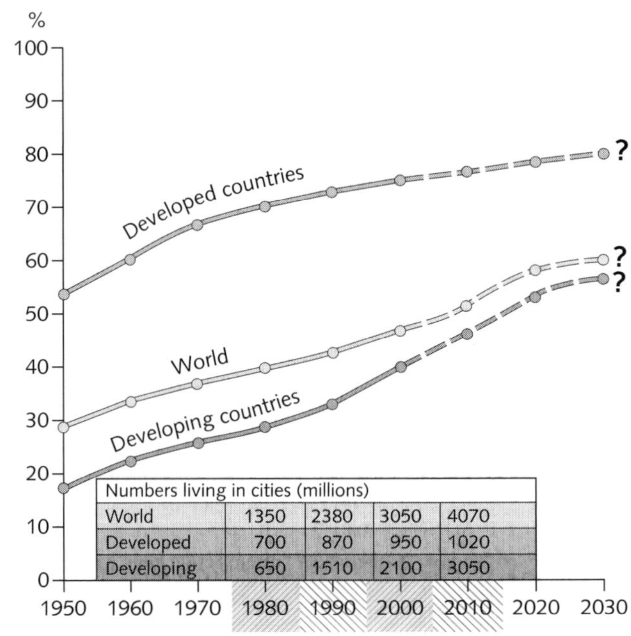

Figure 8.7 World urban population

Least urbanised	
Rwanda	6%
Bhutan	8%
Burundi	9%
Malawi	12%
Niger	12%
Uganda	12%
Ethiopia	15%

Most urbanised	
Singapore	100%
Belgium	97%
Hong Kong	96%
Kuwait	95%
Iceland	93%
Bahrain	92%
Venezuela	91%
Israel	91%
Luxembourg	91%
Uruguay	90%
UK	**89%**
Netherlands	89%

Figure 8.7 shows the proportion of the total population of each country living in towns and cities:

- MEDCs (North America, Western Europe and Oceania) are usually those with the highest proportion
- LEDCs in Africa and South-east Asia have the lowest proportions
- South America, the most economically advanced of the developing continents, is an exception as several of its countries have an urban population exceeding 75 per cent.

Another feature of urbanisation has been the growth of very large cities with a population exceeding 1 million – **millionaire cities**. In 1850 there were only two – London and Paris. This number had increased to 70 by 1950 and an estimated 405 in 2002. A **megacity** is a place with a population in excess of 10 million. Before 1950, most of the millionaire cities were in MEDCs in temperate latitudes north of the equator (i.e. 40–50°N in Europe and North America). Since then there has been a dramatic increase in millionaire cities in developing countries, the majority of which lie between the tropics.

Key words to know

Millionaire city
Megacity

Figure 8.8 The world's largest cities

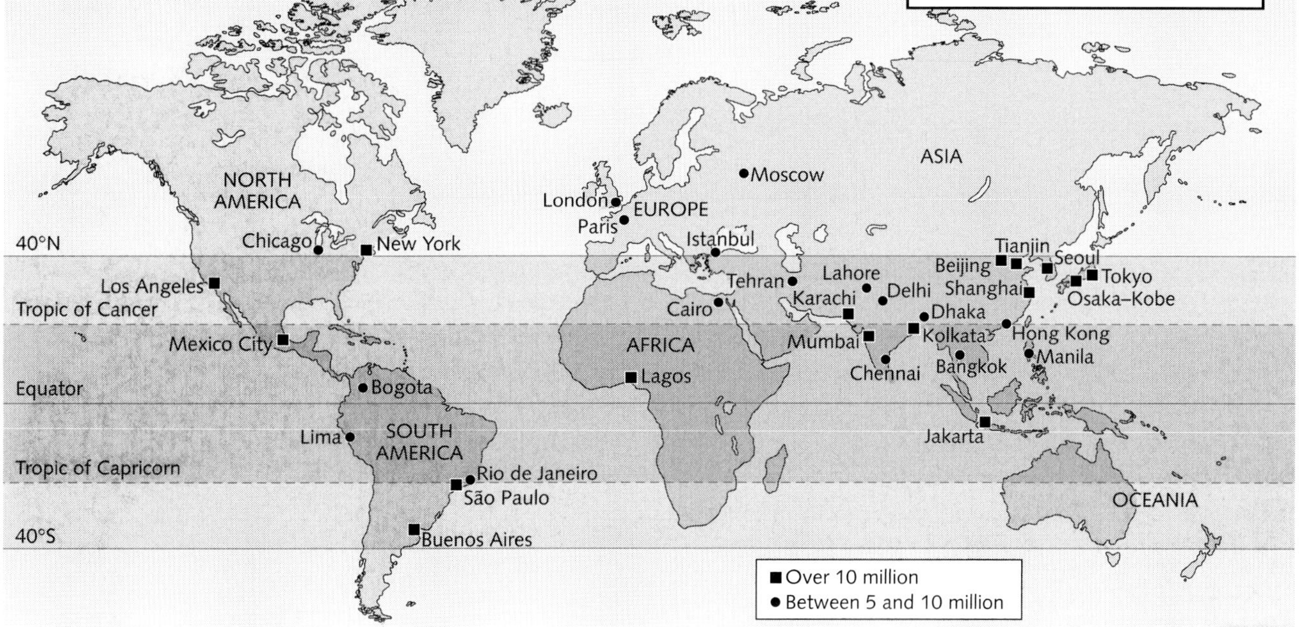

From the 1970s the two fastest-growing urban areas were São Paulo and Mexico City. At present the fastest-growing cities are in southern Asia. The population of Dhaka (Bangladesh) doubled between 1895 and 1995 and those of Karachi, Delhi and Bangkok doubled between 1985 and 2000.

Check this!...

1 Describe the world distribution of people living in towns and cities.

2 What is:
a) a millionaire city
b) a megacity?

Reasons for rapid growth

The rapid growth of people living in towns and cities is due to:

- high birth rates
- rural–urban migration.

The movement of people to cities in developing countries began in the early twentieth century. This has been largely due to high rates of growth in LEDCs, caused by falling death rates but still high birth rates. Since then the growth rate has accelerated so that many places are expanding at a rate of over 25 per cent every decade. The movement from country areas to towns and cities is called **rural–urban migration**. This movement is due partly to **rural push** factors (bad things about the countryside which force people to leave) and **urban pull** factors (perceived attractions of urban areas which draw people to them in search of a better quality of life).

In most developing countries the 'pull' factors are often greater than the 'push' factors. Many of these pull factors are people's perceptions

Back to ...

Figure 2.1 on page 16 of this book, which shows the rapid growth in the world's population.

Key words to know

Rural–urban migration
Rural push
Urban pull

Figure 8.9 Rural push and urban pull factors

Rural push

- Extreme physical conditions such as aridity, drought, rugged mountains, cold, heat and dense vegetation
- Overgrazing by animals leading to soil erosion
- Pests eat crops and cause ill-health
- Floods
- Farming is hard work with long hours and little pay
- Farm machinery replaces workers leading to unemployment
- Lack of job opportunities caused by mechanisation
- Crops are grown for export, not local use
- Large families
- Not enough land for each heir
- Many do not own land
- High birth rate leading to overpopulation
- Poor seeds, poor tools, little fertiliser, low output and insufficient food which create malnutrition and starvation
- Remoteness from services

Urban pull factors

- Better-paid jobs in industry; factory workers get about five times the wages of farm labourers
- Urban dwellers expect to be housed more comfortably and have a higher quality of life
- Better services: schools, hospitals, shops and entertainment
- Attraction to 'bright lights'
- More reliable sources of food
- Religious and political activities can be carried on more safely in larger cities

of the urban area but the reality is often very different. Many of the new arrivals are unlikely to have much money and will be unable to rent or buy a house. They usually have to make a cheap shelter using any materials available.

Results of rapid growth

The rapid growth of many towns and cities in LEDCs has created severe shortages of adequate housing, leading to an extreme contrast between the living conditions of the well-off, who usually live near the city centre, and those of the poor, who are forced to live towards the city boundary.

Case Study

Rio de Janeiro, Brazil

Back to ...

The New Wider World **pages 86–87** for this case study of the problems caused by rapid growth in Rio de Janeiro; and **page 82** which has more detail on the favelas typical of cities in Brazil.

Using your case study

You can use this case study to show how rural–urban migration has led to the rapid growth of a city in an LEDC and the appearance of large numbers of **favelas**. Make sure you can describe some specific problems of housing in terms of their construction and location.

Key word to know

Favela

Update

Go to *The New Wider World Coursemates* website for a link (search for 'Rio de Janeiro') that will direct you to several articles about how Rio's problems are being addressed.

Learn it!

1 Where is Rio de Janeiro and how has it grown?

2 Describe the problems caused by the rapid growth of Rio's:
a) housing
b) crime.

Check this!...

1 List the push factors which encourage people to leave rural areas.

2 List the pull factors which encourage people to migrate to urban areas.

Back to ...

The New Wider World **pages 82–83** for information on housing in another Brazilian city, São Paulo; and **pages 84–85** for information on problems created when cities grow too quickly – in this case Kolkata.

Managing rapid growth

Over 100 million people living in developing cities have no shelter of any kind, while over one-third live in **squatter settlements** – sites that are only vacant because they are subject to flooding, landslips or industrial pollution. Although most local authorities would probably prefer to remove shanty settlements from their cities, few can find the

Key words to know

Squatter settlement

necessary resources that would be needed to provide alternative accommodation. As a result, shanty settlements become permanent.

Self-help schemes

Self-help schemes are often the only hope for squatters to improve their homes. The most immediate needs of the poor are often simple: a plot on which to build, a small loan to improve or extend the house, cheap building materials and basic services. Figure 8.10 shows a self-help scheme in São Paulo – similar schemes operate in Rio de Janeiro.

Figure 8.10 A self-help housing scheme in São Paulo

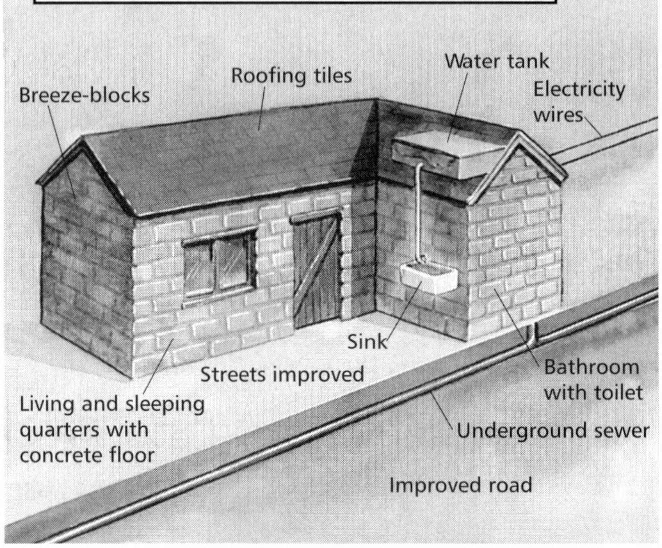

Under a self-help scheme, groups of people are encouraged to help build their own homes. Each group will do basic work such as digging ditches to take the water and sewage pipes. The local authority will then provide breeze-blocks and roofing tiles, and the group provides the labour. The money which this saves can be used by the authorities to provide amenities such as electricity, a clean water supply, tarred

Case Study

Roçinha, Rio de Janeiro

Back to ...

The New Wider World **page 87** for a case study of one specific self-help scheme.

Using your case study

You should make sure you know how the residents themselves have transformed this favela and how they have been helped to do this by the authorities.

Update

Go to *The New Wider World Coursemates* website for a link to The People and Planet website which has information about Roçinha.

Learn it!

1 Where is Roçinha and what were living conditions like in this favela?
2 What have the residents of Roçinha done to improve their favela?
3 What have the local authorities done to help them?

roads and a community centre. The advantages of self-help schemes are that they can be done in stages, they can create a community spirit and, as the cost of building is relatively cheap, more houses can be provided.

Case Study

The Favela Bairro project in Rio de Janeiro

Back to ...

The New Wider World **page 88** for information on this £200 million plan to improve some of the mid-size favelas in Rio de Janeiro.

Using your case study

You need to learn some facts and figures about the Favela Bairro project and you need to be able to explain why the authorities chose the mid-sized favelas to improve and exactly what they changed.

Update

Go to *The New Wider World Coursemates* website for a link giving information on several different aspects of the Favela Bairro project, including facts and figures and opinions on the success of the scheme.

Learn it!

1 What changes were made in the Favela Bairro project?

2 How did the local authorities benefit from this scheme?

Check this!...

1 What is a self-help scheme?

2 Describe the role of local authorities in improving housing in favelas.

Local authority schemes

Local authority schemes usually focus on improving the temporary accommodation built by migrants from rural areas.

3 Large urban areas face many challenges

The causes and consequences of noise, air and land-based pollution

Problems of noise and air pollution are similar in both MEDC and LEDC cities. One of the main causes has been the increase in car ownership and the number of people who **commute** (live on the edge of or outside a city and travel into the city each day) – see Figure 8.11.

- In New York, for example, up to 2 million commuters travel into the central area of Manhattan. About 75 per cent of these use public transport, mainly the underground or 'subway'. Roads become blocked with cars, buses and yellow taxis.
- The rivers that surround Manhattan add to the congestion because they need to be crossed by tunnels, bridges and ferries, causing bottlenecks and traffic jams.
- Emissions from car exhausts also create problems as gases such as nitrogen dioxide reduce air quality and pose threats to human health. More cases of asthma are reported today than ever before and many believe this is linked to increased amounts of low-level ozone.

Key word to know

Commute

Figure 8.11 Increase in car ownership in Western Europe, North America and Japan

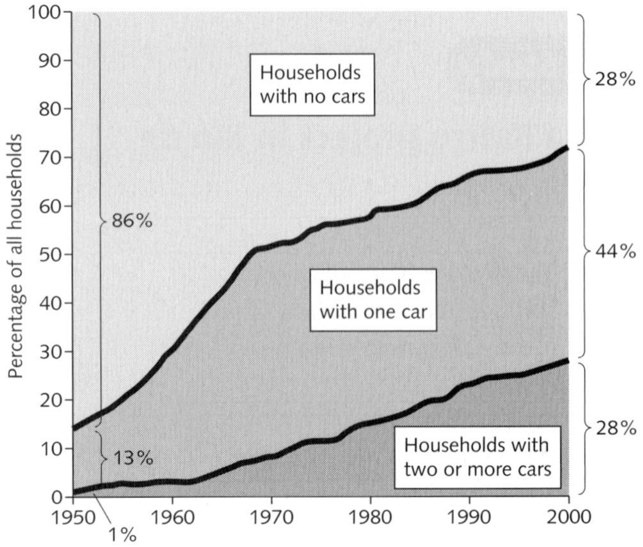

Figure 8.12 Air quality in London, 9 June 1997

	Yesterday's reading	Forecast
Nitrogen dioxide	40 ppb	Very good
Less than 50 = Very good, 50–99 = Good, 100–299 = Poor, 300+ = Very poor		
Ozone	28 ppb	Very good
Less than 50 = Very good, 51–89 = Good, 90–179 = Poor, 180+ = Very poor		
Sulphur	5 ppb	Very good
Less than 60 = Very good, 60–124 = Good, 125–399 = Poor, 400+ = Very poor		

Air quality is calculated in ppb (parts per billion)

London Evening Standard, 9 June 1997

Back to ...

The New Wider World **page 66** Figure 4.21, a photograph of smog over Los Angeles.

- Under high pressure, anticyclonic weather systems, large amounts of air pollution create a smog over towns and cities which increases risks to human health.
- In Osaka–Kobe, Japan, the large volume of road traffic, smoke from some of the older heavy industries and rubbish incinerated at sea all cause serious air pollution.
- Land pollution in New York is caused by problems of collecting and disposing of the large amounts of refuse produced daily.
- This land-based pollution is a more serious problem in LEDCs such as Rio de Janeiro, where the rubbish in the favelas is unlikely to be collected and its presence on the streets could lead to outbreaks of cholera. Some of the beaches along the coast in Rio have become polluted as waste has been dumped there.

Case Study Extra

Causes and consequences of pollution in Cairo

Air, noise and land pollution are major problems in Cairo.

Figure 8.13 Air, noise and land pollution problems in Cairo

Air pollution	Noise pollution	Land pollution
Causes		
• Large increase in the number of vehicles on the roads combined with a very low provision of road space per capita. • The increase in cars was, in the past, encouraged by government subsidies on fuel and the fact that there was little early investment in public transport, so privately owned passenger car companies grew. • In 1998 there were 530 000 vehicles on the roads but this has more than trebled since then to over 2 million. • 60% of these vehicles are over 10 years old. • Bridges over the Nile add to the problems as bottlenecks and congestion are caused. • There are unregistered lead smelters with no pollution controls.	• Constant traffic jams, car horns and inefficient exhaust systems. • Constant flow of boats on the River Nile. • Noise from the increasing number of discos and floating nightclubs.	• Poor waste management with only 60% of the solid waste produced daily being collected • Unplanned development of former agricultural land for both housing and industry. • Rubbish is often left to collect in tips and may be burnt, adding to the air pollution. • Industrial waste such as scrap metal is often left in backyard dumps. • Hazardous waste from chemical plants is not safely disposed of. • Primitive solid waste recycling methods.
Consequences		
• High levels of suspended air particulates and lead, made worse by wind-blown sand from the Great Western Desert. Particulate material in Cairo is 10 times higher than World Health Organisation guidelines. • Deaths due to respiratory problems estimated at 10 000 a year. • Lead emissions reduce children's IQ by 4 points. • High lead concentrations also cause high blood pressure, kidney problems, infertility and nervous disorders. • Air pollution levels 3 or 4 times above accepted levels with 1 million people living close to industrial areas.	• Bad tempers because of constant gridlock. • Hearing disorders. • Annoyance and nuisance to residents who live near the clubs and discos.	• Large numbers of rats and the threat of outbreaks of disease. • A stockpile of 50 000 tonnes of toxic waste.

Using your case study

You can use the example of Cairo to illustrate the problems of air, noise and land-based pollution in cities today. You need to know the specific causes and consequences of each of the three types of pollution.

Update

Go to *The New Wider World Coursemates* website for a link to find more information on the problems faced by Cairo.

Learn it!

1 Where is Cairo? Draw a sketch map to show its location in Egypt on the River Nile.

2 List the causes of:
a) air pollution
b) noise pollution
c) land-based pollution.

3 List the consequences of:
a) air pollution
b) noise pollution
c) land-based pollution.

Check this!...

1 Explain how increased car ownership has caused air and noise pollution in cities.

2 Give some examples of land-based pollution in towns and cities

Back to ...

The New Wider World **pages 68–69** for an example of improvements to public transport in Lille, France.

The development of sustainable strategies and the attitudes of decision makers

Many types of sustainable strategy are being developed in order to solve environmental problems in urban areas:

- The use of brownfield as opposed to greenfield sites – using land which has already been built on instead of open countryside which further encourages the use of the car and its associated problems.
- Improving public transport – in 1998 the Department of the Environment produced *The New Deal for Transport in the UK* which set out a ten-year development plan to include road-widening schemes, improvements to intercity rail links and inner city light railways, and funding to support local public transport schemes.
- Finding alternative locations for building new houses, e.g. in Osaka–Kobe, Japan, two residential areas – Port Island and Rokko Island – have been reclaimed from the sea in Osaka Bay.
- Clean-up campaigns – Japan has made serious attempts to clear up land-based pollution caused by its earlier industrialisation; newer, high-tech industries are less polluting. Japan is also developing its nuclear power which, despite its risks, causes less air pollution than the use of fossil fuels.

Case Study Extra

Cairo – the development of sustainable strategies

The government of Cairo has taken steps to try to manage the consequences of pollution in a more sustainable way:

- It has set up the Cairo Air Improvement Programme (CAIP). With the help of finance from USAID, 42 air monitoring stations had been set up across the city by 2001.
- The media are used to publicise practices which encourage environmental conservation, such as the use of compressed natural gas engines.
- By 2001 CNG (compressed natural gas) was used in 50 of Cairo's buses.
- The CAIP also set up vehicle emission testing stations across the city in an attempt to reduce the number of older, less efficient cars.
- To reduce industrial pollution, environmentally friendly technology is being developed at lead smelting plants.

- To tackle the problem of land-based pollution a more comprehensive waste management strategy is being developed.
- The underground system is being expanded in an attempt to reduce the number of vehicles on the road.

Using your case study

You need to be able to explain how the government of Cairo is trying to adopt a more sustainable approach to the management of pollution problems. See the previous Case Study Extra on the urban problems in Cairo.

Update

Go to *The New Wider World Coursemates* website for a link giving information on how the government of Cairo is trying to address the problem of pollution.

Learn it!

1. Explain how the government of Cairo is trying to address the problems of pollution in a more sustainable way.
2. Suggest what problems the government of Cairo might face in addressing the problems of pollution.

EXAM PRACTICE

1 Referring to an example you have studied, show how attempts are being made to regenerate declining urban areas. (5)

2 Explain why there are often conflicts over land in the rural–urban fringe. (4)

3 Explain the reasons for rapid urbanisation in LEDCs. (4)

4 With reference to an urban area you have studied:

a) describe the causes of air, noise and land pollution

and

b) explain the consequences of high levels of pollution. (6)

5 Explain some of the strategies used by governments in MEDCs and LEDCs to reduce environmental problems such as pollution and the increasing development of the countryside. (6)

EXAM TIPS

Urban management case studies cover several different aspects and only some of these may be addressed by an exam question. Candidates often waste time and lose marks by giving detailed information which is not required. For example, question 1 does not ask you to describe the decline of urban areas – you are only asked to include detail of regeneration strategies such as redevelopment and the work of development corporations.

Back to ...

The New Wider World Coursemates website to check your answers to the exam practice questions.

9 Skills

1 Map skills

2 Interpreting photographs and observing landscapes

3 Graphical skills

4 Looking for patterns

1 Map skills

Map scales

All maps should include a scale. This shows how distance on the map (in cm or mm) relates to real-life distance on the ground.

On a map, scale is shown in two ways (see Figure 9.1). Whenever you use a map you should try to use the scale to get an idea of the real-life distance between places.

Figure 9.1 Map scales

Linear scale

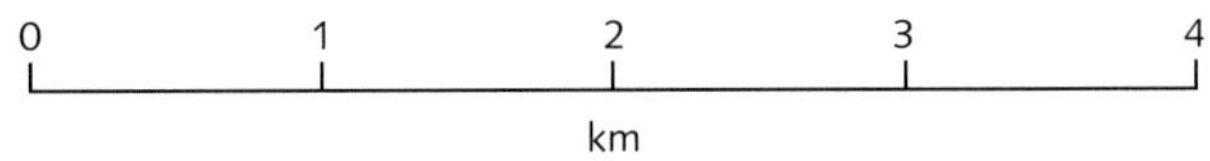

Ratio scale

e.g. 1 : 50 000

This means that one unit on the map is equal to 50 000 units on the ground, i.e. 1 cm on a map = 50 000 cm (0.5 km) on the ground.
Thus, on a 1:50 000 map *2 cm = 1 km* (as shown on the linear scale above)

Back to ...

The New Wider World **pages 41, 292** and **320** for examples of 1:50 000 OS maps.

The New Wider World **inside back cover** to see a copy of the 1:50 000 OS map key.

There are many different scales of map. The larger the scale (e.g. 1:10 000), the more detail is shown; the smaller the scale (e.g. 1:1 million), the less detail is shown. **Large-scale** maps can show road layouts in towns, individual buildings and fields. **Small-scale** maps, like country maps in atlases, cover huge areas but give very little fine detail.

At GCSE you will come across two scales of Ordnance Survey (OS) maps: the 1:50 000 (2 cm = 1 km) and the more detailed 1:25 000 (4 cm = 1 km). You should take time to learn how to use both of these scales.

Ordnance Survey map symbols

Maps contain a huge amount of information. This is made possible by using symbols instead of written labels, which would take up far too much space. Many symbols are clear in their meaning but they are always explained in a key. The key is usually found at the base or to the side of a map.

Key words to know

Large-scale
Small-scale
Eastings

Finding grid references

OS maps have gridlines drawn on them to enable locations to be given. The lines that run 'up and down' and increase in value from left to right (west to east), are called **eastings**. Those that run across the map and increase in value from bottom to top (south to north), are called **northings**.

To locate a grid square on a map, we use a **four-figure grid reference**. The first two digits refer to the easting value and the second two digits to the northing value.

To locate a point rather than a grid square, each grid square is split into 'tenths' to give a **six-figure grid reference**.

When giving a grid reference it is perfectly reasonable to estimate the 'tenths' but you can always use a ruler to be more precise.

Key words to know

Northings
Four-figure grid reference
Six-figure grid reference

Back to ...

The New Wider World **page 41** Figure 3.18: find the village of Thorngumbald. Most of the village is in grid square 2026.

The New Wider World **page 41** Figure 3.18: locate the Post Office (P) in the village of Thorngumbald. Its six-figure grid reference is 208266. Notice how the eastings value is represented by the three digits 208 and the northings value is represented by the digits 266. It is the third digit of each set that is the 'tenths' value. Thus, the eastings value is 20 and 8/10ths and the northings value is 26 and 6/10ths.

The New Wider World **page 41** Figure 3.18. When answering an exam question, be sure to express a compass direction carefully and precisely. For example, on this OS map Thorngumbald is to the south-east of Hedon, and Hedon is to the east of Salt End.

Giving compass directions

Figure 19.2 shows the compass directions. Usually on a map the direction north is 'straight up', but it is very important that you check the key when examining maps and diagrams. This is why it is also good practice to include a north point on all maps and diagrams that you draw.

Figure 9.2 Points of the compass

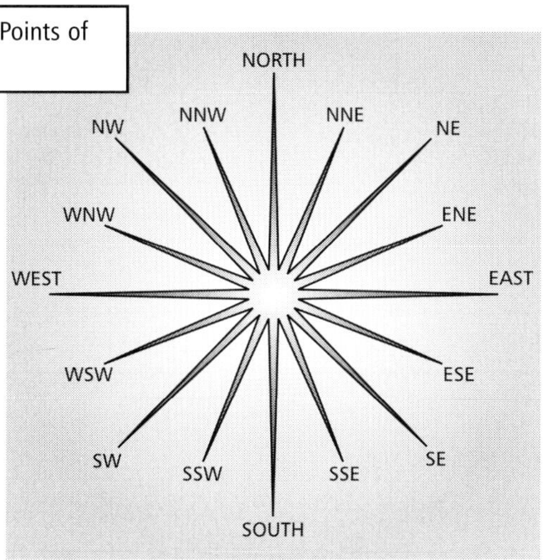

Measuring distances

Every map should have a scale, usually in the form of a measured line (called a *linear scale*) with distances written alongside. To calculate a straight-line distance, you simply measure the distance on the map between the two points in question, using a ruler or the straight edge of a piece of paper. You then line up your ruler or paper alongside the linear scale to discover the actual distance on the ground in kilometres or miles.

A curved distance takes rather longer to work out. The best technique is to use the straight edge of a piece of paper to mark off sections of the curved line, effectively converting the curved distance into a straight-line distance. Look at Figure 9.3 on page 108 to see how this technique works.

Remember to always give the units, for example kilometres, when writing your answer.

Figure 9.3 Measuring a curved distance

1. Place the straight edge of the paper alongside the route. Mark on the start (S). Look along the edge of the paper and mark off the point where the curved line no longer runs alongside the paper.

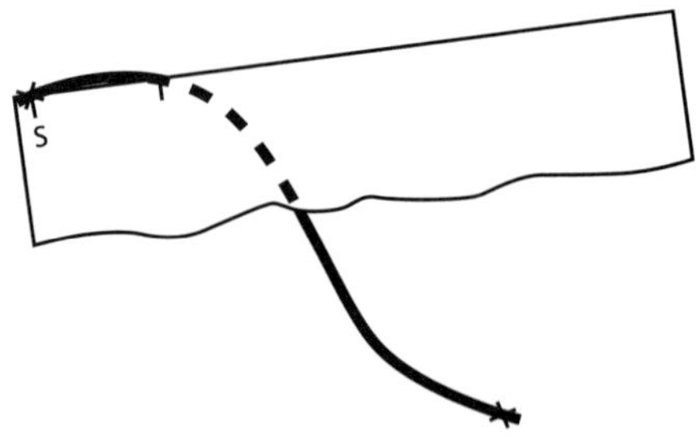

2. Carefully pivot the paper at this point until the curved line once again runs alongside. Continue along the curved line marking off the straight segments until you reach the finish. Mark this on the paper (F).

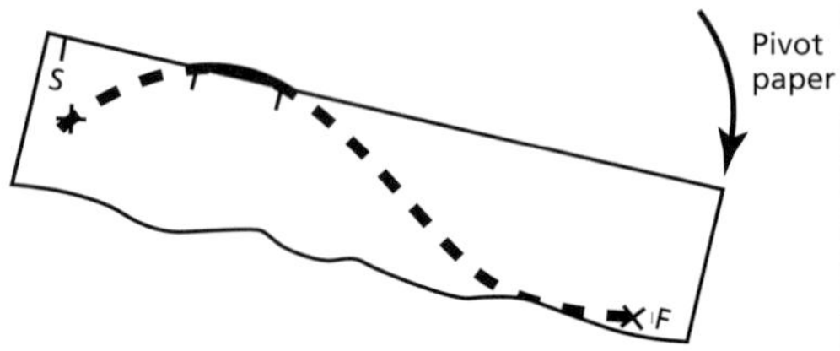

3. Measure the total straight-line distance using a ruler and convert to kilometres using the linear scale on the map.

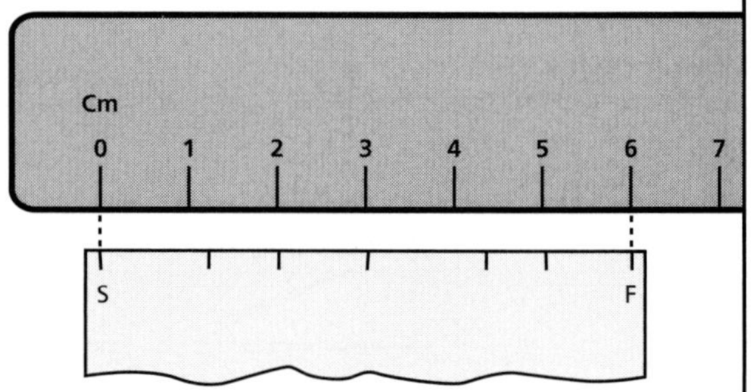

Key words to know

Sketch map

Drawing sketch maps

A **sketch map** is a simplified map that is not drawn absolutely to scale. However, it is important to add a scale even if it is just an approximation.

A sketch map is very useful because the person drawing it can decide what to include and what to leave out. It may be that only information about the physical landscape is needed or, alternatively, just the settlements and roads.

A sketch map can be drawn from any kind of map, including OS maps, maps taken from atlases, or those based on maps seen on the internet.

To draw a sketch map you should follow these steps:

- Start by drawing a frame. Make sure that the shape of the frame matches the shape of the area on the original map. It might be a square or a rectangle. Make your frame bigger or smaller than the original if you want to enlarge or reduce it.
- Now carefully transfer the information that you require from the original map onto your sketch map. You could use grid lines to help you – this is easy if your original map is an OS map – or simply draw one or two major guiding features, such as roads or rivers.
- Once complete, you can use colour and shading if you wish, although black-and-white sketches are often the most successful.

- Label and annotate as required (see below), and don't forget to include an approximate scale, a north point and a title.

Labels

Labels are often single words identifying, for example, physical features or names of places.

Annotations

Annotations are usually short sentences giving a description or explanation. They are more detailed and often more useful than labels.

Remember that most of the credit for a sketch map will relate to your labels and annotations, which show your ability to interpret the map.

Key words to know

Label
Annotation
Cross-section

Drawing a cross-section

A **cross-section** is an imaginary slice through a landscape. It is very useful because it helps you to visualise what a landscape actually looks like.

To draw a cross-section you need a piece of scrap paper, a sharp pencil, a ruler and an eraser. The stages of construction are shown in Figure 9.4.

Figure 9.4 Drawing a cross-section

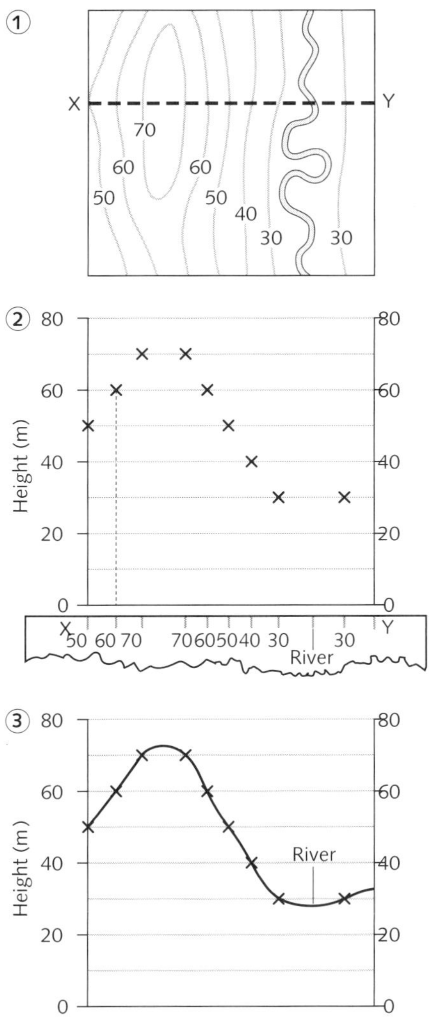

- Place the edge of a straight piece of paper along the line of section and mark off the contours and other details.
- Place the paper along the horizontal base of a graph.
- Choose an appropriate vertical scale.
- Mark off contours on to the graph.
- Join points with a curved line and continue to the axes.

As you complete your cross-section, bear in mind the following points:

- Double-check that you have written down the correct height values.
- Make your vertical scale as realistic as possible – don't exaggerate it so much that you create a totally unreal landscape.
- Complete the cross-section to both vertical axes by carrying on the trend of the landscape.
- Label any features.
- Complete axes labels and give grid references for each end of your cross-section.
- Give your cross-section a title.

A *long profile* is very similar to a cross-section, although it usually involves marking off contour values along a curved distance (see 'Measuring distances' on pages 107–108). Long profiles are most commonly drawn to show changes down a river valley.

Key words to know

Relief
Drainage

Describing the physical landscape

It is very likely that you will be asked to describe aspects of the physical landscape on an OS map. Mostly this involves describing the relief and drainage.

Relief is the geographical term used to describe the lie of the land. To gain the most marks in an exam you should comment on:

- The height of the land, using actual figures taken from contours or spot heights to support your points. Using words like 'high' and 'low' is fairly meaningless, without the use of actual figures. Refer to different areas or parts of the map using compass directions to enable you to be precise.
- The slope of the land – is the land flat, or sloping? Which way do the slopes face? Are the slopes gentle or steep? Are there bare cliffs exposed? Again, it is important to give precise supporting information such as grid references, compass directions, etc.
- The presence of features such as valleys, etc. Refer to names and use grid references.

Drainage is all about the presence (or absence) of water. When describing the drainage of an area try to comment on the following:

- Are there rivers on the map and which way are they flowing (look at the contours)? Is there a dense network of rivers?
- Are the rivers single or multi-channelled? Give names of the rivers, and use distances, heights and directions to add depth to your description.
- If there are no surface rivers, it may well be that the rock is permeable and that water has passed underground. If this is the case look for evidence of springs or wells.
- Can you see a pattern to the rivers (see Figure 9.5)?
- Are there any lakes, artificial or man-made?
- Is there evidence of the influence of people on drainage channels, for example straightened channels, built embankments, etc? Straight channels are rare in nature and usually indicate human intervention.

Back to ...

The New Wider World **page 278** Figure 17.2: the River Exe drainage basin is a very dense network.

The New Wider World **page 291** Figures 17.36 and 17.37 which show what happens when rivers are artificially straightened.

Figure 9.5 River patterns

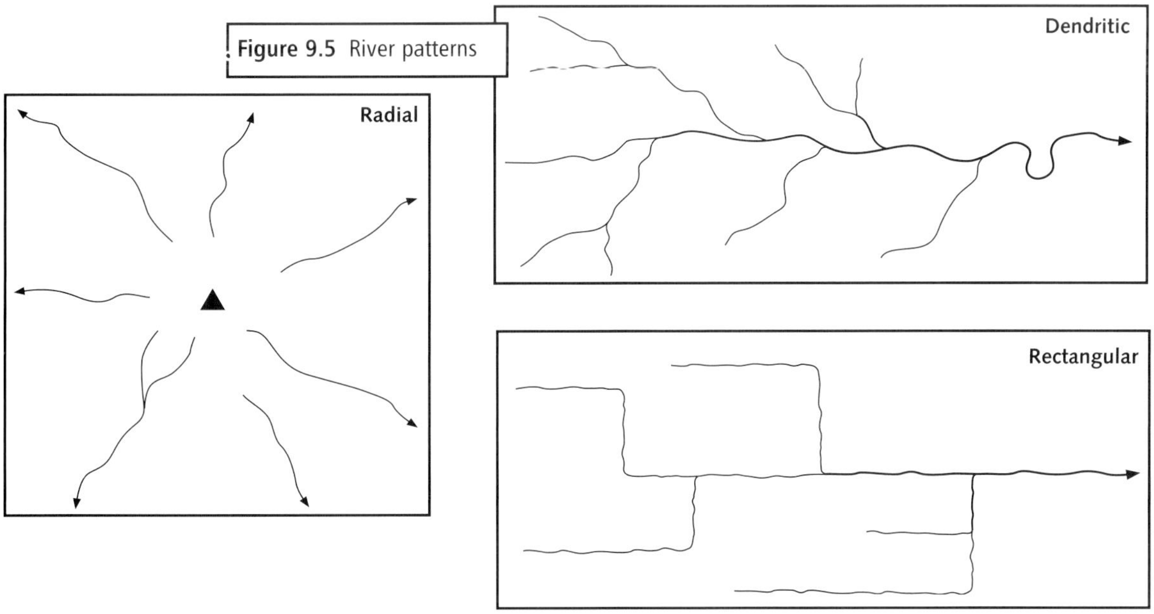

Describing the human landscape

Ordnance Survey maps contain a lot of information about aspects of human geography, for example roads, settlements, functions and industry.

- **Roads** Different colours are used to show the various types of road. When describing road networks, refer to the type of road and use road numbers whenever possible. For example, the main road passing through Thorngumbald (2026) is the A1033. Use compass directions when describing the pattern of roads. Look out for roads that might be intended to act as by-passes, such as the A1033 to the south of Hedon. Road networks are clearly visible in settlements and it is possible to identify patterns. Notice how in grid square 1430 the roads tend to form a regular grid pattern, suggesting that they are probably part of an older terraced housing area. A more modern housing area, with curved roads and cul-de-sacs, can be found in grid square 1432.
- **Settlements** The pale pink/brown colour on the map shows the extent of the built-up areas. This is where the houses and shops are. The white spaces in between are areas of open ground, such as parks. Some important buildings such as schools – you can see several of these on the outskirts of Hull – are shown separately. The shapes of settlements can be readily identified.
- **Functions** There are several functions and services shown on the map. In Preston just to the north of Hedon, there is a Post Office, a public house, several places of worship, a school and a sports centre. Not all functions, particularly shops, are shown on OS maps.
- **Industry** Industrial buildings are usually large and are often arranged in a regular pattern. A good example is the Works to the south of Salt End in grid squares 1627 and 1628. It has easy access to main roads and, in this case, has a jetty into the river. You can see other industrial buildings alongside the A1033 to the west of Salt End.

Back to ...

The New Wider World **page 41** Figure 3.18: study the roads, settlements, functions and industry.

Describing patterns on specialist maps

In addition to OS maps, there are many specialist maps, e.g. geological maps, weather maps, etc.

- Geological maps show the different types of rock below the ground surface.
- Weather maps (synoptic charts) show weather information.

To interpret specialist maps you should make good use of the key, which will tell you the meaning of the symbols. In describing what the maps show, apply all the principles of good practice described above. Refer to specific locations, give facts and figures, refer to distances and compass directions, etc. You may be asked to relate a specialist map to an OS map.

Back to ...

The New Wider World **page 305** Figure 18.18 which is an example of a geological map.

The New Wider World **pages 205–206** Figures 12.13, 12.15 and 12.16 which are all examples of weather maps.

The New Wider World **page 305** Figures 18.17 and 18.18. A geological map appears alongside an OS map. In an exam you may be asked to relate the rock types to the landscape. In this case, notice, for example, that The Foreland (a geographical feature known as a headland) corresponds with the resistant rock chalk.

2 Interpreting photographs and observing landscapes

Interpreting ground photographs

Ground photographs are photographs taken by someone standing on the ground. They show what a place looks like as we would see it if we were standing on the ground.

To interpret a ground photograph you need to look at it closely and look for clues to help you understand what is happening. For example, if trees are in leaf and people are wearing shorts then it was probably taken in the summer.

Back to ...

The New Wider World **page 150** Figures 9.33–9.34, which show some features of recycling and appropriate technology in LEDCs. In an exam, you could be asked to describe in detail what the people are doing.

The New Wider World **page 88** Figure 5.26, which is an oblique aerial photograph of the new town Barra di Tijuca near Rio de Janeiro.

Interpreting aerial photographs

Aerial photographs give us much the same view of an area as we would see when looking out of an aeroplane window. Vertical aerial photographs look directly down on an area much as a map does. Oblique aerial photographs look down at an area at an angle.

Aerial photographs are excellent in showing what an area looks like. They can help us understand and bring to life the detail shown on a map.

You may well be required to relate an aerial photograph to a map extract. Usually you will be asked to work out which way the camera is pointing. To do this, you first need to locate on the map extract some of the features shown at the bottom, middle and top of the photograph. This gives you a line of sight. Then use the compass directions on the map to help you work out which way the photograph faces.

Key words to know

Aerial photograph

Interpreting satellite images

Satellites can provide us with very accurate and detailed images often covering large areas of the Earth's surface. Many modern maps are produced using satellite images because they are so accurate and up to date.

Computers can create satellite images that use false colours to help identify features of interest for example green crops, surface water or settlements.

Back to ...

The New Wider World **page 216** Figure 13.13, which is a satellite image of a hurricane to the west of Florida.

Drawing a sketch from a photograph

It is important to realise that the purpose of a **sketch** is to identify the main geographical characteristics of the landscape. It is not necessary to produce a brilliant artistic drawing; clarity and accuracy are all that is needed. Examiners reward accurate labels and annotations.

To draw a sketch, you first need to draw a frame to the same general shape of the photograph. Then draw one or two major lines that will subsequently act as guidelines for the rest of your sketch. You could draw the profile of a slope or a hilltop, or a road or river, for example. Consider what it is that you are trying to show and concentrate on these aspects; it may be river features or the pattern of settlements. Don't take time drawing a lot of detail that is not required and only serves to confuse.

Always use a good sharp pencil and don't be afraid to rub things out as you go along.

Finally, remember to label or annotate (detailed labels) your sketch to identify the features, and give your sketch a title.

Key word to know

Sketch

Figure 9.6 Annotated sketch of a photograph of Flamborough Head

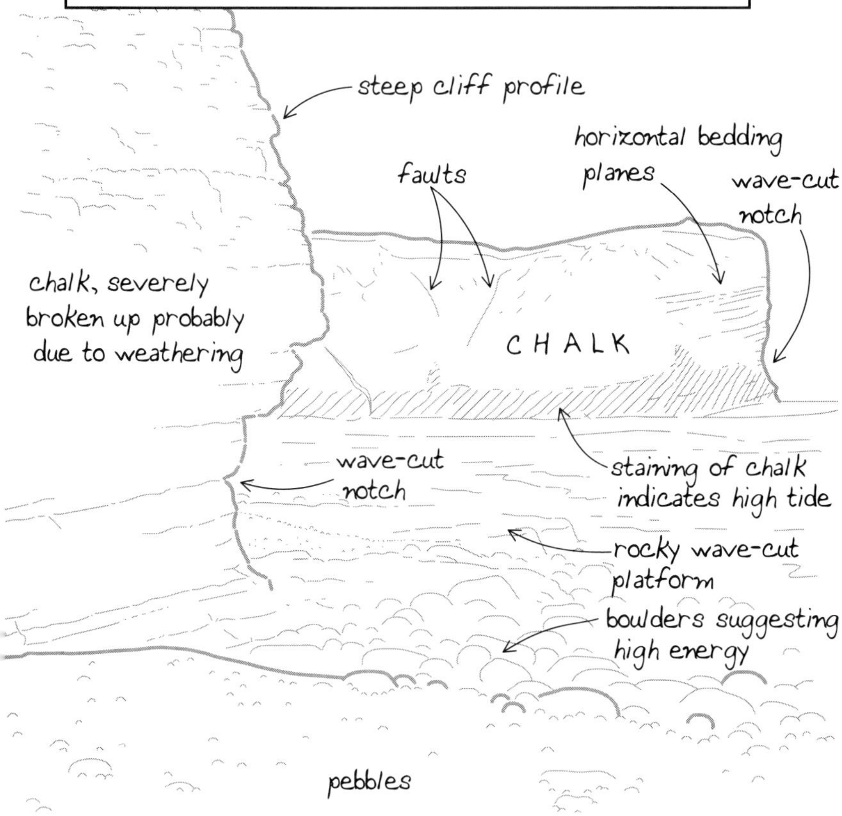

Back to ...

The New Wider World **page 300** Figure 18.5, which shows several features of coastal erosion. Figure 9.6 is an annotated sketch of this photograph.

Drawing field sketches

A **field sketch** is a sketch drawn outside (in the field) to show a particular view. Field sketches are often used to show aspects of the physical landscape, for example a waterfall or cliff. However, they can also be used to show features of the human landscape, for example aspects of village architecture or farming land use.

To draw a field sketch, you should follow the guidelines in 'Drawing a sketch from a photograph' above. Decide how large an area you wish to sketch and draw a frame to the appropriate size and shape. Take time

Key word to know

Field sketch

to represent the landscape accurately within your frame but avoid the temptation to strive for a work of art! It is the labels and annotations that are most valuable.

3 Graphical skills

Drawing line graphs

A **line graph** shows continuous changes over a period of time, for example stream flow or population change. It is a very common and effective technique to use, but it is important to remember that time, which is shown on the horizontal axis, must have an equal spacing, for example from year to year.

Back to ...

The New Wider World **page 10** Figure 1.10, which is a line graph showing the growth in world population since 1800. Notice that the points have been joined up with a freehand curve, which is usually the case with such graphs.

The New Wider World **page 164** Figure 10.15, which is a rainfall climate graph and is an example of a histogram. The monthly rainfall values form part of the total annual rainfall, so they can be drawn as 'touching' bars.

The New Wider World **page 14** Figure 1.17 which is a composite bar chart showing the differences between male and female life expectancy in selected countries.

Key words to know

Line graph
Bar graph
Histogram

Drawing bar graphs and histograms

Bar graphs and histograms are one of the most common methods used to display statistical information. However, they are not exactly the same.

- A **bar graph** is used to show the frequency or amount of a number of different categories, such as types of goods bought from a supermarket. The bars are drawn with a gap between them and they are coloured or shaded differently because they are unconnected (see Figure 9.7).

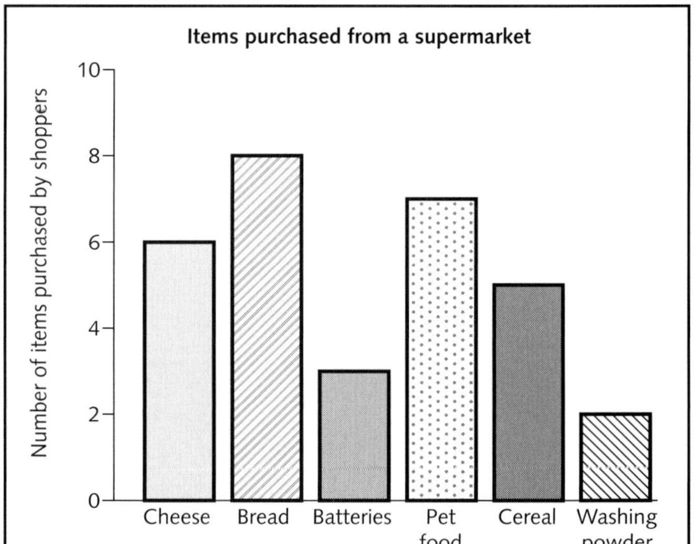

Figure 9.7 A bar graph

- A **histogram** also uses blocks but with no gaps between them. This is because a histogram is drawn when there is continuous data (such as daily rainfall values over a period of a month) or the values are all part of a single survey, for example the sizes of particles in a sediment sample. As the bars are effectively connected, a single colour or type of shading is used.

It is possible to use multiple bar charts and 'split' or composite bar charts to show two or more pieces of information at the same time.

Drawing pie graphs

A **pie graph** is quite simply a circle divided into segments, rather like slicing a cake! It is usually drawn to show the proportions of a total, for example the number of shoppers visiting a supermarket each day during one week. Pie graphs work best when they have between 4 and 10 segments; pie graphs with only one segment are a waste of time and those with many segments become too confusing.

When drawing a pie graph, remember to convert your values into degrees (for percentages multiply by 3.6).

Drawing triangular graphs

A **triangular graph** enables three values to be plotted at the same time to produce a single point. The values take the form of percentages that add up to 100. They are commonly used to show soil texture, employment and types of mass movement.

Figure 9.8 Rose diagram showing the orientation of corries

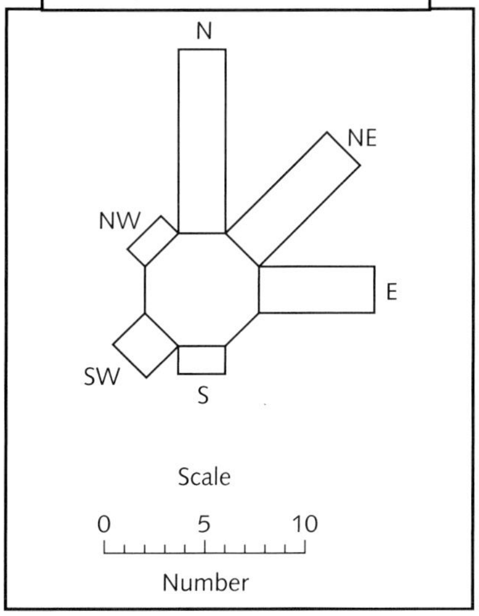

Drawing rose diagrams

A **rose diagram** shows the orientation of observed data, for example wind direction or the orientation of corries (Figure 9.8). Bars are drawn from an octagonal central shape to represent the number or frequency of each direction.

Drawing proportional symbols

Proportional circles are very effective ways to show data, particularly on a base map where spatial variations can be seen. However, they are rather tricky to draw and you will need to choose your scale carefully.

Select a scale for the radius of your circle. As it is the *area* of the circle that needs to be proportional, you must use the square root value as your radius distance.

Drawing scattergraphs

If you think that two sets of data are related, then the information can be plotted on a graph called a **scattergraph**. To complete a scattergraph you should work through the steps on the next page.

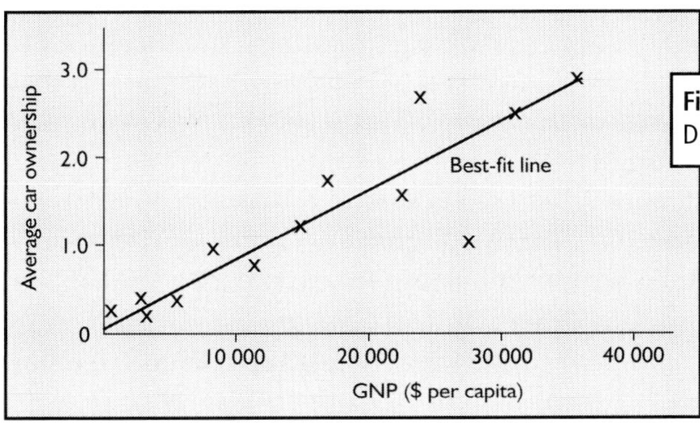

Figure 9.9
Drawing a scattergraph

Back to ...

The New Wider World **page 173** Figure 10.36 which uses pie graphs to show statistics for the Lake District National Park.

The New Wider World **page 186** Figure 11.11 which compares types of trade for a number of different countries.

The New Wider World **page 93** Figure 6.4 which shows how employment structure data can be displayed on a triangular graph.

The New Wider World **page 93** Figure 6.3: proportional circles are used very effectively to show regional variations in employment structures in the UK. Notice how the circles are also used as pie charts to show the different types of employment. This complex method of data presentation will score highly in any coursework that you undertake.

Key words to know

Pie graph
Triangular graph
Rose diagram
Proportional circle
Scattergraph

Key words to know

Best-fit line
Flow line
Choropleth map
Isopleth map

- Draw two graph axes in the normal way, but try to put the variable that is thought to be causing the change in the other (called the *independent variable*) on the horizontal (x) axis. In Figure 9.9, the wealth of a country (GNP) is thought to be responsible for the number of cars owned by a family.
- Use each pair of values to plot a single point on the graph using a cross.
- Use a **best-fit line** to clarify the trend of the points if there is one (see Figure 9.9). Your best-fit line should pass roughly through the centre of the points so that there is approximately the same number of points on either side of the line. Use a ruler to draw a straight line. The best-fit line does *not* need to pass through the origin.

The resultant pattern can now be described.

Drawing flow lines

Flow lines are an excellent way to show movement, for example where people visiting a particular country have come from. Each line is drawn with its width proportional to its value, for example 1 cm = 10 million tourists. Flow lines are most effective when drawn on a base map.

Drawing choropleth maps

A **choropleth map** is a map that uses different colours or density of shading to show the distribution of data categories.

Notice the following key features in Figure 1.2 on page 5 of *The New Wider World*:

- The base map shows regions or areas, in this case countries.
- Data is divided into a number of groups or categories. Ideally there should be between four and six categories. Notice that the category values do not overlap.
- The darker the shading, the higher the values.
- The map has a powerful and immediate visual impact; it is an effective form of mapping.

Back to ...

The New Wider World **page 178** Question 4 which includes a flow map showing the numbers of tourists travelling to Spain. Notice that the largest number of tourists come from France.

The New Wider World **page 201** Figure 12.3 which uses isotherms to show average July temperatures in the UK. Figure 12.4 on the same page uses isotherms to show January temperatures.

Drawing isopleth maps

An **isopleth map** is a map that uses lines of equal value to show patterns. Contours are a good example of isopleths, and are usually drawn at intervals of 10 metres.

Some of the most common isopleth maps are drawn to show aspects of weather and climate, e.g. isobars show pressure, and isotherms show temperature.

Whilst isopleth maps are rather difficult maps to draw, they are very effective at showing patterns, particularly when they are superimposed on a base map.

To draw an isopleth map, you need to mark your observed data onto a base map or sheet of tracing paper/acetate. You then need to consider how many lines to attempt to draw and at what intervals you will draw them. This decision is largely 'trial and error' and you may need to have a go in rough first.

Look at Figure 9.10 to see how isopleths are drawn. Notice how they pass between values that are higher and lower than the value of the line. Just remember that all values to one side of a line will be higher, and all those to the other side will be lower.

There is a degree of individual determination and decision-making, so do not worry if your map turns out to be slightly different from those of your neighbours.

Figure 9.10 An isopleth map showing a pedestrian count

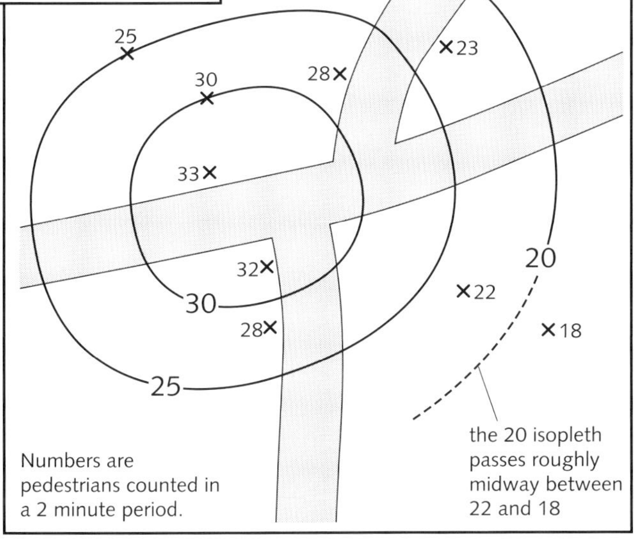

Drawing topological maps

A **topological map** is a map that is not drawn to a true distance scale. Whilst it shows where places are relative to each other, it often appears distorted.

Figure 9.11 shows the Newcastle Metro system. Whilst stations are located correctly according to their links, no attempt has been made to draw the map to a true distance scale.

Back to ...

The New Wider World **page 201** Figures 12.3 and 12.4, in which the isotherms have been drawn at 1° intervals.

Key words to know

Topological map
Describe

Figure 9.11 Newcastle Metro system

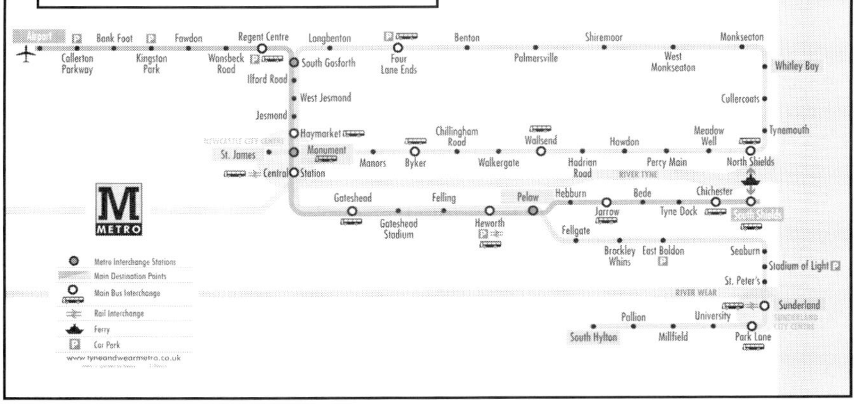

Topological maps can be very effective and can stimulate discussion, such as those drawn to a sacle of time taken rather than distance.

4 Looking for patterns

How to 'describe'

To **describe** a map, photograph or diagram you need to put into words what it shows. Start by describing the overall picture or pattern. Refer to the information available on the map, photograph or diagram and give actual facts and figures to support your statements. Then, if appropriate, look for any exceptions (called *anomalies*) to the general pattern. The most important thing is to be as precise and detailed as you can. Also, avoid giving reasons unless you are specifically asked to 'explain'.

Back to ...

The New Wider World **page 4** Figure 1.1: a description of the distribution of world population as shown here might be as follows:

'World population is unevenly distributed. In some parts of the world, for example north-west Europe, India, eastern China and south-east Africa, there is a dense population distribution. However, large parts of the world have a relatively low population density, for example Canada, much of the Russian Federation, north Africa and much of Australia.'

How to 'compare' and 'contrast'

To **compare** or **contrast**, you need to write about similarities and differences, for example between two areas on a map. It is essential to make comparisons all the way through your answer, so you should use words like 'whereas' or 'compared with'. Avoid the temptation to write separate paragraphs on the two areas under discussion.

As with making a description, you should refer to places and data wherever possible.

How to 'explain' or 'give reasons'

To **explain** patterns on maps or diagrams you need to try to think of reasons why they exist. This is much more difficult and will test your understanding of geography. You may need to refer to other maps and diagrams to help you. Log on to *The New Wider World Coursemates* website. This gives examples of answers which 'explain' and 'give reasons'.

How to 'analyse'

An analysis is very similar to an explanation except that it usually involves more detail and a much greater use of facts and figures. When conducting your coursework you will probably be required to **analyse** your data.

How to 'synthesise'

A synthesis involves the 'pulling together' of a variety of different forms of information to give a general overview. It is a kind of conclusion, pulling together all the different aspects that have been studied. Whilst you are unlikely to be asked to **synthesise** in an exam, it is possible that you will be required to do so in your coursework.

Back to ...

The New Wider World **pages 268–269**: a comparison between the two volcanic eruptions shown in these photographs might read as follows:

'In Figure 16.20 the volcano is erupting large quantities of red-hot lava, whereas the volcano in Figure 16.22 is erupting dense black clouds of ash and pyroclastics. An ash cloud is rising into the atmosphere from the volcano in Figure 16.22, whereas there is no ash cloud in Figure 16.20. Both eruptions look very dramatic and dangerous.'

Key words to know

Compare and contrast
Explain
Analyse
Synthesise

Back to ...

The New Wider World **page 81** Figure 17.8: an analysis of this complex hydrograph is given in the Case Study box. Notice that it involves a detailed study of the graph together with an interpretation of the effects of drainage basin characteristics on river flow.

The New Wider World **pages 272–273**: the case study of the Afghanistan earthquake of 1998 is a good example of a synthesis. Several different pieces of information, including tectonic details, the physical geography of Afghanistan, and economic and social characteristics of the population, are used to account for the impact of the earthquake.

A
aid 80
air masses and UK weather 46–53
anticyclones 50–3
arable farming, East Anglia 39–40

B
bar graphs 114
birth rates 17, 19–20, 22
brownfield sites 91, 92–3, 104

C
CBDs (Central Business Districts) 29, 30
choropleth maps 116
cliff recession 10–11, 61–3
climate 46, 53–4
  and vegetation 55–8
coasts
  coastal management 62–4
  coastal processes 9–14, 61–2
compass directions 107
coniferous trees 57, 58
corries 7, 8
cross-sections, drawing 109–10
cyclones 71–2, 75–6

D
death rates 17, 19–20, 22
deltas 5
demographic transition model 19–20
dependency ratio 23–4
deposition process 3, 13–14
depressions (weather) 49–50

E
earthquakes 72–4, 77–8
economic systems 34–6
  farming 36–40
  industry 41–4
ecotourism 84, 86–7
employment structures 34–6
erosion
  by ice 6–7, 8
  by rivers 2, 4
  coastal 9–11

F
farming 36–40
field sketches, drawing 113–14
floodplains 4, 5
floods, river 64–8
flow lines 116
forests 55–9
frontal rainfall 49

G
glaciation 6–8
graphs 114–16
greenfield sites 93, 94–5
grid references 106–7

H
hazards, natural 71–80
high-tech industries 42
histograms 114
housing 89, 90–1, 93–4, 100
hurricanes 71–2, 75–6

I
industry 41–4
  impact of tourism on 82–3
inner cities 89–91
interlocking spurs 3
isopleth maps 116–17

L
land use models 28–9, 32
LEDCs (less economically developed countries)
  aid 80
  economic systems 36, 43–4
  farming 37
  natural hazards 76, 78
  population 17, 21, 23, 24–5
  tourism 82
  urban areas 32, 96–101
levées 4, 5
line graphs 114
longshore drift 13

M
maps
  describing 110–12, 117–18
  map skills 106–10
  types of 108–9, 116–17
meanders 4, 5
MEDCs (more economically developed countries)
  farming 37
  industries 36, 41–2
  natural hazards 76, 78
  population 17, 21, 23, 25
  tourism 82, 83
  urban areas 28–31, 89–95, 97
migration 18, 98–9
moraine 7

O
organic farming 37–8
ox-bow lakes 4, 5

P
photographs 112, 113
pie graphs 115
plates (Earth's crust) 73–4
pollution 101–5
population
  change 16–20
  settlements 26–32
  structure 21–5
proportional circles 115

R
rainfall in the UK 47–9
rapids 3
relief rainfall 48
rivers
  floods 64–8
  processes and landforms 1–5
rose diagrams 115
rural-urban migration 98

S
satellite images 52–3, 112
scales, map 106, 107
scattergraphs 115–16
settlements 26–32
sketch maps, drawing 108–9
sketches, drawing 113–14
spits 13–14
squatter settlements 99–100
suburbanisation 93
sustainable development 69
  sustainable tourism 86–7
  tropical rainforests 57, 59
synoptic charts 51, 52–3

T
taiga 57
topological maps 117
tourism 82–7
transnational corporations (TNCs) 44
transportation process 2, 13
triangular graphs 115
tropical rainforests 56–7, 57, 59
tropical storms 71–2, 75–6

U
urban areas
  environmental issues 101–5
  LEDCs 32, 96–101
  MEDCs 28–31, 89–95, 97

V
valleys
  glaciation and 6–8
  river 1–3
volcanic activity 72–4, 77–8

W
waterfalls 3
waves 9–11, 13
weather 46
  patterns and climate 53–4
  UK weather 46–53
weathering 11–12

Notes

Notes

Notes